MILITARY FLIGHT
APTITUDE
TESTS

MILITARY FLIGHT APTITUDE TESTS

3rd Edition

LearningExpress®

NEW YORK

Library of Congress Cataloging-in-Publication Data:
Military flight aptitude tests.—3rd ed.
    p. cm.
  ISBN-13: 978-1-57685-688-8 (pbk. : alk. paper)
  ISBN-10: 1-57685-688-7 (pbk. : alk. paper) 1. Air pilots, Military—Training of—United States. 2. United
States—Armed Forces—Officers. 3. United States—Armed Forces—Examinations. 4. United States—Armed
Forces—Recruiting, enlistment, etc. I. LearningExpress (Organization)
UG638.M55 2009
358.400973—dc22   2008052184

Printed in the United States of America
9 8 7 6 5 4 3 2
Third Edition

ISBN-10: 1-57685-688-7
ISBN-13: 978-1-57685-688-8

Regarding the Information in This Book
We attempt to verify the information presented in our books prior to publication. It is always a good idea,
however, to double-check such important information as minimum requirements, application and testing
procedures, and deadlines, as such information can change from time to time.

For more information or to place an order, contact LearningExpress at:
  2 Rector Street
  26th floor
  New York, NY 10006

Or visit us at:
  www.learnatest.com

About the Contributors

Patti Courville is a Long Island–based photographer. Aside from aerial photography, she photographs artists, musicians, gardens, and landscapes.

Jason Foley, formerly a collegiate flight instructor, is now flying for a regional airline.

Lt. Col. Michael France recently retired from the U.S. Air Force. He is a graduate of the U.S. Air Force Fighter Weapons School, with more than 3,000 hours in military aircraft, including 2,800 hours in the F-16 Fighting Falcon. He holds a bachelor of science in engineering science from the U.S. Air Force Academy and a master's of science in engineering from Arizona State University.

Marcella Gallardo is a graphic artist and illustrator whose work includes everything from industrial schematics to children's book illustrations. She lives in Massachusetts.

Major Doug Hadley is a member of the U.S. Air Force. He is an F-16 instructor pilot with more than 2,200 flight hours and more than 1,200 hours of instructor pilot time.

Chris Kirschman, a captain in the U.S. Air Force, is a graduate of the U.S. Air Force Weapons School. He has 10 years of experience flying combat aircraft and is currently training EC-130H students at Davis-Monthan Air Force Base in Tucson, Arizona.

Montgomery Knott is a freelance project editor. Besides making music, he is currently finishing his first feature-length film in Williamsburg, Brooklyn.

James D. MacDonald was born in White Plains, New York, and now lives in New Hampshire. He is a published novelist and a former naval officer.

CDR Bill Paisley is a former F-14 Tomcat radar intercept officer with 25 years active and reserve service. He holds two undergraduate degrees in education and a master's of arts in national security. He lives in northern Virginia and works as a modeling and simulation professional for the U.S. Navy.

Toni Saul, who made the flight arrangements for the Cyclic Orientation section, is director of flight programs at Dowling College in Oakdale, New York.

Diann Thornley is a novelist and reserve Air Force officer who lives in Houston, Texas.

LCDR John Wickham is an active-duty officer in the U.S. Navy with more than 17 years of service in the submarine and maritime patrol communities. He is a P-3C "Orion" instructor pilot with more than 2,000 hours of flight time.

Special thanks to Chief Warrant Officer Dan McClinton, Master Sgt. John E. Lasky, Scott A. Thornbloom, Master Sgt. David Richards, Master Sgt. Fernando Serna, Mass Communication Specialist First Class Erik Hoffmann, CDR Bill Paisley, and the U.S. Army and Navy for providing us with many of the beautiful images used in the book.

Contents

MILITARY FLIGHT APTITUDE TESTS

1 ▶ Becoming a Military Aviator

Congratulations on taking the first step toward a career as a military flight officer! As you prepare for your test, know that you have come to the right place for up-to-date information on the entire process. This chapter describes the different aviator jobs available in the military and the programs for becoming an officer that are offered by the Air Force, Army, Navy, and Marine Corps. Simply put, you will find all the facts you need to achieve your career goals. In addition, information about the benefits of becoming an officer and the opportunities available in the military reserves is included.

Let's begin by exploring the positions of airplane pilot, helicopter pilot, flight navigator, and naval flight officer. All of these jobs require a high level of expertise and are very challenging. While it is obvious that the Air Force has jobs for aviators, in fact, all five branches of the armed forces have jobs and training programs available for aviators. Keep in mind that the Navy and the Marine Corps call their aircraft navigators *flight officers*. We will examine each position on the pages that follow.

Airplane Pilots

The exciting and highly sought-after job of a military airplane pilot is one that has been glamorized by Hollywood, and indeed it is one to which many people aspire. Although the reality of being an airplane pilot is different from the movie version, it is an extremely intense and exciting career.

If you choose to become an airplane pilot in the military, you will have several areas of specialization to choose from, based on the needs of the service. Take a look at this sampling:

Types of Pilots
Airlift Pilot
Astronaut
Bomber Pilot
Experimental Test Pilot
Fighter Pilot
Reconnaissance/Surveillance/Electronic
    Warfare Pilot
Special Operations Pilot
Tanker Pilot
Instructor Pilot
Other specialties as needed by the service

Airplane Pilot Duties
Depending on the branch of the military you choose, your daily duties will vary. However, you can expect to do any or all of the following:

- Fly airplanes in all weather conditions in peace and wartime
- Plan and execute missions over targeted hostile areas
- Deploy new technologies involving long-range missiles and satellite defenses

Naval Flight Officer

- Plan and prepare for missions
- Supervise and direct navigation, in-flight refueling, and cargo deliveries
- Brief crewmembers and ensure the operational readiness of your crew
- Develop flight plans
- Advise commanders
- Communicate with air traffic controllers
- Perform combat maneuvers
- Take photographs
- Patrol areas to carry out flight missions
- Monitor planes' fuel, flight control, electrical, and weapons systems
- Practice emergency and normal operating procedures
- Fly missions alone, as part of a group of airplanes, or as copilot of a large airplane

A Choice of Planes

When you become a pilot, you will start your career in a flight squadron made up of 10 to 25 airplanes, and you will be working with the crews trained to fly and maintain them. You will specialize in one type of airplane, so you can fully master it. Examples of the different types of planes are:

- Supersonic jet fighters, fighter bombers, or ground-attack planes
- Long-range strategic bombers
- Large tanker airplanes that provide in-flight refueling
- High-altitude reconnaissance planes
- Medium- or long-range antisubmarine patrol planes
- Long-range multiengine heavy transport planes
- Lightweight utility planes
- Airborne command and control platforms

Physical Demands

The physical demands placed on military airplane pilots are intense. Modern jet aircraft are powerful machines and the g-forces generated during routine missions require the aircrew to be in excellent physical condition. Excellent vision is another requirement—exact vision standards vary depending on the service. You must have a controlled and quick reaction time when maneuvering at high speeds. In addition, you will need to pass strict height and weight requirements, which vary among the military branches, to ensure that you can easily fit into the cockpit or ejection seat of the plane you will be flying.

Ways to Prepare

In addition to getting into excellent physical condition, you can study on your own or take courses in the following areas to help you prepare for becoming a military airplane pilot:

Aerodynamics
Airplane Systems
Meteorology
Federal Flight Rules and Regulations
Physics
Aerospace Engineering
Electrical Engineering
Mechanical Engineering

Once you become an airplane pilot, many additional opportunities will arise for you to expand your knowledge and gain additional flight experience. Indeed, continued education is one thing you can bet on if you become a military pilot, so it is a good idea to develop excellent study habits.

To learn more about specific qualifications needed to become a military pilot, read the second half of this chapter, which covers how to become a commissioned officer or a warrant officer. You will have to hold one of these positions in order to become a military pilot. Chapter 2 will give you more details about airplane pilot and navigator/flight officer jobs and training opportunities in each branch of the military. While the road to becoming a pilot is long and highly competitive, once you make it, you will have the satisfaction of knowing that you have accomplished an incredible feat.

Transition to Civilian Life

Military airplane pilots who desire to make the transition into civilian life have excellent career opportunities available as commercial pilots. Historically, most commercial pilots were military-trained, although more and more are getting their training from private companies. You could also get a civilian job as a flight instructor, a crop duster, or a pilot for a private company.

Helicopter Pilots

All five branches of the armed forces utilize helicopter pilots. The job of a helicopter pilot is similar to that of an airplane pilot, and the selection process for helicopter pilots is also very competitive. As a helicopter pilot, you could be stationed at military bases in the United States or on an aircraft carrier or smaller naval vessel. You need to be in excellent physical shape, just as airplane pilots do, and you should study the same list of topics shown in the previous section to prepare for a career as a helicopter pilot.

Helicopter Pilot Duties

Your daily duties will vary depending on which branch of service you serve. However, you can expect to do any of the following:

- Fly helicopters in all weather conditions in peace and wartime
- Prepare flight plans showing air routes and schedules

- Conduct search and rescue missions
- Perform combat maneuvers
- Patrol areas to carry out missions
- Monitor gauges and dials located on cockpit control panels
- Practice emergency and normal operating procedures
- Consult weather reports to learn about flying conditions

Transition to Civilian Life

Military helicopter pilots who desire to make the transition into civilian life have excellent career opportunities available in a variety of settings. You could become a helicopter pilot for a police force, a firefighting unit, a private business, a news organization, or a local commuter service. Other jobs available to you include helicopter flight instructors, crop dusters, and traffic spotters.

AH-64 Apache Helicopter

Flight Navigators/ Naval Flight Officers

Navigators are needed in the Air Force, Navy, Marine Corps, and occasionally in the Coast Guard. The Army doesn't have positions for aircraft navigators—their pilots handle their own navigation. In the Navy and Marine Corps, these aviation experts are called *naval flight officers*. However, navigators and naval flight officers perform many of the same functions. Here's a look at different types of navigator specialties:

Aircraft Navigator

Types of Navigator Positions
Airlift Navigator
Bomber Navigator
Experimental Test Navigator
Fighter Navigator
Reconnaissance/Surveillance/Electronic Warfare Navigator
Special Operations Navigator
Tanker Navigator
Trainer Navigator

If you have an ability to read maps and charts, and can respond quickly to emergencies, you will be one step ahead of the competition vying for the position of navigator. Attention to detail and the ability to perform work with a high degree of accuracy on a consistent basis will also help you achieve the goal of becoming a navigator or flight officer.

Navigator/Flight Officer Duties

If you become an airplane navigator or flight officer, you will operate complex, state-of-the-art electronic navigation, communication, and weapon systems that will allow you to bring your aircraft safely and successfully through its missions. Here are several duties of an airplane navigator/flight officer:

- Direct aircraft course using radar, sight, and other navigation methods
- Locate and track aerial, submarine, or surface targets
- Operate communications equipment to send and receive messages
- Operate weapons systems
- Plan missions and tactics with pilots, considering weather, fuel, and aircraft load
- Conduct preflight inspections of navigation and weapons systems
- Guide tanker and other airplanes during in-flight refueling operations
- Conduct fuel consumption projections
- Provide pilots with instrument readings, fuel usage, and other flight information
- Practice normal and emergency operating procedures

Physical Demands

You need not only be in top physical shape to become a navigator, but also in top mental shape to handle the intense level of concentration needed to operate sophisticated equipment for long periods of time. Tactical fighter aircraft can pull up to six g's, or six times the force of gravity, making even the easiest task in a cockpit a physical exertion. Concentration and the ability to perform under pressure are essential during strenuous flight maneuvers.

Ways to Prepare

To gain an edge on the competition, you can study the following topics to prepare for a career as a navigator or flight officer:

Flight Theory
Air Navigation
Meteorology
Flying Directives
Aircraft Operating Procedures
Cartography
Geography
Surveying

To learn more about specific qualifications needed to become a military navigator or flight officer, read the second half of this chapter, which covers how to become a commissioned officer or a warrant officer. You will have to become a commissioned officer in order to become a navigator.

How Can I Become an Officer?

The first step in the process of starting a career as a military pilot, navigator, or flight officer is to decide if you want to become a commissioned officer or a warrant officer.

All military pilots, navigators, and flight officers are either commissioned officers or warrant officers of the armed forces of the United States. One of the main differences between a commissioned and a warrant officer is that a commissioned officer must have a four-year college degree from an accredited institution. A warrant officer is promoted from an enlisted position, which requires only a high school diploma or the equivalent. Before 2005, the only service that has a pilot program for warrant officers was the Army. That year, however, the Navy began their own warrant officer aviation program called the Flying Chief Warrant Officer program. This new program, calling on an experienced group of military professionals, supplements the current officer aviation force by placing qualified CWOs in the cockpit as pilots and naval flight officers (NFOs). The Army's program is called the Warrant Officer Flight Training Program, which is described in Chapter 2. With the exception of these two programs for warrant officers, all pilots, naval flight officers, and navigators must be commissioned officers of the armed forces of the United States.

The following table shows the basic eligibility requirements for becoming a commissioned officer.

Age	**AGE REQUIREMENT IS BASED ON SELECTED PROGRAM:** **OCS/OTS (OFFICER CANDIDATE SCHOOL/OFFICER TRAINING SCHOOL):** Between 19 and 29 years **ROTC (RESERVE OFFICERS TRAINING CORPS):** Between 17 and 21 years **SERVICE ACADEMY:** Between 17 and 22 years (but have not passed 23rd birthday) If age 17, parent's signed consent is required.
Citizenship	Must be a U.S. citizen
Physical Condition	**MALES:** Height 5'0" to 6'8' **WEIGHT** 100 lbs. to 255 lbs. **FEMALES:** Height 4'10" to 6'8" **WEIGHT** 90 lbs. to 227 lbs.
Vision	Must have at least 20/200 vision corrected to 20/20 with eyeglasses or contact lenses. Depth perception and color blindness are also tested.
General Health	Must be able to pass a medical exam
Education	Must have a four-year college degree from an accredited institution. Some officer occupations require advanced degrees or four-year degrees in a specialized field.
Aptitude	Must qualify for enlistment on an officer qualification test. Each service uses its own officer qualification test with the exception of the U.S. Coast Guard, which uses the Navy's ASTB aptitude test.
Background Investigation	Must pass a background investigation that shows you are of strong moral character
Marital Status and Dependents	**OCS/OTS, ROTC, or direct appointment:** May be either single or married. **Service Academy:** Must be unmarried, not pregnant, and without legal obligation to support children or other dependents. **For** other officer programs, the number of allowable dependents varies by branch of service.

Fortunately, there are a variety of ways to become a commissioned officer, and each branch of the armed forces has programs designed to help you. Let's begin by discussing the five ways in which you can become a commissioned officer.

Reserve Officer Training Corps (ROTC)

The most common way to land an officer's commission in the armed forces is to graduate from a program called the Reserve Officer Training Corps, also known as ROTC. Indeed, more than 44% of new officers gain their commission through an ROTC program each year. The Navy receives more than 40% of its flight students from ROTC programs. More than one thousand colleges and universities throughout the United States offer ROTC programs. If you choose this route, you may be able to get full scholarships for tuition and fees as well as a monthly paycheck for other expenses. You just have to agree to enlist for two-, three-, or four-year ROTC programs, depending on the service branch you choose.

Then you will learn military skills in addition to your college course of study, and you will be expected to undertake military exercises for several weeks each summer. After you graduate, you can become a commissioned officer and go on active duty or you can become a member of a reserve or National Guard unit.

Officer Candidate/ Training Schools

The second most common way to become a commissioned officer is to gain admittance to an Officer Candidate School (OCS) or Officer Training School (OTS), depending on the branch of service. Close to 21% of the military's officers earn their commission through these schools each year. While a majority of Air Force OTS graduates go on to flight training, the Navy's OCS program provides nearly 20% of their flight students.

You must have a four-year college degree from an accredited institution before you can enter one of these schools. The training programs offered at these schools vary in length from 14 to 20 weeks, depending on the branch of service. To request an application or to obtain more information about this option, contact your local military recruiter.

Officer Candidate School Commissioning Ceremony

Service Academies

The third most common way to become a commissioned officer is to graduate from a service academy. About 13% of newly commissioned officers each year are graduates of service academies. This route carries a high level of prestige, because it is difficult to gain entrance to an academy. The four service academies are:

Army:	U.S. Military Academy West Point, NY
Air Force:	U.S. Air Force Academy Colorado Springs, CO
Navy and Marine Corps:	U.S. Naval Academy Annapolis, MD
Coast Guard:	U.S. Coast Guard Academy New London, CT

You don't have to pay any tuition at these academies; in fact, room and board are also free. Plus, you get a monthly paycheck. With all these benefits, you can be sure that competition to gain entry is fierce. The basic eligibility requirements are listed here:

- Be at least 17 years old
- Be a citizen of the United States
- Have good moral character
- Be able to pass a physical aptitude exam
- Be able to pass a medical exam

In addition to these basic requirements, you need a nomination from an elected official to attend all but the U.S. Coast Guard Academy, which bases acceptance on merit only. You can request help from the service academies for obtaining one of these coveted nominations from your U.S. representative, one of your two U.S. senators, or another eligible official. If you graduate from a service academy, you must serve on active duty for at least five years.

Direct Appointment

The military offers some direct commissioning programs for becoming an officer. While these appointments are mainly open to medical, legal, engineering, and religious professionals, you may want to discuss the direct appointment option with your local recruiter if you have prior military experience or other aviation training. Direct appointments account for about 11% of newly commissioned officers.

Enlisted Commissioning Programs

Depending upon which branch of the military you want to join, you may be eligible for a program that helps enlisted personnel become commissioned officers. These programs vary in length and type, but they all lead to one of the previously discussed routes to becoming a commissioned officer. One example of a program for enlisted personnel is called BOOST, which stands for Broadened Opportunity for Officer Selection and Training. This program gives enlisted personnel specific academic preparation that helps increase their chances of getting into the U.S. Naval Academy or the Marine Corps Enlisted Commissioning Education Program or of landing a Navy or Marine Corps ROTC scholarship. Enlisted commissioning programs account for about 11% of the military's new officers each year.

Benefits of Becoming an Officer

As a military pilot, navigator, or flight officer, you will receive the same great benefits that all officers in the military receive. Most of them are described here.

A Good Paycheck

As an officer, you can expect to receive a respectable amount of pay, which will increase with your years of service and demonstrated skills. One benefit you can take advantage of right now is that officer pay grades are published for the whole world to see. Therefore, you can get an idea of the amount of money you can make before you even begin the process of becoming an officer. See the table on the following pages for the monthly dollar amounts of officers' basic pay, based on years of service. If you are a commissioned officer, you will most likely be starting out at pay grade O–1. You will probably move up to pay grade O–2 within your first two years of service and to pay grade O–3 a few years later. As you climb the pay-grade ladder, promotions become increasingly competitive. One reason for the competition is that Congress limits the number of officers in the very highest pay grades. Warrant officers start out at the W–1 pay grade and move up to W–5.

2009 MILITARY MONTHLY BASE PAY RATES

Commissioned Officers

Pay Grade	Years of Service														
	Under 2	Over 2	Over 3	Over 4	Over 6	Over 8	Over 10	Over 12	Over 14	Over 16	Over 18	Over 20	Over 22	Over 24	Over 26
O–10	–	–	–	–	–	–	–	–	–	–	–	14,688.60	14,688.60	14,688.60	14,688.60
O–9	–	–	–	–	–	–	–	–	–	–	–	12,846.90	13,032.00	13,299.30	13,765.80
O–8	9,090.00	9,387.60	9,585.30	9,640.50	9,887.10	10,299.00	10,395.00	10,786.20	10,898.10	11,235.30	11,722.50	12,172.20	12,472.50	12,472.50	12,472.50
O–7	7,553.10	7,904.10	8,066.40	8,195.40	8,429.10	8,660.10	8,926.80	9,192.90	9,460.20	10,299.00	11,007.30	11,007.30	11,007.30	11,007.30	11,063.10
O–6	5,598.30	6,150.30	6,553.80	6,553.80	6,578.70	6,860.70	6,897.90	6,897.90	7,290.00	7,983.30	8,390.10	8,796.60	9,027.90	9,262.20	9,716.70
O–5	4,666.80	5,257.20	5,621.40	5,689.80	5,916.60	6,052.80	6,570.60	5073.30	6,853.80	7,287.30	7,493.40	7,697.40	7,928.70	7,928.70	7,928.70
O–4	4,026.90	4,661.40	4,972.20	5,041.80	5,330.40	5,640.00	6,325.50	4930.20	6,534.30	6,654.00	6,723.30	6,723.30	6,723.30	6,723.30	6,723.30
O–3	3,540.30	4,013.40	4,332.00	4,722.90	4,948.80	5,197.20	5,622.30	4441.20	5,759.70	5,759.70	5,759.70	5,759.70	5,759.70	5,759.70	5,759.70
O–2	3,058.80	3,483.90	4,012.50	4,148.10	4,233.30	4,233.30	4,233.30	3344.10	4,233.30	4,233.30	4,233.30	4,233.30	4,233.30	4,233.30	4,233.30
O–1	2,655.30	2,763.60	3,340.50	3,340.50	3,340.50	3,340.50	3,340.50	2638.50	3,340.50	3,340.50	3,340.50	3,340.50	3,340.50	3,340.50	3,340.50

Commissioned Officers with More Than Four Years of Active Service as an Enlisted Member or Warrant Officer

Pay Grade	Years of Service														
	Under 2	Over 2	Over 3	Over 4	Over 6	Over 8	Over 10	Over 12	Over 14	Over 16	Over 18	Over 20	Over 22	Over 24	Over 26
O–3E	–	–	–	4,722.90	4,948.80	5,197.20	5,358.00	5,622.30	5,844.90	5,972.70	6,146.70	6,146.70	6,146.70	6,146.70	6,146.70
O–2E	–	–	–	4,148.10	4,233.30	4,368.30	4,595.70	4,771.50	4,902.30	4,902.30	4,902.30	4,902.30	4,902.30	4,902.30	4,902.30
O–1E	–	–	–	3,340.50	3,567.60	3,699.30	3,834.30	3,966.60	4,148.10	4,148.10	4,148.10	4,148.10	4,148.10	4,148.10	4,148.10

Warrant Officers

Pay Grade	Years of Service														
	Under 2	Over 2	Over 3	Over 4	Over 6	Over 8	Over 10	Over 12	Over 14	Over 16	Over 18	Over 20	Over 22	Over 24	Over 26
W–5	–	–	–	–	–	–	–	–	–	–	–	6,505.50	6,835.50	7,081.20	7,353.60
W–4	3,658.50	3,935.70	4,048.80	4,159.80	4,351.20	4,540.50	4,732.20	5,021.10	5,274.00	5,514.60	5,711.40	5,903.40	6,185.70	6,417.30	6,681.90
W–3	3,340.80	3,480.30	3,622.80	3,669.90	3,819.60	4,114.20	4,420.80	4,574.70	4,731.90	4,904.10	5,213.10	5,422.20	5,547.30	5,680.20	5,860.80
W–2	2,956.50	3,236.10	3,322.20	3,381.60	3,573.30	3,871.20	4,018.80	4,164.30	4,341.90	4,480.80	4,606.80	4,757.10	4,856.40	4,935.00	4,935.00
W–1	2,595.30	2,874.00	2,949.60	3,108.30	3,286.50	3,572.70	3,701.70	3,882.30	4,059.90	4,199.40	4,328.10	4,484.40	4,484.40	4,484.40	4,484.40

2009 MILITARY MONTHLY BASE PAY RATES (continued)

Enlisted

Pay Grade	Years of Service														
	Under 2	Over 2	Over 3	Over 4	Over 6	Over 8	Over 10	Over 12	Over 14	Over 16	Over 18	Over 20	Over 22	Over 24	Over 26
E–9	–	–	–	–	–	–	4,420.50	4,520.70	4,646.70	4,795.50	4,944.90	5,185.20	5,388.00	5,601.90	5,928.30
E–8	–	–	–	–	–	3,618.60	3,778.80	3,877.80	3,996.60	4,125.00	4,357.20	4,474.80	4,674.90	4,785.90	5,059.50
E–7	2,515.50	2,745.60	2,850.60	2,990.10	3,098.70	3,285.30	3,390.30	3,577.50	3,732.60	3,838.50	3,951.30	3,995.40	4,142.10	4,221.00	4,521.00
E–6	2,175.60	2,394.00	2,499.60	2,602.20	2,709.30	2,950.80	3,044.70	3,226.20	3,282.00	3,322.50	3,369.90	3,369.90	3,369.90	3,369.90	3,369.90
E–5	1,993.50	2,127.00	2,229.60	2,334.90	2,499.00	2,670.90	2,811.00	2,828.40	2,828.40	2,828.40	2,828.40	2,828.40	2,828.40	2,828.40	2,828.40
E–4	1,827.60	1,920.90	2,025.00	2,127.60	2,218.50	2,218.50	2,218.50	2,218.50	2,218.50	2,218.50	2,218.50	2,218.50	2,218.50	2,218.50	2,218.50
E–3	1,649.70	1,753.50	1,859.70	1,859.70	1,859.70	1,859.70	1,859.70	1,859.70	1,859.70	1,859.70	1,859.70	1,859.70	1,859.70	1,859.70	1,859.70
E–2	1,568.70	1,568.70	1,568.70	1,568.70	1,568.70	1,568.70	1,568.70	1,568.70	1,568.70	1,568.70	1,568.70	1,568.70	1,568.70	1,568.70	1,568.70
E–1 >4	1,399.50	1,399.50	1,399.50	1,399.50	1,399.50	1,399.50	1,399.50	1,399.50	1,399.50	1,399.50	1,399.50	1,399.50	1,399.50	1,399.50	1,399.50
E–1 <4 w/less than 4 months	1,294.50														

Note: Basic Pay for O7–O10 is limited to level III of the executive schedule.
Note: Basic Pay for O6 and below is limited to level V of the executive schedule.

In addition to your basic pay, as shown in the previous table, you may be eligible to receive incentive pay, called flight pay. Here is a table showing additional incentives paid each month to aviators in the military:

AVIATION CAREER INCENTIVE PAY

Years of Aviation Service	Amount
2 or less	$125
More than 2	$156
3	$188
4	$206
6	$650
14	$840
22	$585
23	$495
24	$385
25	$250

Housing and Food Allowances

One of the opportunities afforded military personnel is the ability to live free of charge in military housing on your assigned base. Just think of it—no rent or mortgage payment to pay every month! However, since military housing is limited, not all officers get this benefit. If you can't get housing at the base, you can live off-base and get a monthly housing allowance to offset your rent or mortgage payments. A new law just went into effect that increases the basic housing allowance for most military personnel. The exact amount of the allowance depends on the price for housing in the geographic area in which you are stationed. For example, if you are a new officer in pay grade O–1 stationed in Pensacola, Florida, your monthly allowance would be $1,143 if you have dependents or $1,081 if you don't have dependents.

In addition to generous housing allowances, the military also offers a monthly food allowance called a subsistence allowance. You can get about $223 each month to help pay for your food. While you can't buy a lot of caviar on that budget, it is tax-free money and a good benefit.

Other Benefits

Life as a military officer has several other benefits, too. You get free health and dental care, low-cost life insurance, generous vacation time of 30 days per year, a 20-year retirement plan, tuition assistance that often covers from 75% to 90% of education costs, legal assistance that includes several free legal services for personal matters, shopping privileges at base commissaries and exchanges, recreation programs, and membership in prestigious officers' clubs. Plus, the post–9/11 GI Bill provides expanded benefits for qualified military personnel.

Are the Military Reserves for You?

If you don't see yourself having a full career as an active-duty full-time military officer, perhaps a career in the military reserve or National Guard aviation program is for you. In the reserves or National Guard, you get to enter the same exciting aviation careers as your active-duty counterparts, but do so on a part-time basis. Your active-duty time will count toward your retirement income and benefits. While there will always be the possibility your unit will be called to active duty, you will usually serve only one weekend a month and one two-week active-duty tour each year.

The Benefits

As a reserve or National Guard officer, you will get to enjoy some of the same benefits as active-duty officers. They include:

- 20-year retirement plans
- Commissary and exchange privileges
- Membership in officers' clubs
- Tuition assistance and access to GI Bill benefits
- Exciting career assignments

Here's a closer look at several benefits that a career in the military reserves offers.

SAME RANK

If you enter the reserves directly from active duty, in most cases you will do so at the same rank you left the active force. This ensures you will continue on a competitive career path with promotions and increased responsibilities that match your active-duty service mates.

RESERVE FORCES MILITARY PAY RATES

Commissioned Officers

Pay Grade	Years of Service														
	Under 2	Over 2	Over 3	Over 4	Over 6	Over 8	Over 10	Over 12	Over 14	Over 16	Over 18	Over 20	Over 22	Over 24	Over 26
O-7	1,007.08	1,053.88	1,075.52	1,092.72	1,123.88	1,154.68	1,190.24	1,225.72	1,261.36	1,373.20	1,467.64	1,467.64	1,467.64	1,467.64	1,475.08
O-6	746.44	820.04	873.84	873.84	877.16	914.76	919.72	919.72	972.00	1,064.44	1,118.68	1,172.88	1,203.72	1,234.96	1,295.56
O-5	622.24	700.96	749.52	758.64	788.88	807.04	846.88	876.08	913.84	971.64	999.12	1,026.32	1,057.16	1,057.16	1,057.16
O-4	536.92	621.52	662.96	672.24	710.72	752.00	803.36	843.40	871.24	887.20	896.44	896.44	896.44	896.44	896.44
O-3	472.04	535.12	577.60	629.72	659.84	692.96	714.40	749.64	767.96	767.96	767.96	767.96	767.96	767.96	767.96
O-2	407.84	464.52	535.00	553.08	564.44	564.44	564.44	564.44	564.44	564.44	564.44	564.44	564.44	564.44	564.44
O-1	354.04	368.48	445.40	445.40	445.40	445.40	445.40	445.40	445.40	445.40	445.40	445.40	445.40	445.40	445.40

Commissioned Officers with More Than Four Years Active Duty Service as an Enlisted Member or Warrant Officer

Pay Grade	Years of Service														
	Under 2	Over 2	Over 3	Over 4	Over 6	Over 8	Over 10	Over 12	Over 14	Over 16	Over 18	Over 20	Over 22	Over 24	Over 26
WO-3E	–	–	–	629.72	659.84	692.96	714.40	749.64	779.32	796.36	819.56	819.56	819.56	819.56	819.56
O-2E	–	–	–	553.08	564.44	582.44	612.76	636.20	653.64	653.64	653.64	653.64	653.64	653.64	653.64
O-1E	–	–	–	445.40	475.68	493.24	511.24	528.88	553.08	553.08	553.08	553.08	553.08	553.08	553.08

Warrant Officers

Pay Grade	Years of Service														
	Under 2	Over 2	Over 3	Over 4	Over 6	Over 8	Over 10	Over 12	Over 14	Over 16	Over 18	Over 20	Over 22	Over 24	Over 26
W-5	–	–	–	–	–	–	–	–	–	–	–	867.40	911.40	944.16	980.48
W-4	487.80	524.76	539.84	554.64	580.16	605.40	630.96	669.48	703.20	735.28	761.52	787.12	824.76	855.64	890.92
W-3	445.44	464.04	483.04	489.32	509.28	548.56	589.44	608.68	630.92	653.88	695.08	722.96	739.64	757.36	781.44
W-2	394.20	431.48	442.96	450.88	476.44	516.16	535.84	555.24	578.92	597.44	614.24	634.28	647.52	658.00	658.00
W-1	346.04	383.20	393.28	414.44	439.48	476.36	493.56	517.64	541.32	559.92	577.08	597.92	597.92	597.92	597.92

A PAYCHECK

You will earn good pay for your two days a month of training plus 15 days of annual active duty, plus compensation for any additional days you choose to put in. Your pay will also be adjusted automatically for cost-of-living increases. What's more, you will get pay increases for every two years of accumulated service and additional pay if you are on flight status. Your accomplishments in the military reserves will also be recognized through awards, decorations, and promotions. A chart showing monthly reserve pay is on the previous page.

TUITION ASSISTANCE

If you have your mind set on college or trade school, there is financial assistance through the Montgomery GI Bill, which offers eligible reservists money for a college education. And because there are reserve units all over the country, there's a good chance you can attend college or trade school and still train two days a month and two weeks a year near your school.

OTHER BENEFITS

Other benefits include getting low-cost servicemember group life insurance, medical care while on duty, a noncontributory retirement program, free flights on military aircraft when space is available, and reemployment rights that enable you to return to your civilian job after being ordered to active duty for training or during a national emergency. Additionally, you can use a military reserve base's recreational facilities, gym, tennis courts, libraries, commissary, and exchange.

Air Force Reserve and Air National Guard

If you do not have any prior military experience, you will incur an eight-year service obligation when becoming a reservist. These eight years are broken down into two segments. The first six years you will be an active participating member. The last two years, if you choose, you will be in the inactive ready reserve.

During this time, you still will be subject to recall in the event of a national emergency or in time of need.

Reserve aircrews operate unit-equipped aircraft or, through the reserve's associate program, fly active-duty aircraft. Some crews provide long-range worldwide airlift, and others perform shorter-range transport of troops and cargo.

About half of the reserve's airlift units fly the C-130 Hercules. Its speed, range, load-carrying characteristics, and capability to operate under difficult terrain conditions make it a valuable and versatile aircraft. It is strong enough to deliver its cargo on unimproved landing strips. Other missions involve aeromedical evacuation and special air support operations. In wartime, the Air Force Reserve Command provides 23% of the Air Force's C-130 airlift force.

In Air Mobility Command associate units, reservists train with active-duty units and fly active-duty aircraft. Six different types of aircraft are flown to support the associate airlift mission: the C-141 Starlifter, C-5 Galaxy, C-9 Nightingale, C-17 Globemaster III, KC-135 Stratotanker, and KC-10 Extender. Because they have dual capability as aerial refueler or cargo transport, the KC-10 and KC-135 are used to meet the Air Force's refueling and airlift requirements. For more information about the Air Force reserve and National Guard, and the numerous fighter and units encompassed within each, you can contact the following:

Websites
www.afreserve.com
www.goang.af.mil

Telephone Recruiting
1-800-257-1212 (Reserve)
1-800-TO-GO-ANG (National Guard)

Army Reserve and National Guard

If you enlist in the Army reserve or National Guard, you will choose one of the available Military Occupational Specialties (MOS) for which you have demonstrated an aptitude. You will be scheduled to attend Advanced Individual Training (AIT) in that MOS after you complete basic training. As with basic training, you will travel at government expense to the Army post that teaches the specialty for which you qualified.

In AIT, you will receive intense, comprehensive classroom and hands-on training in the skill you selected. You will get the same training your active-duty counterparts receive. Most AIT courses last approximately 12 weeks, but actual training duration depends on your specialty. Once your training is complete, you will have numerous opportunities to enhance your skills during drills and annual training periods.

The Army reserve or National Guard is a good part-time career if you have prior military service. Regardless of your branch of previous active-duty service, the time you have invested can work to your advantage. Depending on your branch, your military skill, the length of time since your last discharge, and your unit's needs, you can enter the Army reserve or National Guard at, or close to, your last pay grade. Your active-duty time will count toward reserve or Guard retirement income and benefits. You may not be required to attend the usual initial training period because of your experience in a specialty. You may also have an opportunity to learn a new specialty. There are some opportunities, depending on location, for training in a new specialty and assignment to a unit where that specialty is needed.

Along with standard aviation opportunities, the National Guard also has Special Forces, the elite Green Berets, who specialize in unconventional warfare.

For more information about the Army reserve or National Guard, you can contact the following:

Websites
www.goarmyreserve.com (Reserve)
www.1800goguard.com (National Guard)

Telephone Recruiting
1-800-USA-ARMY (Reserve)
1-800-GO-GUARD (National Guard)

Marine Corps Reserve

The Marine Corps Reserve offers many opportunities to reservists. Here are a few:

THE SELECTED RESERVE INCENTIVE PROGRAM (SRIP)

The SRIP currently offers a monetary incentive to qualified applicants to help maintain a reserve unit's strength. Up to $4,000 is available for a Marine reservist who enlists to serve in a critical unit or job. Check with a local Marine recruiter for availabilities and qualifications.

THE INCREMENTAL INITIAL ACTIVE DUTY FOR TRAINING PROGRAM (IIADT)

The IIADT program is designed especially for college students. It allows you to become a Marine reservist without interrupting your college education. If you qualify, you can enlist in the reserve while still a high school senior. You attend recruit training and become a Marine after high school graduation. As a Marine reservist, you will earn your regular pay and be eligible for GI Bill educational benefits while attending college. As a college student and a Marine reservist, you will attend one weekend drill per month. Depending on your MOS, you will attend one or two summer training sessions to complete your MOS training, then continue your summer training with two-week drills.

THE RESERVE OPTIONAL ENLISTMENT PROGRAM (ROEP)

The Marine reserve offers four drill status options. These options let you decide on the amount of time spent in full-drill status and in the Individual Ready Reserve (IRR). With the 6x2 ROEP, you will drill for six years and spend the last two years in the IRR. This is the most popular option and the one that qualifies you for the GI Bill educational benefits. Other ROEPs include 5x3, 4x4, and 3x5. You can tailor your drill participation to fit your personal needs.

Website

www.marforres.usmc.mil

Telephone Recruiting

If you have never served in the Marine Corps or have served in any other branch of the military, call 1-800-MARINES to speak to a recruiter about joining the Marine reserves.
If you are a Prior Service Marine, call 1-800-255-5082, ext. 3061 to speak with a Prior Service Recruiter.

Navy Reserve

If you are a college graduate and possess the specialty qualifications sought by the Naval reserve, you can be directly appointed as a Naval reserve officer for the purpose of performing that specialty with minimal training.

Most direct-appointment Naval reserve officers attend a two-week indoctrination course at the Naval Air Station in Pensacola, Florida, to learn about the Navy and the Naval reserve. Monthly weekend duty is performed at a naval activity near home, while the two weeks of annual training are usually served at a naval base, air station, Navy or Naval reserve ship, or, in some cases, overseas. For more information about the Navy reserves, you can contact the following:

Website

www.navy-reserve-jobs.com

Telephone Recruiting

1-800-USA-USNR

Aviation Opportunities in Each Branch of the Military

Now that you have found out the basics about becoming a military aviator, it's time to get down to specifics. This chapter explains the aviation programs and training opportunities offered by the Air Force, Army, Navy, Marine Corps, and Coast Guard. Following the requirements listed in this chapter for your particular service is key to success as a military aviator.

Air Force

After you become a commissioned officer, the next step on the road to becoming an Air Force pilot or navigator is meeting the entrance requirements for getting into the Air Force pilot training program. Here are the specific requirements:

1. You must have a bachelor's degree and be a commissioned officer. (See Chapter 1 for information about how to become a commissioned officer.)
2. You must undergo a simple background investigation to determine suitability for duty and must be eligible to obtain a secret security clearance.
3. You must pass a flight physical and meet the Air Force comparative height and weight minimum requirements.

4. The vision requirements are 20/50 (ROTC candidates) or 20/70 (Air Force Academy candidates) for pilots. Navigators must have distance visual acuity no worse than 20/200 and near visual acuity no worse than 20/40 in either eye. Vision for both must be correctable to 20/20. Navigators must also have normal color vision. Applicants who have had their vision corrected through photorefractive keratectomy (PRK), radial keratotomy (RK), or laser in-situ keratomileusis (LASIK) are ineligible for aviation duty.

5. For navigators and fighter pilots, you must be between 64 inches and 77 inches standing and between 34 inches and 40 inches sitting, and you cannot weigh more than 232 pounds.

6. Your date of birth must be after April 1, 1979.

7. Your total active federal commissioned service date must be after April 1, 2005.

8. You must attain minimum required Air Force Officer Qualifying Test (AFOQT) scores—the 25th percentile or higher in the respective category (pilot or navigator-technical) composite. The combined total score of the pilot and the navigator composites must be at least the 50th percentile.

9. Pilot applicants must complete the Test of Basic Aviation Skills (TBAS), formerly the Basic Attributes Test (BAT).

Pilot Training

Once you have met the previous requirements, you will be ready to start pilot training. Pilot training takes approximately one year to complete and is accomplished at various bases around the country, including Vance Air Force Base, Oklahoma; Laughlin Air Force Base, Texas; Columbus Air Force Base, Mississippi; Sheppard Air Force Base, Texas; as well as naval air training bases, depending on your program. After you complete pilot training, you and your fellow students will be placed in rank order based on your performance in undergraduate training. You will then be offered a list of available aircraft from which to choose your desired aircraft. The list is based on how you were ranked and on the needs of the Air Force at the time.

FLIGHT SCREENING

The Air Force screens both pilot and combat systems officer candidates before admitting them to its training program. This screening process is called Initial Flight Screening (IFS). The purpose of this program is to increase the success rate of officers entering Specialized Undergraduate Pilot Training (SUPT). All active-duty, Air National Guard, and Air Force reserve SUPT candidates begin IFS about six months before they start Specialized Undergraduate Pilot Training (SUPT).

The Air Force IFS program is based at Pueblo Memorial Airport in Pueblo, Colorado, and is administered by Doss Aviation. Candidates learn their initial aviation skills in a Diamond DA-20 aircraft, and their training includes the following requirements:

If you do not have a private pilot's license, you must:
1. Complete 25 hours (19 total flight/2 solo program) of flying
2. Complete 83 hours of officer development and ground school/aeronautical training

If you do have a PPL (or higher), you must:
Fly a specified number of hours with a FAA-certified flight instructor; the number of hours to be flown is determined by assessing the amount of time between your last flight review and the date when you will start SUPT.

IFT Program Eligibility

To be eligible for the IFT program you must:

- Be a commissioned officer on active duty in the Air Force awaiting SUPT or be a senior Air Force ROTC cadet who was categorized by the Air Force ROTC Pilot Categorization Board. Air National Guard and Air Force Reserve SUPT candidates must contact their respective command representatives to determine eligibility.
- Have an Air Force–assigned SUPT class date and have been assigned an SUPT base or be a senior Air Force ROTC cadet who was categorized by the Air Force ROTC Pilot Categorization Board.
- Not have been contacted to participate in IFS under the 40-hour program.
- Not be on medical/administrative hold, which would prevent you from attending SUPT.

SPECIALIZED UNDERGRADUATE PILOT TRAINING (SUPT)

Once you successfully complete the IFT program, you can begin the next phase of aviation training, SUPT. Some Air Force aviation students will enter a training program with students from the Navy and Marine Corps called Joint Specialized Undergraduate Pilot Training (JSUPT). While both the Air Force and the naval services also conduct their own, separate flight training programs, JSUPT is a joint service effort to train pilots together by utilizing trainer aircraft, facilities, installations, and instructors from both the Navy and the Air Force.

The SUPT and JSUPT programs are similar; each one lasts about a year and will culminate with your being awarded pilot's wings—provided you remain committed to the task and finish all phases of the program. Undergraduate pilot training consists of intense training and many 12-hour days. However, for most pilot students, the sacrifice is worth it because of their intense desire to fly.

T-6A Texan Used in Air Force Pilot Training

Currently, undergraduate pilot training begins in either the soon-to-be retired T-37 Tweet or the new T-6A Texan II, the first joint training aircraft the Air Force and Navy have used in decades. The T-6A's high power-to-weight ratio, its modern cockpit, zero-zero ejection seat, ease of maintenance, and low operating cost make it a strong replacement for the Air Force T-37 and the Navy T-34 training workhorses. Additionally, it can fly at speeds in excess of 270 knots true air speed. Its certified ceiling is 31,000 feet, and it has a range of more than 900 nautical miles.

The first phase of SUPT/JSUPT, which lasts five weeks, is mostly academics. You will first learn general aerodynamics and engine systems, then flying rules and procedures, safety, egress training, and emergency procedures. And with Navy and Marine students now in the JSUPT course, phase one of JSUPT includes swimming training and water survival tests.

Phase two of SUPT/JSUPT is on the flight line, and it lasts about five months. During this phase, you will team up with an instructor pilot. You will get more schooling on how to fly the T-37 or T-6A and the procedures for flying in a base's busy airspace. Then you will get in the aircraft for your first flight. You can expect to get about 80 hours of flight and 30 hours of simulator time during phase two. It is during phase two training, in the thirteenth week of training when you have about 20 hours of flight time when you will solo.

At the end of phase two, it's evaluation time. Instructors and flight commanders rate your and your fellow students' progress since day one. Scores go into a computer, and the computer creates the class ranking. Then instructors decide which airplane each student will fly in the third phase. They do take into account what kind of plane you want to fly, but "the needs of the service" are always the priority.

Then it is time for phase three of SUPT/JSUPT, which is the specialized advanced track. Phase three lasts approximately five to seven months, depending on the track. Phase three also consists of more ground training for your selected aircraft type. If you are chosen to fly a fighter or a bomber, you will fly the supersonic T-38 Talon. Airlift and tanker troops fly the T-1A Jayhawk. Students who will be flying the C-130 will go to the Naval Air Station in Corpus Christi, Texas, to train in the T-44. Some students will go to the Army base in Fort Rucker, Alabama, for joint helicopter training in the UH-1

Total SUPT/JSUPT training includes between 193 flying hours (for the airlift/tanker track) and 208 flying hours (for the bomber/fighter track).

Students electing to fly fighters are given an introductory course in fighter fundamentals. This training is conducted at Randolph, Columbus, and Sheppard Air Force bases. After this training, students bound for training in the F-15 aircraft are trained at Tyndall Air Force Base, Florida. At Tyndall, different courses are offered for pilots who have never flown a fighter aircraft, experienced pilots converting to or requalifying in the F-15, and pilots selected to become F-15 instructor pilots. Similar training is conducted at Luke Air Force Base, Arizona, for F-16 pilots.

Airlift training for C-5, C-17, C-141 and KC-135 pilots is conducted at Altus Air Force Base, Oklahoma.

Special operations training for pilots in the MC-130 aircraft and the MH-53J and HH-60G helicopters is conducted along with UH-1 training at Kirtland Air Force Base, New Mexico.

Note Regarding Euro-NATO Joint Jet Pilot Training

Euro-NATO Joint Jet Pilot Training is an international effort conducted by the Air Force and its North Atlantic Treaty Organization (NATO) allies. This 55-week program with the 80th Flying Training Wing at Sheppard Air Force Base, Texas, trains pilots from NATO countries as well as some U.S. Air Force pilots. Primary training is conducted in the T-37 and T-6A, while advanced training takes place in the T-38.

TOURS OF DUTY

After completing your pilot training, you have several assignment possibilities available to you. Positions are available worldwide. The assignment officer, along with your squadron commander, will help guide you to different jobs and locations, depending on the needs of the Air Force and your individual desires.

Flight Navigator Training

The Air Force has a joint training program with the Navy and the Marine Corps for the training of Air Force navigators. For information about this training program, see the section titled "Naval Flight Officer/Navigator Training," under the heading "Navy and Marine Corps" that appears toward the end of this chapter.

SUPT/JSUPT Terms to Know

Dollar ride: Rookie pilot's first plane ride. By tradition, when a student makes that ride, he or she has to decorate a dollar bill with highlights of the flight and give it to the instructor. If not, the instructors will hunt the student down and demand payment.

Down: The Navy's "hook" (see below). Only it's a bit more severe. The Air Force gives a hook for any part of a ride. The Navy gives a down to an entire flight. Three downs and you're out.

FAIP: First-assignment instructor pilot. Once a four-letter word, but now respected for bravery. Same as an instructor pilot, but usually younger and better looking.

Hook: A rookie's bad move. What an IP or FAIP gives a student who flunks part of a flight, like making a wheels-up landing. How used: "He hooked that flight rudely."

IP: Instructor pilot. Rookie's mentor, teacher, friend—mom.

Kid: Any new student. Some FAIPs are older kids.

The old man: The wing, group, or flight commander—or anybody who outranks a student, which is just about everybody.

Skipper: The commanding officer of a ship or of a naval aircraft in flight.

Solo: Rookie pilot's first flight without his or her IP or FAIP. Can cause sweats. And it's still a hookable flight.

For More Information

Here are resources for gaining more information about aviation opportunities in the Air Force:

Website
www.af.mil

Telephone Recruiting
1-800-423-USAF

Army

The Army has two routes to becoming a pilot—by becoming a commissioned officer or a warrant officer. As discussed in Chapter 1, one of the big differences between a commissioned and a warrant officer is that a commissioned officer must have a four-year college degree from an accredited institution, whereas a warrant officer is promoted from an enlisted position, which requires only a high school diploma or equivalent.

Commissioned Officers

Here are the basic eligibility requirements for Army aviation training selection for commissioned officers:

1. You must take the Alternate Flight Aptitude Selection Test (AFAST). A score of 90 or higher is required on the AFAST in order to qualify for further processing of an applicant for flight training. Applicants who fail to score 90 may be retested only once, at least six months after first testing.
2. You must meet established medical fitness standards established by the Army and undergo a thorough flight duty medical exam.
3. You must be older than 18, but not more than 33 years of age before the Accession Board convenes. If you have prior service, you will have considerable latitude for an age waiver.

4. Your uncorrected vision must be no worse than 20/50 in each eye and correctable with spectacle lenses to 20/20 in each eye.

5. You must meet certain measurement requirements in your total arm reach, sitting height, and crotch height.

Commissioned aviation officers in the Army normally are selected for one of the following areas of concentration:

> Combined Arms Operations
> Tactical Intelligence
> Logistics

The majority of aviation officers are commissioned through ROTC or the U.S. Military Academy. Some lieutenants are commissioned through the OCS. These officers normally are former aviation warrant officers.

Commissioned Officer Pilot Training

Once you become a newly commissioned officer, you will take the Aviation Officer Basic Course (AVOBC), which includes Initial Entry Rotary Wing (IERW) training, at the U.S. Army Aviation Center in Fort Rucker, Alabama. During your time at Fort Rucker, you will obtain the following types of training:

- Basic Flight
- Aerodynamics
- Meteorology
- Aeromedical
- Instrument Flight
- Combat Skills Training
- Night Vision Goggle Training

The pilot flight training is conducted in three phases, as described here.

PHASE I: TWO-WEEK INTRODUCTORY PHASE

Phase I includes verification of commissioning source programs and integration into the Army and Army aviation. In this phase, you will learn the expected performance standards for lieutenants in the aviation program. Physical fitness and readiness are highly emphasized throughout the course and begin during Phase I. The common core curriculum consists of leadership training, military law, Army and aviation organizations, combined arms doctrine, and the Army safety program. A platoon trainer gives instruction in professionalism, military bearing, appearance, and professional ethics. Additionally, platoon trainer time focuses on student/trainer interaction regarding the roles of a commissioned officer in the Army aviation program. You cannot go on to Phase II training unless you successfully pass the physical training test given in Phase I.

PHASE II: THIRTY-TWO WEEKS OF FLIGHT TRAINING

Phase II is also referred to as Initial Entry Rotary Wing (IERW) training and lasts approximately nine months. The Aviation Training Brigade supports all flight training you will receive in IERW. However, specific subjects instructed during IERW's, approximately 118 program-of-instruction hours are considered AVOBC instruction and focus on tactical training/education, which you must receive prior to assuming duties in the field. Topics include adjustment of field artillery, signal-operating procedures, additional combined arms doctrine, threat identification, and logistics. In other words, training to be an army aviator is not all aviation related. Physical training, managed and monitored by the IERW Phase Commander, continues during Phase II five days a week to ensure the total officer concept is maintained. Senior leaders from the chain of command will provide you with a professional development program each month, focusing on professional responsibilities and what is expected of a lieutenant and officer in the Army. Training progresses from the preflight through the primary and instrument-qualification phases in TH-67 aircraft. You will be tracked into either aeroscout or assault programs during IERW in Phase II.

PHASE III: SIX WEEKS OF WAR-FIGHTING AND LEADERSHIP TRAINING

Phase III is the final phase of AVOBC, and the emphasis of training shifts from individual tactical skills to collective tactical skills. The objective of Phase III is to develop a tactically proficient and effective platoon leader. Upon arrival at Phase III, you will be divided into two platoons: Cavalry/Assault and Attack/Assault. You will be placed in a platoon that matches your aircraft qualification and the future tour of duty needs of the Army. Each platoon is led by a captain platoon trainer during this six-week phase. Physical fitness training in Phase III is designed to illustrate that there are many demanding physical training events that provide variety and excitement for unit physical training once you get into the field. In the Phase III classroom, you will receive instruction on the following topics:

- Aircrew Training Program
- Force Protection
- Aviation Brigade and its Subordinate Units
- Threat Identification and Examination
- Battle-Focused Training
- Operational Terms and Graphics
- Battlefield Operating System
- Aviation Logistics

Practical exercises reinforce all classroom instruction, led by the platoon trainers on terrain boards or in the visual simulator at the aviation test bed. You will be given the opportunity to plan, rehearse, and execute your own mission based on a battalion order provided by the cadre. You will focus on threat vehicle and aircraft identification, risk assessment, fratricide prevention, rehearsals, after-action reviews, and delegation of responsibilities (Mission Planning Cells).

Phase III culminates in a six-day field exercise that incorporates all previous training, including:

- Executing an alert
- Mission brief
- Precombat inspection
- Deployment planning
- Quartering-party operations
- Tactical road march
- Occupation of an assembly area
- Tactical mission planning
- Downed-aviator recovery procedures
- Recovery operations
- After-action review

During Phase III, you will most likely go into Basic Combat Skills and Night Vision Goggles programs in the OH-58C. However, depending on sitting height, taller officers may be required to go through the UH-1H Basic Combat Skills and Night Vision Goggles track. Once you make it through all three pilot training phases successfully, you will be awarded the Army Aviator Badge—that is, your "wings."

AIRCRAFT QUALIFICATION COURSE

After getting your wings, you will attend an advanced Aircraft Qualification Course (AQC) prior to your first assignment. The principle qualification courses are OH-58D(I) Kiowa Warrior, AH-64A Apache, UH-60 Blackhawk, and CH-47 Chinook. In addition, the AH-64D Longbow Apache AQC has recently become available at Fort Rucker, Alabama. You may also request to attend any of these military specialty schools:

- Airborne
- Air Assault
- Master Fitness
- Pathfinder

Officers who attend initial entry flight training will incur a six-year obligation on completion of the course or voluntary termination of attendance.

OH-58 Kiowa Helicopter Used in Army Pilot Training

Warrant Officers

As a warrant officer pilot, you can earn pay and privileges that are much the same as those of a commissioned officer. Warrant officers not only command approximately 80% of the aircraft cockpits in the Army, but they also lead the majority of aircraft flights. You do not need to have any college credits, prior military experience, or flight training to get into the Warrant Officer Flight Training Program. Here are the basic eligibility requirements:

1. You must be at least 18 years of age at the time of the selection board and not have passed your 33rd birthday before the board convenes. High school seniors who will be 18 when they graduate may also apply. If you are not yet 39 years of age, you may request an age waiver.

2. You must score 90 or higher on the revised Alternate Flight Aptitude Selection Test (AFAST). AFAST test results are valid indefinitely as long as verifiable official records exist. No waivers are available for failure to meet the minimum AFAST score.

3. You must earn a minimum 110 General Technical (GT) score on the Armed Forces Vocational Aptitude Battery (ASVAB). This requirement is also nonwaivable. The GT score is one component of the ASVAB results.

4. You must meet the Army's screening height and weight standards.

5. You must take a complete physical exam at a Military Entrance Processing Station (MEPS) and meet entry medical fitness standards as determined by military medical authorities no more than 18 months prior to the date of your application. You must also undergo a Class 1A flight physical examination in addition to the one conducted at the MEPS and have results approved by flight surgeons at Fort Rucker, Alabama, prior to the selection board. The flight physical must also be less than 18 months old.

6. You must be able to obtain secret security clearance.

7. If you have prior military experience, then you must not have more than 10 years of active federal service when appointed as a warrant officer.

Warrant officer candidates earn Sergeant (E–5) pay while in the Warrant Officer Candidate School (WOCS) and are appointed as warrant officers (WO–1) once they graduate; they maintain that status throughout flight school at Fort Rucker.

If you previously served in any branch of the U.S. military, including the U.S. Army reserve and Army National Guard, you are also eligible for this program.

Warrant Officer Pilot Training

If you do not have any prior military experience and are accepted for the WOCS enlistment option, you will attend basic combat training as an enlisted soldier for nine weeks prior to attending the Army WOCS in Fort Rucker, Alabama. If you are an active-duty enlisted member of any of the armed services, you can apply for and go straight to WOCS without having to attend basic combat training.

The WOCS is a six-week course (four for those with prior service) that trains qualified people to serve as warrant officers in the Army. All active Army WOCS graduates are obligated to serve at least six years in warrant officer flight status on active duty. Although applicants are selected from both the Army reserve and Army National Guard, there is currently no reserve component warrant officer flight training option available.

After you finish WOCS, you will begin IERW training at the Army Aviation Center in Fort Rucker, Alabama. During your IERW training, you will be trained alongside newly commissioned officers as well as your fellow warrant officers.

Training to become a warrant officer and fully trained helicopter pilot takes about a year from start to finish. Initial qualification for all warrant officers will be in the TH-67 training helicopter. Upon completion of instrument training, you will transition (qualify) in one of the Army's combat aviation helicopters (such as the OH-58 Scout).

Upon completion of initial flight training, you may receive training in other Army aircraft. Some newly appointed warrant officer aviators will serve an initial utilization tour in the aircraft in which they were last qualified while attending flight school. Most, however, will transition into other systems such as the CH-47 Chinook, AH-64 Apache, OH-58D Kiowa Warrior, or UH-60 Black Hawk in an advanced AQC. A few warrant officer pilots are selected for multiengine fixed-wing training by the Total Army Personnel Command.

Successful completion of the IERW course is a prerequisite to attending the Aviation Warrant Officer Basic Course (AWOBC). The Aviation Warrant Officer Basic Course consists of five major phases of instruction taught over a four-week period:

1. A comprehensive academic program
2. A four-day field training exercise with emphasis on assembly area operations, mission planning, and execution
3. A company/troop-level flight simulation exercise (SIMNET)
4. Weapons familiarization (squad live fire) and 9 mm qualification
5. Survival/Evasion/Resistance Exercise (SEREX)

Completion of the AWOBC will qualify you to earn your wings and be designated as an Army Aviator and will make you eligible for further promotion to Chief Warrant Officer 2 (CW–2). You will receive a commission as a Chief Warrant Officer in the Army.

For More Information

Here are some resources for gaining more information about aviation opportunities in the Army:

Website
www.army.mil

Telephone Recruiting
1-800-USA-ARMY

Navy and Marine Corps

Since the Marine Corps is technically a branch of the Navy, the training for pilots and naval flight officers is similar for both services. Indeed, if you are a Marine student aviator, you will report to the Naval Air Station in Pensacola, Florida, just like the Navy student aviators. The main difference is that Marine student aviators check in with and get support from the Marine Aviation Training Support Group (MATSG), which is located at the Naval Air Station.

Two specialists make up the naval aviation team: the pilot and the naval flight officer. After 12 weeks at OCS or after selection for the aviation program when you are commissioned from the Naval Academy or ROTC, you'll begin flight training as a Navy or Marine Corps officer and then continue training as either a pilot or flight officer.

As a student pilot, you will study aerodynamics, aircraft engine systems, air navigation, flight planning, and meteorology before beginning basic flight training in a high-performance turboprop aircraft. By the time you've successfully completed intermediate and advanced pilot training, you will have achieved the rank of pilot. You will go on to perform a variety of missions, from strike and intercept to surveillance, collection of photographic intelligence or tracking of submarines.

As a student naval flight officer, you will receive specialty training on advanced tactical systems and complex communications equipment. Your course of study will be similar to that of the pilot, including aerodynamics, aircraft engine systems, and air navigation; you will also train in a specialized area such as radar intercept, weapon systems, advanced radar navigation, airborne tactical data systems, or advanced navigation.

After the successful completion of your training, you will be designated as a naval flight officer and will report to a fleet readiness squadron for training in your specific type of fleet aircraft before ultimately reporting to your first operational squadron.

Introductory Flight Screening (IFS)

In 2001 the Navy began a new program designed to better prepare their flight students for the rigors of flight training. The Introductory Flight Screening (IFS) program provides prospective naval aviators and naval flight officers with 25 hours of flight instruction from Federal Aviation Administration–certified flight instructors prior to commencing the Navy's flight training program. Graduation from Navy IFS is mandatory to continue in the flight program.

Aviation Preflight Indoctrination (API)

The next phase of your training is called the Aviation Preflight Indoctrination (API) program. The API division provides commissioned officers in the Navy, Marine Corps, and Coast Guard, as well as selected international military students, with the basic skills and knowledge needed for primary flight training and basic naval flight officer training. Successful completion of this course is a prerequisite for primary pilot flight training and primary naval flight officer training. Aviation Preflight Indoctrination consists of 231 hours of instruction over a six-week period in the following areas:

- Aerodynamics
- Aircraft Engines
- Air Navigation
- Meteorology
- Flight Rules and Regulations
- Aviation Physiology
- Physical Conditioning
- Land and Water Survival Training

Pilot Training

Upon completion of API, you will be assigned to one of five Navy training squadrons for primary pilot flight training using the T-6A Texan II, a single-engine turboprop aircraft. Primary flight training includes the basics of contact, instrument, formation, and aerobatic flying.

T-6A Texan II Used in Navy Pilot Training

After successfully completing primary training, you will be selected for your aviation pipeline and move on to the intermediate phase. Selection is based on personal preference, individual flight performance, and the needs of the service at the time. Student pilots will be selected for one of five pipelines described later in this chapter. Upon completion of your intermediate training, you will be awarded your wings and will then proceed to specific fleet readiness squadrons for specialized training in either a fixed-wing or rotary wing aircraft. Here's a list of the aircraft in each type:

Fixed-Wing	Rotary Wing
F-35 Joint Strike Fighter (expected introduction to the fleet in 2016)	V-22 Osprey (USMC only)
F/A-18 Hornet	SH-60 Seahawk
EA-6B Prowler	H-53 Sea Stallion
P-3 Orion	H-46 Sea Knight
C-130 Hercules	
C-2 Greyhound	
E-2C Hawkeye	

Now let's take a closer look at each phase of pilot training.

PRIMARY FLIGHT TRAINING

Primary flight training is the initial stage of training, in which all students study the same curriculum. In this program, you will learn the fundamentals of flight using the T-6A Texan II Turbomentor turboprop aircraft. The majority of primary training takes place at Whiting Field Naval Air Station in Milton, Florida.

At the end of primary training, you will enter one of five aircraft pipelines for intermediate training.

Where Most Primary Pilot Training Is Conducted— Whiting Field

Selection is based on your grades in primary training and the needs of the service. The options are:

- Jets
- Carrier-based props
- Maritime props
- Helicopters
- E-6 strategic support

INTERMEDIATE AND ADVANCED JETS

Intermediate jet flight training follows primary training if you are selected to fly jets. You will complete intermediate and advanced strike (i.e., jet) training at either Kingsville, Texas, or Meridian, Mississippi, and will learn the basics of jet flight in the two-seat Boeing T-45 Goshawk. You will prepare for carrier qualification through field carrier landing practices.

Advanced jet flight training is the final stage for all jet students. In addition to carrier qualification, you will learn principles such as aerial combat maneuvering (dogfighting) and weapons delivery. Upon completion of advanced jet flight training, you will be awarded your wings of gold.

TYPES OF JETS YOU WILL FLY

Navy tactical jet pilots fly carrier-based aircraft. Skill in carrier operations is what separates jet naval aviators from other pilots. Landing a 25-ton jet on an aircraft carrier in heavy seas demands the ultimate in precision and skill. Marine jet pilots fly traditional missions in support of Marine ground troops, but are also well integrated into the aircraft carrier airwing mission.

The F/A-18 Hornet strike fighter has air-to-ground attack capability in addition to handling air-to-air fighter operations. This single- and dual-cockpit jet is in wide use in both the Navy and the Marine Corps and will also take over the role of the Navy's primary electronics countermeasures jet (EF-18G), replacing the Grumman EA-6B in 2009.

INTERMEDIATE AND ADVANCED CARRIER-BASED PROPS

If you are selected into the carrier-based props pipeline, you will move to Corpus Christi, Texas, for intermediate training after you have completed primary flight training. You will have the opportunity to qualify in multiengine flying using the T-44 Pegasus.

During the advanced stage of carrier-based prop training, you will go to Pensacola, Florida. In this stage, you and all other student aviators who are designated to fly carrier-based prop aircraft will study the same curriculum. You will learn the basics of flight, culminating in carrier landings. You will fly the T-45 Goshawk aircraft. At the end of the advanced stage, you will receive your wings as a naval aviator and proceed to the fleet.

TYPES OF CARRIER PROPS YOU WILL FLY

Carrier prop pilots fly either the E-2C Hawkeye or the C-2A Greyhound. The E-2C is an airborne-early-warning aircraft that provides services for fleet forces under all weather conditions. The C-2 serves as the carrier-on-board delivery aircraft. It transports mail, supplies, and passengers.

INTERMEDIATE MARITIME PROPS AND HELICOPTERS

The intermediate phase of training for the maritime props and helicopter students is identical. It takes place at Whiting Field in the T-34C or the T-6A Texan II, the same aircraft used in the primary training phase. You will accumulate experience in flights devoted to more advanced instrument work, day and night navigation, and airways navigation. Upon successful completion of intermediate training, you will progress to the next step in your respective pipeline, either advanced maritime prop flight training or transition and advanced helicopter flight training.

ADVANCED MARITIME PROPS

The final stage for students in the maritime pipeline takes place at Corpus Christi, Texas, where you will fly the T-44 Pegasus. You will become familiar with the peculiarities of a twin-engine airplane, including single-engine operation. You will also qualify for your instrument ratings during this stage. Finally, the coveted wings of gold are awarded, and you get to report to the fleet for training in your specific aircraft.

TYPES OF MARITIME PROPS YOU WILL FLY

The P-3 Orion is a land-based aircraft with capabilities in all-weather antisubmarine, surveillance, mine warfare, and maritime air-to-surface attack operations. The Marine Corps's logistics support/transport aircraft is the C-130 Hercules.

TRANSITION AND ADVANCED HELICOPTERS

The transition and advanced rotary wing training stages will teach you to fly helicopters. Training is accomplished at Whiting Field utilizing the TH-57 Jet Ranger. After you complete this advanced training phase, you will receive your wings of gold.

TYPES OF HELICOPTERS YOU WILL FLY

Navy and Marine helicopter pilots may fly one of several helos. One example is the CH-53 Sea Stallion, which is configured for minesweeping operations, search and rescue, logistic transport, and vertical replenishment. Marine CH-53s also transport personnel and supplies for landing forces in amphibious operations. Marines fly the UH-1N Huey light helicopter. It provides airborne battlefield command, troop insertion, fire support coordination, and other functions. The SH-60 Seahawk is a light airborne multipurpose system. It provides all-weather antisubmarine warfare and antiship surveillance, in addition to targeting operations. The CH-46 Sea Knight serves in search and rescue and vertical replenishment in support of fleet requirements. The CH-46 is flown by both the Navy and the Marine Corps. As a U.S. Marine Corps rotary-wing pilot, you will also have the new MV-22 Osprey tilt-rotor platform as a type of aircraft you may fly. This vertical-short take-off and landing (VSTOL) aircraft fulfills many multimission operational requirements, both in combat as well as logistical support.

INTERMEDIATE AND ADVANCED E-6s

Earlier this decade, the Navy transitioned to a joint pilot flight training program with the Air Force. Presently, some Navy students receive primary training in the Air Force T-37 trainer, while some Air Force students undergo primary training in the T-6A Texan II at Whiting Field. Navy pilots who are selected for the E-6 pipeline receive their advanced stage training at Tinker Air Force Base in Oklahoma City, Oklahoma. You will get to fly the E-6A Mercury, which is an electronic strategic support aircraft in a Boeing 707 airframe. It performs the Take Charge and Move Out (TACAMO) mission, which provides a communication link from the National Command Authority to all strategic forces.

Naval Flight Officer/ Navigator Training

The Navy and Marine Corps have a joint training program with the Air Force for the training of naval flight officers and navigators; it's called Joint Undergraduate Navigation Training (JUNT). The training program consists of three phases: primary, intermediate, and advanced. These three phases of training take place at Sherman Field at the Naval Air Station in Pensacola, Florida, at the Naval Air Station at Jacksonville, Florida, and at Tinker Air Force Base in Oklahoma City, Oklahoma. The naval flight officer/navigator training squadrons train hundreds of students each year. The instructors for the joint training programs come from the Navy, Marine Corps, and Air Force.

PRIMARY NAVAL FLIGHT OFFICER/ NAVIGATOR TRAINING

The primary phase of training for flight officers/navigators lasts 17 weeks at the Naval Air Station in Pensacola, Florida. In this phase, you will fly seven familiarization flights in the T-6 Texan and 15 airways navigation flights. You will spend the first three weeks learning the basics of air navigation, T-6 systems, meteorology, flight regulations, and emergency procedures.

After simulator training, you will sit in the front seat of a T-6 for seven familiarization flights. This portion of your training is much like pilot training, because you need to know what pilots deal with while commanding an aircraft. The biggest difference from the pilot primary training phase is that you will not fly alone. While in the air, you will get to orient yourself to the three-dimensional world of flight. During the airways navigation portion of primary training, you will learn how to fly from point A to point B without violating any FAA regulations.

At the end of the primary phase, you may be selected to go on to advanced panel navigator training at either the Naval Air Station in Jacksonville, Florida, (if you are selected for the P-3 or EP-3 pipeline) or Tinker Air Force Base (if you are an Air Force flight student or if you are a Navy E-6 platform selectee), or you will continue through the intermediate naval flight officer/navigator training at the Naval Air Station in Pensacola, Florida.

About 60% of the students will be selected for the jet syllabus and will remain at the Naval Air Station for intermediate training. If you are selected for advanced panel navigator training, you will eventually fly in Navy P-3, EP-3, and E-6A aircraft or Air Force KC-135, RC-135, C-141, and any variant of the C-130 aircraft, depending on your branch of service.

INTERMEDIATE NAVAL FLIGHT OFFICER/ NAVIGATOR TRAINING

The intermediate phase of training consists of nine weeks in Pensacola, Florida. In this phase, you will continue to fly the T-6 for 10 airways navigation flights, four visual navigation flights, two formation flights, and one combined airways/visual navigation checkflight. Upon completing T-6 training, you will go on to fly the T-1A Jayhawk for four airways navigation flights, three visual navigation flights, and one combined airways/visual navigation checkflight. Upon completing the intermediate phase, you will be selected for Navy E-2C training or the Electronic Warfare Officer (EWO) school for the Air Force's B-52, RC-135, and EC-130 aircraft. Remaining students not selected for either E-2C or EWO training will continue to advanced naval flight officer/navigator training.

ADVANCED NAVAL FLIGHT OFFICER/ NAVIGATOR TRAINING

Advanced training for naval flight officers and navigators is conducted at the Naval Air Station in Pensacola and at Columbus Air Force Base. The advanced training in Pensacola is handled by Training Squadron 86, and the advanced training at Columbus is handled by the Twelfth Flying Training Wing. During the advanced stage of training, you will refine your navigational techniques and learn about radar navigation and intercepts.

Strike and Strike-Fighter Advanced Training

Advanced training in VT-86 lasts from 20 to 28 weeks in Pensacola. This is the only training program where you can train in the T-39 Sabreliner and the T-45 Goshawk aircraft. After 10 weeks of initial training in the advanced squadron, you will be selected to either the Strike syllabus or Strike-Fighter syllabus. After continued training, Strike students will earn their wings and go on to fly Navy EA-6B Prowlers, or Air Force B-52 Stratofortresses or B-1B Lancers. Strike-Fighter students will eventually earn their wings after continued advanced training and go on to fly the Navy/Marine Corps F/A-18 Hornet or Air Force F-15E Strike Eagle.

Panel Navigator Advanced Training

The advanced panel navigator training program takes place at Randolph Air Force Base and is handled by the Twelfth Flying Training Wing, which conducts undergraduate training for Air Force, Navy, and Marine Corps personnel in the JSUNT program and the Marine Aerial Navigation School. The largest of the wing's training programs, these courses offer you the opportunity to earn your wings and an aeronautical rating as a navigator, electronic warfare officer, or naval flight officer. In this phase of training, you will fly the T-6A Texan, the T-1A Jayhawk, the T-39 Sabreliner, and the T-43 (a modified Boeing 737-200).

The JSUNT program is 32 weeks long and is divided into academic, T-45 simulator, and T-43 flight instruction. This program trains navigators and naval flight officers headed for heavy aircraft such as the KC-135, E-3, C-130, E-6A, C-141, and P-3.

The Electronic Warfare Officer Training School moved to Randolph Air Force Base from the Naval Air Station in Pensacola in May 1999. It provides specialized training for undergraduate navigator students selected to train as electronic warfare officers and weapon systems officers.

The Marine Aerial Navigation School is 24 weeks long and offers academic, T-45, and T-43 training. This program is staffed by Marine Corps instructors and prepares navigators to fly C-130 cargo aircraft.

T-43 Used in Navigator and Flight Officer Training

For More Information

Here are some resources for gaining more information about aviation opportunities in the Navy and Marine Corps:

Navy Website
www.navy.mil

Navy Telephone Recruiting
1-800-327-NAVY

Marine Corps Website
www.usmc.mil

Marine Corps Telephone Recruiting
1-800-MARINES

Coast Guard

The use of aircraft to support Coast Guard missions has resulted in career paths with significant potential for aviation officers. In fact, nearly 15% of the Coast Guard officer corps wear the gold wing. Officers entering this specialty can expect to spend the greater portion of their career applying aviation skills while performing a variety of missions in Coast Guard aircraft.

As the nation's only branch of the armed forces with domestic law enforcement authority, the Coast Guard is involved daily in enforcing federal law in the areas of drug interdiction, immigration, marine environmental protection, marine safety, fisheries, and general federal laws applicable in the maritime environment.

There are four ways one can become a Coast Guard aviator—via acceptance to the U.S. Coast Guard Academy and being selected for the aviation program, through USCG Officer Candidate School (OCS) and being accepted for aviation training, through the USCG Blue 21 Program (OCS with a guarantee of flight training), or via direct commissioning from another service.

All these paths to becoming a Coast Guard aviator include the following basic eligibility requirements:

1. You must be a U.S. citizen.
2. You must be over 21 and under 32 years of age (34 for the Direct Commissioning Program).
3. You must meet physical standards prescribed by the Coast Guard.
4. You cannot be on active duty in the military (except for the Coast Guard) at the time of commissioning, or you must submit a letter of resignation from your current service with your application.
5. You cannot have more than 10 years of active-duty experience (six years of active-duty experience for OCS and the Blue 21 Program).
6. You must have full-time military or civilian flight experience within two years of the published application deadline (direct commissioning program only).
7. You need to have a bachelor's degree or to have completed 30 semester hours (45 quarter hours) at an accredited college or university.
8. You must have served a minimum of two years as either a warrant officer in the Army or a commissioned officer in any of the armed forces (direct commissioning program only).
9. You must present evidence of being a military-rated pilot with a minimum of 500 flight hours (direct commissioning program only).

The USCG uses the U.S. Navy's Aviation Selection Test Battery (ASTB) as its aptitude test for selection to its aviation programs.

Pilot Training

The USCG uses the U.S. Navy's Aviation Selection Test Battery (ASTB) as its aptitude test for selection to its aviation programs. After being selected for flight training and qualifying physically, an academy or OCS graduate enters Coast Guard flight training at the Naval Air Training Command in Pensacola, Florida. Based on current service needs, you may pursue a course of study leading to qualification as a rotary-wing (helicopter) or fixed-wing (multiengine) aviator. If you successfully complete the advanced phase of flight training, you will be designated as a Coast Guard aviator—you must meet the same standards and achieve the same qualifications to wear the same wings as your Navy and Marine Corps counterparts. Upon graduation, you will be obligated to serve eight years in addition to any other educational or training-related service obligation you had before entering flight training.

Specific Coast Guard aviation training is conducted at the Aviation Training Center in Mobile, Alabama, the Aviation Technical Training Center in Elizabeth City, North Carolina, and at the Coast Guard Air Station at Clearwater, Florida. Lasting between 18 and 24 months, Coast Guard flight training prepares officers for aviation duty. Naval flight training consists of ground school courses (academics, aircraft systems, land and sea survival) followed by primary and intermediate flight training in basic fixed-wing aircraft. Advanced flight training involves specializing in fixed-wing aircraft or helicopters while continuing ground school courses in advanced navigation and overwater operations. Following completion of flight training and designation as a Coast Guard aviator, you can move on to complete transitional training in a Coast Guard aircraft.

The Coast Guard Aviation Training Center is located at the Regional Airport in Mobile, Alabama; it provides training for Coast Guard pilots in the HH-60 Jayhawk, the HH-65 Dolphin, and the HU-25A Falcon. This center is the largest air unit in the Coast Guard, with more than 575 personnel. It provides initial and recurrent training to all Coast Guard HU-25, HH-65, and HH-60 pilots in addition to conducting aircrew training and ensuring that Coast Guard air stations and flight-deck-equipped Coast Guard cutters are mission ready. If you become a jet or helicopter pilot in the Coast Guard, you will receive an initial transition into Coast Guard aircraft and return once a year for a week of intensive refresher training on one of three flight simulators, including the $25 million HH-60 Jayhawk simulator.

HH-60 Jayhawk Used in Coast Guard Pilot Training

TYPES OF AIRCRAFT YOU WILL FLY

Coast Guard aircraft cover the entire profile of Coast Guard operations. From helicopters operating off flight-deck-equipped cutters supporting law enforcement and search-and-rescue missions to long-range patrols in fixed-wing aircraft supporting the International Ice Patrol to high-speed jets intercepting airborne drug smugglers, Coast Guard aircraft are involved in every mission area. Aviation support must be available day or night, regardless of weather; therefore, Coast Guard aviators must be accomplished all-weather pilots.

Direct Commission Aviator Program

In addition to officers sent to flight training, the Coast Guard may grant direct commissions (at the lieutenant junior grade or ensign level) to individuals who have completed a military flight training program in another service. The application and selection process for these officers is managed through Coast Guard recruiting. If this applies to you, you can bypass boot camp, OCS, and flight training and go straight to a four-week indoctrination course at the Coast Guard Academy in New London, Connecticut. This four-week course offers you an introduction to the history, roles, and missions of the Coast Guard. From there you will receive a transition into a Coast Guard aircraft prior to reporting to your first duty station.

You will be commissioned as an ensign (O–1) if you are a prior Army warrant officer aviator or as a lieutenant (junior grade, O–2) if you are a prior commissioned officer from another service. The Coast Guard has the same rank structure as the Navy. The rank of ensign corresponds to the rank of second lieutenant in the Army, Air Force, and Marine Corps.

Your first duty station assignment will be at one of the Coast Guard's 26 aviation units. Your background (fixed-wing or rotary) and the needs of the service will determine your exact duty station.

Tour of Duty

Once you become a Coast Guard aviator, you may have a rotation out-of-specialty (sometimes called a rotational tour) after your first or second aviation tour. These rotational tours may include career-broadening assignments in district command centers or on various staffs at the district, area, and headquarters level. An aviator rotating out-of-specialty while in the grades of lieutenant or lieutenant commander can normally expect to return to a duty-standing aviation tour.

For More Information

Here are some resources for gaining more information about aviation opportunities in the Coast Guard:

Website
www.uscg.mil
www.gocoastguard.com

Telephone Recruiting
1-877-NOW-USCG

Aviation Program
Aviation Assignment Officers
1-202-267-6025 or 1-202-267-1680

Office of Aviation Management
1-202-267-0952

3 ▶ Test Maneuvers: Explanation of Military Flight Aptitude Tests

Each branch of the U.S. armed forces that has an aviation component—Army, Navy, and Air Force—has its own aptitude or qualifying test that emphasizes job-related skills within that service, but the academic sections of those tests are fairly standard to all the Armed Forces. Because of that, some portions of the tests, such as Instrument Comprehension and Mechanical Knowledge, will be much the same from one service to the next. The U.S. Marine Corps and the U.S. Coast Guard both use the Navy's Aviation Selection Test Battery (ASTB) as their aptitude or qualifying test.

The practice exam in Chapter 4 is a combination of the subject areas most commonly tested in the selection of pilots and aviation officers. Taking it will help you get a feel for any of the services' qualifying tests.

Each service has different requirements for taking its test, and being familiar with those requirements is as important as having a knowledge of the subject matter. Specific information about each test follows.

Air Force Officer Qualifying Test

The Air Force Officer Qualifying Test, or AFOQT, is a standardized test that resembles the SAT and ACT. You must achieve minimum scores in each of its 12 sections in order to become an officer and to be accepted into training in the career field of pilot or navigator. You also must pass the test in order to attend field training between your sophomore and junior years of college.

Cadets are allowed to take the AFOQT only twice during their college years. If you have already completed at least a bachelor's degree, you will take the AFOQT as part of your application process for acceptance into the 12-week officer commissioning program, Officer Training School (OTS). For additional information about the OTS option, contact your local Air Force recruiter or talk to an officer at a nearby university's Air Force ROTC program.

If you fail the test the first time, you may take it again following a six-month waiting period. This gives you an opportunity to review and study those areas in which you may be weak or less confident. If someone fails the test on the second try, he or she is removed from the ROTC program.

The AFOQT is made up of 12 subtests. The subtests and the time allotted for each follow.

Subtest	# of Questions	Time Limit
Verbal Analogies	25 questions	8 minute
Arithmetic Reasoning	25 questions	29 minutes
Instrument Comprehension	20 questions	6 minutes
Block Counting	20 questions	3 minutes
Word Knowledge	25 questions	5 minutes
Table Reading	40 questions	7 minutes
Math Knowledge	25 questions	22 minutes
Aviation Information	20 questions	8 minutes
Rotated Blocks	15 questions	13 minutes
General Science	20 questions	10 minutes
Hidden Figures	15 questions	8 minutes
Self-Description Inventory	220 items	40 minutes

The scores from each of these subtests are combined to create five composite scores, which are used to help determine your aptitude for the various career fields within the Air Force. The five composite scores cover the areas of pilot, navigator-technical, academic aptitude, quantitative, and verbal. All cadets take the complete test whether they are seeking to become a pilot or to enter any of the Air Force's other career specialties. The five composite blocks are described as follows.

Pilot

This area gauges knowledge and abilities that are necessary to complete pilot training successfully. This composite includes subtests that measure your verbal ability, your knowledge of aviation and mechanical systems, your ability to determine aircraft altitude and attitude by instruments, your understanding of aeronautical concepts, your ability to read scales and interpret tables, and some spatial comprehension.

Navigator-Technical

This block measures knowledge and abilities necessary to complete navigator training successfully. It shares many of the subtests included in the pilot composite, but the subtests measuring verbal ability, determination of aircraft altitude, and knowledge of aeronautical concepts are not included. Subtests that measure your quantitative aptitude, some spatial or visual abilities, and your knowledge of general science are added instead.

Academic Aptitude

This composite measures verbal and quantitative knowledge and abilities. The academic composite combines all of the subtests used to score both the verbal and quantitative composites.

Verbal

This area measures a variety of verbal abilities and knowledge. This composite includes subtests measuring your abilities to reason, to recognize relationships between words, to read and understand paragraphs on a wide range of topics, and to understand synonyms.

Quantitative

This block measures a number of quantitative abilities and knowledge. This composite shares several subtests with the navigator-technical composite described previously. It includes subtests that measure your ability to understand and reason with arithmetic relationships, to interpret data from graphs and charts, and to apply mathematical terms, formulae, and relationships.

Army Alternate Flight Aptitude Selection Test

Like the AFOQT, the Army's Alternate Flight Aptitude Selection Test, or AFAST, is a test that measures your specific aptitudes, personality traits, and characteristics. It is used to help predict your likelihood of succeeding in the Army's helicopter flight training program. It is *not* an intelligence test; it simply determines your aptitudes. The AFAST is part of the Army Personnel Testing (APT) program. It is the prime tool used for determining eligibility for aviation-specific programs.

Becoming an Army aviator requires you to have special skills. The most important of these include the ability to comprehend complex processes, to adapt quickly to spatial relation situations, and to process large amounts of information rapidly. Because flight training is very expensive and there are limited quotas for new students, it is necessary to screen applicants to ensure that only those with the capabilities to succeed in flight school are accepted for training. The AFAST has been developed to assist in the selection process.

The AFAST has a total of 200 questions divided into seven subtests, each of which has its own instructions and time limits. The seven subtests are listed here with the number of questions and time limit allowed to complete the subtest.

Subtest	# of Questions	Time Limit
Self-Description	75 questions	25 minute
Background Information	25 questions	10 minutes
Instrument Comprehension	15 questions	5 minutes
Complex Movements	30 questions	5 minutes
Helicopter Knowledge	20 questions	10 minutes
Cyclic Orientation	15 questions	5 minutes
Mechanical Functions	20 questions	10 minute

Your application for flight training will be considered only if your AFAST score is equal to or higher than the qualifying (cutoff) score. The current cutoff score is 90 out of a possible 176. If you meet or exceed the cutoff score, you may not retest. Because of this, it's to your advantage to earn as high a score as you can on the test.

Applicants who score below the established cutoff score may retest only once. As with the AFOQT, you must wait six months after testing the first time. This six-month waiting period cannot be waived.

You can't really study for the AFAST, because it is an aptitude test. This means, however, it will be helpful for you to become familiar and comfortable with the information in each of the subtest areas. This will help you decrease the time it takes for you to answer the questions and improve your overall score.

You are required to read DA PAM 611-256-2, the AFAST information pamphlet, prior to taking the AFAST. To obtain a copy of this pamphlet, you can contact your local Army recruiter, the Army ROTC detachment at any university, or download it off the internet. The pamphlet is designed to provide general information and a clearer understanding of the test before you take it. You will be required to verify on block 11 of the AFAST answer sheet that you have had sufficient time to review DA PAM 611-256-2 prior to taking the test. This is very important, as you will not be allowed to retest if you claim you didn't have sufficient time to review the pamphlet once you have filled in block 11 on the answer sheet.

Retaking the AFAST is not authorized for the purpose of improving a qualifying score. You can retest only if you receive a nonqualifying score. A third attempt at the test is not allowed.

Navy Aviation Selection Test Battery

The Aviation Selection Test Battery, or ASTB, was developed by the Bureau of Medicine and Surgery (BUMED) in conjunction with the Naval Aerospace Medical Institute (NAMI) in Pensacola, Florida. All midshipmen and all potential U.S. Coast Guard personnel considering aviation as a career must pass this exam. It is used by the naval aviation (including USMC) community and the USCG in the selection of potential naval aviators and flight officers and is based on the characteristics of successful officers within the aviation community. It is also a significant part of your service selection ranking against other potential aviators.

The ASTB consist of six subtests, listed as follows with the number of questions and time limit allowed to complete the subtest:

Subtest	# of Questions	Time Limit
Math Skills Test (MST)	30 questions	25 minutes
Reading Skills Test (RST)	27 questions	25 minutes
Mechanical Comprehension Test (MCT)	30 questions	15 minutes
Spatial Apperception Test (SAT)	25 questions	10 minutes
Aviation and Nautical Information Test (ANIT)	30 questions	15 minutes
Aviation Supplemental Test (AST)	34 questions	25 minutes

Six scores are taken from your ASTB test. The first five areas are graded on a curve, with one (1) being the minimum score and nine (9) being the highest. The OAR portion is irrelevant for Navy ROTC midshipmen. These are the categories and possible scores:

Academic Qualification Rating (AQR) 1–9
Pilot Flight Aptitude Rating (PFAR) 1–9
Flight Officer Flight Aptitude Rating (FOFAR) 1–9
Officer Aptitude Rating (OAR) 20–80

The AQR, PFAR, and FOFAR scores predict a candidate's future performance.

Midshipmen from all Navy ROTC units nationwide compete for the available aviation billets. An aviation service selection score is computed for all physically qualified midshipmen who would like to go into naval aviation. The top candidates are then selected. The service selection criteria include a number of the following functional areas and the weighted values from each area differ based on your commissioning source:

■ Cumulative Grade Point Average (GPA)
■ Adjusted Aptitude (fall of first year only)
■ Academic Major
■ Subjective Evaluation (assigned by Commanding Officer [CO])
■ Academic Qualification Rating (AQR)
■ PFAR (for pilots) or FOFAR (for Naval Flight Officers [NFOs])

Past ASTB tests included a Biographical Inventory (BI) section; however, that portion was removed when, after student attrition data was analyzed, it was apparent the BI's ability to predict program completion had declined over the years.

Obviously, the way to get the best score is to get a 4.0 (4.0 grading scale) in a technical major, get a 4.0 fall evaluation, and score well on the ASTB. If you are not a midshipman in a Navy ROTC program and have already earned at least a bachelor's degree, you may be eligible to apply through the Navy's OCS program. Contact your local Navy recruiter or the testing officer at the Navy ROTC detachment of a nearby university for additional information.

You *must* take the ASTB in order to apply for an aviator billet in the Navy. The test is a large part of your ranking against other Navy ROTC midshipmen and OCS candidates in the service selection process.

A full 40% of your ranking will be based on this two-and-a-half-hour test, so you can see how critical it is to your selection. If you *are* a midshipman in a Navy ROTC program, take the ASTB early, as official scoring takes time. Take the test for the first time during the spring of your junior year, and take it the second time during September or October of your senior year.

One major change to the ASTB that occurred in June 2004 was the establishment of a three-test lifetime limit. You can still take the test more than one time; however, you must wait 30 days between tests, and you can take the test only three times.

Most midshipmen improve on the second attempt taking the ASTB. Take notes on the portions you found most challenging immediately after you finish the first test, review those areas, and then take it again. **If you take the test a second time, remember that the second test is the only one that counts.** If your scores are good on the first try, you may not want to take it again. **Once you pass, your scores are good for life! You *must* pass this test to become an aviator.**

It may be helpful to you to know that none of these tests has a penalty for guessing if you are not certain of the answers. With multiple-choice questions, it is usually easy to quickly eliminate at least one and often two choices (known as "distracters") as obvious wrong answers. Doing this increases your chances of choosing the correct answer in cases where you may be uncertain. Some tests are given on computerized systems, however, which will not allow you to skip questions and go back to them later. If you are taking this sort of test, you will have to guess on answers you are unsure of in order to get any credit at all for those questions.

Now that you are familiar with each service's specific requirements, go ahead and take the short sample test. This will help you get a feel for the kinds of questions asked, and allow you to see how well you would do if you were to take any of these tests today. After you are familiar with the types of questions, you will be able to use the full-length practice tests to improve your score.

C H A P T E R

Sample Military Flight Aptitude Test Questions

The sample test in this chapter consists of 18 different sections common to at least two if not all three of the aviation selection tests. For these sample questions, don't worry about time limits. Just work at a steady, relaxed pace. The answers and rationale are provided in Chapter 5.

Section 1: Verbal Analogies

DIRECTIONS: This part of the test measures your ability to reason and see relationships between words. Choose the answer that best completes the analogy developed at the beginning of each question. The best way to approach this type of test is to look for patterns or comparisons between the first phrase and the choices available to you.

1. FLIGHT STATION is to AIRPLANE as BRIDGE is to
   a. tunnel
   b. road
   c. ship
   d. mountain
   e. highway

2. RACQUET is to COURT as
   a. tractor is to field
   b. blossom is to bloom
   c. stalk is to prey
   d. plan is to strategy
   e. moon is to planet

3. SWEATER is to CLOTHES as
   a. bottle is to cork
   b. hand is to finger
   c. shoe is to foot
   d. rose is to flowers
   e. dog is to cat

4. ROW is to BOAT as SAIL is to
   a. ocean
   b. navigate
   c. rudder
   d. ship
   e. travel

5. FLY is to AIRPLANE as
   a. drive is to stake
   b. skate is to slide
   c. push is to fall
   d. swim is to float
   e. rod is to hook

Section 2: Arithmetic Reasoning

DIRECTIONS: This section of the test measures mathematical reasoning and problem solving. Each problem is followed by five possible answers. Decide which one of the five answers is correct. A method for attacking each of these questions is given in the answer block in Chapter 5.

1. A field with an area of 420 square yards is twice as large in area as a second field. If the second field is 15 yards long, how wide is it?
   a. 7 yards
   b. 14 yards
   c. 28 yards
   d. 56 yards
   e. 9 yards

2. A passenger plane can carry two tons of cargo. A freight plane can carry five tons of cargo. If an equal number of both kinds of planes are used to ship 105 tons of cargo, and each plane carries its maximum cargo load, how many tons of cargo are shipped on the passenger planes?
   a. 15 tons
   b. 30 tons
   c. 42 tons
   d. 52.5 tons
   e. 75 tons

3. A fighter jet was scheduled to fly four sorties. The average duration of the sorties flown was 93 minutes. If sortie one and two were canceled, what was the duration of sortie four?
   a. 288 minutes
   b. 93 minutes
   c. 168 minutes
   d. 195 minutes
   e. 126 minutes

4. A recruiting station enlisted 450 people. Of these, 40% were under 22 years old. How many of the recruits were over 22 years old?
   a. 130
   b. 140
   c. 175
   d. 180
   e. 270

5. If an aircraft travels at 330 miles per hour, how far did the aircraft fly in 1,800 seconds?

a. 11 miles

b. 300 miles

c. 30 miles

d. 165 miles

e. 660 miles

Section 3: Reading Skills

DIRECTIONS: This part of the test measures your ability to read and understand paragraphs. For each question, choose the answer that best completes the meaning of the paragraph. Pay close attention as you read, and try to find the point that the author is trying to make. Once you have read the paragraph all the way through, you will find that one or two of the possible answers can be quickly eliminated based on the context.

1. If they are to function effectively, organizations, like other systems, must achieve a natural harmony, or coherence, among their component parts. The structural and situational elements of an effective organization form themselves into a tightly knit, highly cohesive package. An organization whose parts are mismatched, however, cannot carry out its missions. If managers are to design effective organizations, they need to

a. simplify organizational structures.

b. encourage greater specialization of labor.

c. emphasize the fit of organizational parts.

d. introduce more technological innovations.

e. reduce the span of control in the organization.

2. First, *Clostridium botulinum*, the bacterium that produces the poison, must be present. These bacteria are widespread in the environment and are considered by some to be everywhere. Second, the bacterium that produces the deadly toxin must be treated to an atmosphere that's free of oxygen and to temperatures that are just warm enough, but not too warm. These conditions have to be held long enough for the toxin to develop. Acid will prevent the growth of the organism and the production of the toxin. The following condition is necessary for botulism to develop

a. the presence of oxygen.

b. a brief period of time.

c. the presence of acid.

d. warm temperatures.

e. exposure to rare bacteria.

3. Due to our short lifespan of 70-odd years, it is easy for human beings to think of the earth as a planet that never changes. Yet we live on a dynamic planet with many factors contributing to change. We know that wind and rain erode and shape our planet. Many other forces are also at work, such as volcanic activity, temperature fluctuations, and even extraterrestrial interaction such as meteors and gravitational forces. The earth, in actuality, is a large rock

a. in a state of inertia.

b. that is quickly eroding.

c. that is evolving.

d. that is subject to temperature fluctuations caused by interplanetary interaction.

e. that is subject to winds caused by meteor activity.

4. *Mustela nigripes*, the rarely seen black-footed ferret, is often confused with *Mustela putorius*, the common European polecat. It is true that these two mammals resemble each other in some ways. However, they are two distinct and separate species, with differences in color, body form, and other attributes. Who knows how many sightings of the black-footed ferret

   a. were the result of seeing the European polecat running loose?

   b. were of species other than the common European polecat?

   c. were made of a related species of the same form and color?

   d. were instead sightings of *Mustela nigripes*?

   e. were due to the European polecat destroying their habitat?

5. One theory that explains the similarities between Mayan art and ancient Chinese art is called diffusion. This theory evolves from the belief that invention is so unique that it happens only once, and then it is diffused to other cultures through travel, trade, and war. This theory might explain why

   a. the airplane and birds both have wings.

   b. certain artifacts in Central America resemble those found in Southeast Asia.

   c. most great art comes from Europe, where there is much travel between countries.

   d. rivers in South America and Africa have similar features.

   e. England, being so remote in the Middle Ages, is the only country to have castles.

Section 4: Word Knowledge

DIRECTIONS: This part of the test measures your vocabulary. For each question, choose the answer that most closely means the same as the capitalized word. If you are somewhat familiar with the capitalized word, you can quickly eliminate the options that you know are incorrect.

1. CRIMSON
   a. crisp
   b. neatly dressed
   c. reddish
   d. colorful
   e. lively

2. CEASE
   a. start
   b. change
   c. continue
   d. stop
   e. fold

3. BENIGN
   a. harmless
   b. active
   c. dangerous
   d. unfavorable
   e. explosion

4. SULLEN
   a. grayish yellow
   b. soaking wet
   c. very dirty
   d. angrily silent
   e. mildly nauseated

5. TERSE
   a. pointed
   b. trivial
   c. oral
   d. lengthy
   e. raggedy

Section 5: Math Knowledge

DIRECTIONS: This part of the test measures your ability to use learned mathematical relationships. Each problem is followed by five possible answers. You must decide which one of the five answers is correct. The best method for attacking each of these questions is given in the answer block in Chapter 5. When you take the actual test, scratch paper will be provided for working out the problems.

1. The first digit of the square root of 59,043 is
   a. 1
   b. 2
   c. 3
   d. 4
   e. 5

2. The distance in miles around a circular course with a radius of 35 miles is (use pi $= \frac{22}{7}$)
   a. 110 miles.
   b. 156 miles.
   c. 220 miles.
   d. 440 miles.
   e. 880 miles.

3. The expression *4 factorial* equals
   a. $\frac{1}{4}$
   b. $\frac{1}{16}$
   c. 12
   d. $\frac{1}{24}$
   e. 24

4. Solve for x: $\frac{2x}{7} = 2x^2$
   a. $\frac{1}{7}$
   b. $\frac{2}{7}$
   c. 2
   d. 7
   e. 14

5. The reciprocal of 5 is
   a. 0.1
   b. 0.2
   c. 0.5
   d. 1.0
   e. 2.0

Section 6: Mechanical Comprehension

DIRECTIONS: This part of the test measures your ability to understand and reason with mechanical terms. Included in this part of the test are diagrams showing various mechanical devices. Following each diagram are several questions or incomplete statements. Study each diagram carefully, as details do make a difference in how each device operates, and then select the choice that best answers the question or completes the statement.

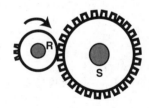

1. If gear R is the driver, at the moment shown, gear S is
   a. not moving.
   b. jammed.
   c. moving at a high speed.
   d. moving in the same direction as R.
   e. moving in the opposite direction as gear R.

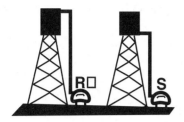

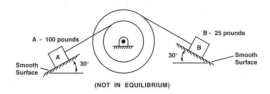

(NOT IN EQUILIBRIUM)

2. Which water wheel will turn for the longer time?

a. R

b. S

c. Both wheels will turn an equal amount of time.

d. Neither wheel will turn at all.

e. This cannot be determined from the figure.

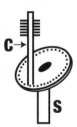

3. As shaft S makes one complete turn from the position shown, C moves

a. left, then right.

b. right, then left.

c. up only.

d. down only.

e. up and down.

4. If weight B is to slide to the right, what change must be made in the diagram?

a. The slope of the inclined plane under A must be increased.

b. The slope of the inclined plane under B must be increased.

c. The radius of the inner pulley must be decreased.

d. The radius of the inner pulley must be increased to a size nearer to that of the outer pulley.

e. The radius of the outer pulley must be twice that of the inner pulley.

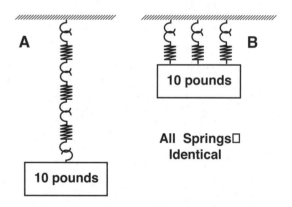

All Springs Identical

5. Ten-pound weights are each suspended from a ceiling by three identical springs. In drawing A, the extension of each spring is

a. nine times greater than in B.

b. three times greater than B.

c. the same as in B.

d. $\frac{1}{3}$ less than in B.

e. $\frac{1}{9}$ less than in B.

Section 7:
Instrument Comprehension

DIRECTIONS: This test measures your ability to determine the position of an aircraft in flight by reading instruments showing its compass heading, its amount of climb or dive, and its degree of bank to right or left. In each test item, the left-hand dial is labeled ARTIFICIAL HORIZON. The small aircraft silhouette remains stationary on the face of this dial, while the positions of the heavy black line and black pointer vary with the changes in the position of the aircraft in which the instrument is located.

The heavy black line represents the HORIZON LINE, and the black pointer shows the degree of BANK to right or left. If the aircraft is neither climbing nor diving, the horizon line is directly on the silhouette's fuselage. If the aircraft has no bank, the black pointer will point to zero (Dial 1).

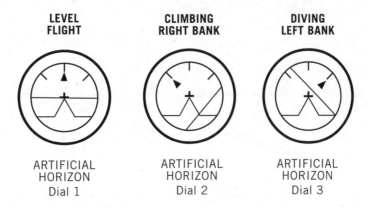

LEVEL FLIGHT

CLIMBING RIGHT BANK

DIVING LEFT BANK

ARTIFICIAL HORIZON
Dial 1

ARTIFICIAL HORIZON
Dial 2

ARTIFICIAL HORIZON
Dial 3

If the aircraft is climbing, the fuselage silhouette is seen between the horizon line and the pointer. The greater the amount of climb, the greater the distance between the horizon line and the fuselage silhouette. If the aircraft is banked to the pilot's right, the pointer will point to the left of zero (Dial 2).

If the aircraft is diving, the horizon line is between the fuselage silhouette and the pointer. The greater the amount of dive, the greater the distance between the horizon line and the fuselage silhouette. If the aircraft is banked to the pilot's left, the pointer will point to the right of zero (Dial 3).

The HORIZON LINE tilts as the aircraft is banked. It is always at a right angles to the pointer.

In each test item, the right-hand dial is the COMPASS. This dial shows the direction in which the air-craft is headed. Dial 4 shows north, Dial 5 is west, and Dial 6 is northwest.

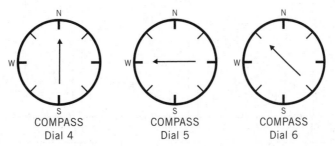

COMPASS
Dial 4

COMPASS
Dial 5

COMPASS
Dial 6

Each item in this test consists of two dials and four silhouettes of aircraft in flight. Your task is to determine which of the four aircraft is closest to the position indicated by the two dials. Remember, you are always looking NORTH at the same altitude as each plane. East is always to the RIGHT as you look at the page.

In the following example, the ARTIFICIAL HORIZON shows no bank and the COMPASS shows southwest. Box C is the silhouette that meets the specifications. (NOTE: B is the rear view of the aircraft, and D is the front view. A is banked right, and B is banked left.)

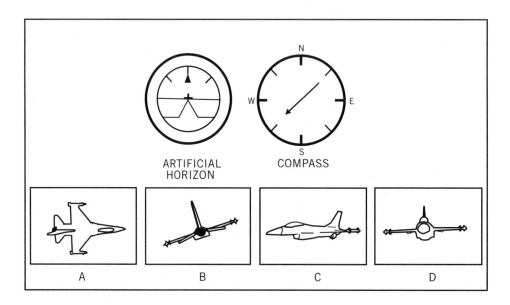

Now work the following examples.

1.

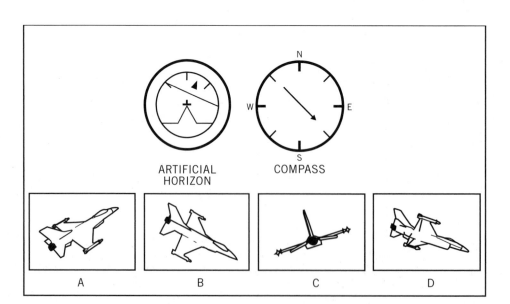

2.

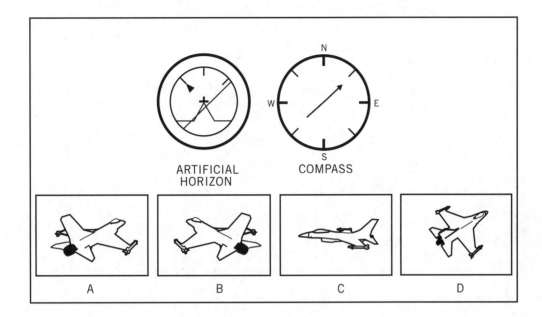

ARTIFICIAL HORIZON   COMPASS

A   B   C   D

3.

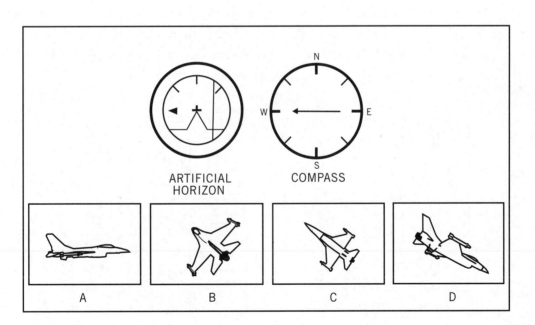

ARTIFICIAL HORIZON   COMPASS

A   B   C   D

4.

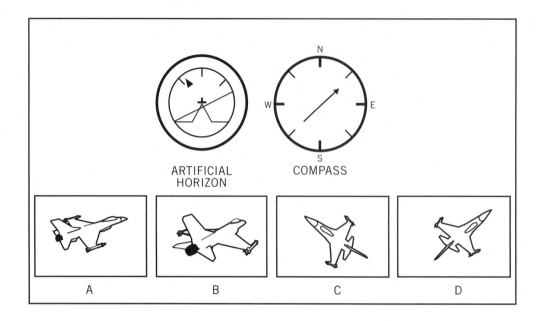

ARTIFICIAL
HORIZON

COMPASS

A   B   C   D

Section 8: Block Counting

DIRECTIONS: This is a test of your ability to see into a three-dimensional stack of blocks to determine how many pieces are touched by the numbered blocks. It is also a test of your abilities to observe and deduce what you cannot specifically see. Closely study the way in which the blocks are stacked. You may find it helpful to remember that all of the blocks in the pile are the same size and shape. While there will be several stacks of blocks on the actual test, for this practice example there is only one.

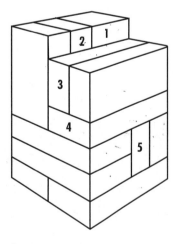

KEY					
Block	**A**	**B**	**C**	**D**	**E**
1	3	4	5	6	7
2	5	6	7	8	9
3	5	6	7	8	9
4	4	5	6	7	8
5	4	5	6	7	8

1. Block 1 is touched by _____ other blocks.

    a. 2

    b. 3

    c. 4

    d. 5

    e. 1

Section 9: Table Reading

DIRECTIONS: This is a test of your ability to read tables quickly and accurately. Look at the following table. Notice that the X values are shown at the top of the table and the Y values are shown at the left of the table. In this test, you are to find the entry that occurs at the intersection of the row and the column corresponding to the values given. On your answer sheet, fill in the letter that corresponds with the number at the intersection of the X and Y values. Accuracy is important.

X VALUE

Y VALUE	-3	-2	-1	0	+1	+2	+3
+3	22	23	25	27	28	29	30
+2	23	25	27	29	30	31	32
+1	24	26	28	30	32	33	34
0	26	27	29	31	33	34	35
-1	27	29	30	32	34	35	37
-2	28	30	31	33	35	36	38
-3	29	31	32	34	36	37	39

	X	Y		a.	b.	c.	d.	e.
1.	0	0		29	31	32	35	34
2.	-3	+3		22	29	30	39	35
3.	+2	-2		25	31	36	30	27
4.	0	+2		33	34	35	27	29
5.	-2	+3		31	38	32	23	22

Section 10: Aviation Information

DIRECTIONS: This part of the test measures your knowledge of aviation. This portion is common to all three services' selection tests, although the number of questions varies from one service to another. Each of the questions or incomplete statements is followed by several choices. You must decide which one of the choices best completes the statement or answers the question. Eliminating any obviously incorrect choices first will increase your chances of selecting the right answer.

1. At 0° angle of attack, a symmetrical airfoil will produce
   a. lift, but less than a positively cambered airfoil.
   b. no form drag.
   c. no induced drag.
   d. no net aerodynamic force.

2. Airport runways are numbered according to
   a. length and width.
   b. wind direction.
   c. the first two digits of compass direction.
   d. order of construction.

3. Which of the following, when doubled, will cause the greatest change in lift?
   a. coefficient of lift
   b. velocity
   c. density
   d. area

4. All motion or changes in aircraft attitude occur about which position?
   a. aerodynamic center (AC)
   b. center of pressure (CP)
   c. center of gravity (CG)
   d. the cockpit

5. What are the colors of the port and starboard running lights?
   a. white/white
   b. red/green
   c. green/red
   d. red/white

6. A pilot is flying under standard day conditions at sea level. His true airspeed will
   a. equal indicated airspeed.
   b. be greater than indicated airspeed.
   c. be less than indicated airspeed.

7. The transponder codes for loss of communication and for emergency are
   a. 7,600 and 7,500.
   b. 7,700 and 7,600.
   c. 7,600 and 7,700.
   d. 7,500 and 7,700.

8. What are the five major components of an airplane?
   a. wings, fuselage, empennage, landing gear, and engine
   b. wings, cockpit, empennage, flaps, and engine
   c. fuselage, rudder, empennage, ailerons, and engine
   d. fuselage, empennage, engine/transmission assembly, vertical stabilizer, and tail rudder

9. Yaw is defined as the motion of the longitudinal axis about which axis?

   a. the lateral axis

   b. the longitudinal axis

   c. the vertical axis

   d. the horizon

10. Vertigo can be described as

   a. the sensation of spinning while stationary.

   b. too little oxygen in the blood stream.

   c. the sensation of feeling no movement.

   d. a form of blackout.

Section 11: Rotated Blocks

DIRECTIONS: This test measures your ability to visualize and manipulate objects in space. For each question in this test, you will be shown a picture of a block. You must find a second block that is identical to the first.

To see how to approach this test, study the following two blocks. Although you see them from different points, you can see that the blocks are exactly alike.

Look at the next two blocks. They are not alike, and they can never be turned so they will be exactly alike.

Now look at the following sample item. Which of the five choices is identical to the first block?

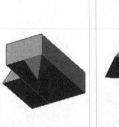  

SAMPLE   **a.**   **b.**   **c.**   **d.**   **e.**

The correct choice in the sample is **a**.

1.

       a.   **b.**   **c.**   **d.**   **e.**

2.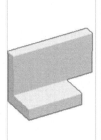

       a.   **b.**   **c.**   **d.**   **e.**

3.

       a.   **b.**   **c.**   **d.**   **e.**

4.

       a.   **b.**   **c.**   **d.**   **e.**

5.

a.   **b.**   **c.**   **d.**   **e.**

Section 12: General Science

DIRECTIONS: This part of the test measures your knowledge in the area of science. Each of the questions or incomplete statements is followed by five choices. You must decide which one of the choices best answers the question or completes the statement. Again, if you are unsure of an answer, use the process of elimination. Remember, there are no penalties for guessing.

1. An eclipse of the sun throws the shadow of the
    a. moon on the sun.
    b. earth on the sun.
    c. sun on the earth.
    d. earth on the moon.
    e. moon on the earth.

2. Substances that hasten a chemical reaction without themselves undergoing change are called
    a. buffers.
    b. catalysts.
    c. colloids.
    d. reducers.
    e. polymers.

3. Lack of iodine in the diet is often related to which of the following diseases?
    a. beriberi
    b. scurvy
    c. rickets
    d. goiter
    e. asthma

4. The chief nutrient in lean meat is
    a. starch.
    b. protein.
    c. fat.
    d. carbohydrates.
    e. Vitamin B.

5. After adding salt to water, the freezing point of the water is
    a. variable.
    b. inverted.
    c. the same.
    d. raised.
    e. lowered.

Section 13: Hidden Figures

DIRECTIONS: This part of the test measures your ability to find a simple figure in a complex drawing. Above each group of questions are five figures, lettered A, B, C, D, and E. Below this set of figures are several numbered drawings. You are to determine which lettered figure is contained in each of the numbered drawings. On the following sample, the lettered figures are:

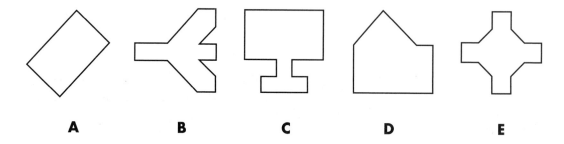

A   **B**   **C**   **D**   **E**

See if you can find one of the five figures in drawing X below.

Now look at drawing Y. It is exactly the same as X, but the outline of figure B has been darkened to show where it is located

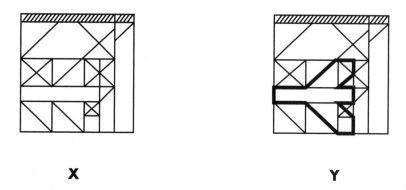

X   **Y**

As you work the following problems, remember that each numbered drawing contains only ONE of the lettered figures. The correct figure in each drawing will always be of the same size and in the same position as it appears in the set of figures. Look at each numbered drawing and decide which one of the five lettered figures is contained in it.

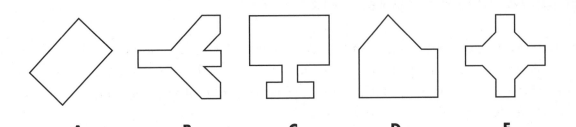

A   **B**   **C**   **D**   **E**

1.

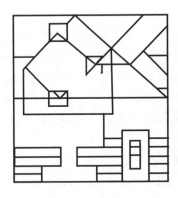

4.

2.

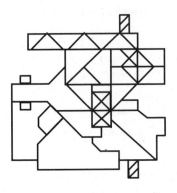

5.

3

Section 14: Complex Movements

DIRECTIONS: The questions in this subtest measure your ability to judge distance and visualize motion. For each question, five pairs of symbols are given representing direction and distance. You need to choose the pair that represents the movement of the black dot into the center of the circle—that is, up or down, left or right, and a short, medium, or long distance.

In the following Direction Key, the symbols are divided into Top row of symbols (left and right movements) and Bottom row of symbols (up and down movements). In the Distance Key, the width of the line is shown to represent length of movement: thin line = small movement, medium line = medium movement, and thick line = long movement.

The easiest rule to follow when answering these questions is: Always look at the Direction Key. First, ask yourself what direction the black dot needs to move to get to the center of the circle (for example, right and up). Then, look at the Direction Key and find the appropriate symbols (including "no move"). Most answers can be eliminated by this first step, but you will still need to figure out the distance of movement required by the thickness of the symbols. (Notice: "No move" has only one width because there is no distance traveled.)

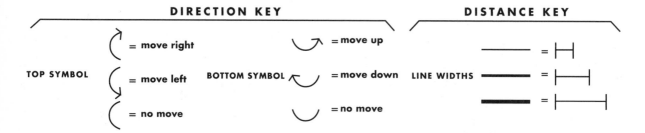

For this sample question, decide which direction the dot needs to travel and then look at the Direction Key. Then, decide how far the dot needs to travel in each direction and match it to the line width of the Top and Bottom symbols. Only one pair of arrows is correct.

In the example, the correct answer is D. To center the dot in the circle, you had to move a medium distance to the left and a long distance down. Now practice with the following problems.

Example

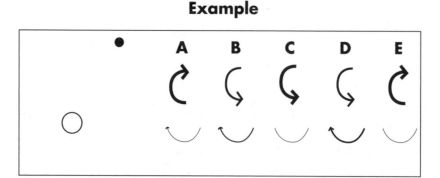

1.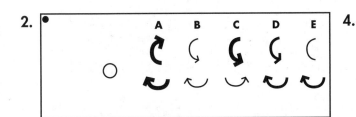

2.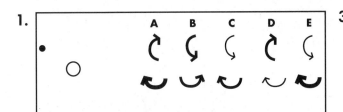

3.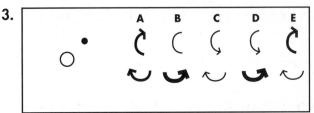

4.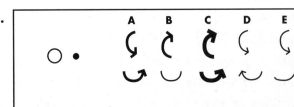

Section 15: Helicopter Knowledge

DIRECTIONS: This segment deals with your understanding of the principles of helicopter flight. It also is found only in the Army and Navy exams. Decide which one of the choices given for each question best answers it or completes the statement.

1. You are in a helicopter in straight and level flight with a constant power setting. When the nose of the helicopter is pulled up, the altitude will
   a. remain the same.
   b. initially increase.
   c. initially decrease.
   d. none of the above

2. When you start up your helicopter, the Ng rises slowly and stabilizes below 50%, and the TOT rises more slowly than normal. These indicate a
   a. starter failure.
   b. igniter failure.
   c. hung start.
   d. hot start.
   e. none of the above

3. A helicopter's anti-icing system is to be used only as a preventive measure. Once ice has accumulated, the anti-ice system cannot be used as a corrective measure.
   a. true
   b. false

4. During daylight operations, you must turn the BRIGHT-DIM switch to DIM and set the instrument lights on LOW because the amber-colored caution lights will be extremely difficult to distinguish.
   a. true
   b. false

5. You are in a helicopter in straight and level flight when the fuel pump caution light comes on and you find you have an indicated fuel pressure of zero. This indicates
   a. you have run out of fuel.
   b. one boost pump has failed.
   c. both boost pumps have failed.
   d. you are decreasing altitude.
   e. none of the above

Section 16: Cyclic Orientation

DIRECTIONS: This is a test of your ability to recognize simple changes in helicopter position and to indicate the corresponding cyclic (stick) movement. You will look at a series of three sequential pictures that represent the pilot's view through the helicopter windshield. The three pictures change from top to bottom, showing the view from an aircraft in a climb, a dive, a bank to the left or right, or a combination of these maneuvers. You will determine how the cyclic (stick) would be positioned in order to perform the maneuver indicated by the pictures.

S1. You are the pilot of a helicopter with a constant power setting. You are going through a maneuver as shown in the following pictures. Look at the pictures from top to bottom to decide what maneuver the helicopter is doing.

Look at the following table, showing the various positions of the cyclic for different maneuvers and the cyclic diagram to determine the cyclic position for the maneuver previously shown. Fill in the circle for the correct cyclic position.

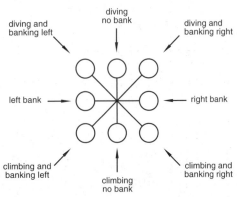

Section 17: Spatial Apperception

DIRECTIONS: This test measures your ability to determine the position of an aircraft in flight in relation to a ship on the water. You are to determine whether it is climbing, diving, in level flight, banking to the right or left, flying straight toward the water (perpendicular to the coast), flying diagonally out toward the water, or any combination of these maneuvers. A sketch of the view seen directly out of the middle of the aircraft windscreen will be shown. You will be required to determine which aircraft below the sketch depicts the correct attitude and flight path shown in the windscreen view sketch. The position of the horizon will indicate if the aircraft is climbing or diving. If the horizon is above the middle of the picture, the aircraft is diving (see the following examples).

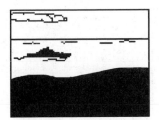

Example 1: diving, left bank   Example 2: diving, no bank   Example 3: diving, right bank

Conversely, if the horizon is below the middle of the picture, the aircraft is climbing (see examples 4–6, following). The angle of the horizon will indicate the aircraft's bank angle. A horizon sloping down to the right indicates left bank (see examples 1, 4, and 7) and a horizon sloping down to the left indicates right bank (see examples 3, 6, and 9).

Example 4: climbing, left bank

Example 5: climbing, no bank

Example 6: climbing, right bank

Example 7: level flight, left bank

Example 8: level flight, no bank

Example 9: level flight, right bank

If the aircraft is in a bank, the position of the center of the horizon in the sketch will indicate if the aircraft is also in a climb or dive or in level flight. If the horizon is above the center, the aircraft is in a dive. The horizon is in the center for level flight and below center for a climb. Example 1 shows an aircraft in a dive and banking left.

The position of the coastline (left or right side of aircraft) will be important in questions when the sketch shows a view of the aircraft course flying parallel to the coast. When the aircraft is flying a diagonal course out to sea, the coastline will slope up to one side, but the horizon will be level. This indicates a diagonal course with the coastline 45° off of the aircraft's flight path and a direction straight out to sea 45° off the other side.

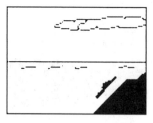
Example 10: level flight, no bank, diagonal heading, coastline on right

Remember that in all sketches the aircraft is flying toward the ocean and not toward land. This should be your first check on all aircraft attitude pictures. Examples of the various aircraft attitudes follow.

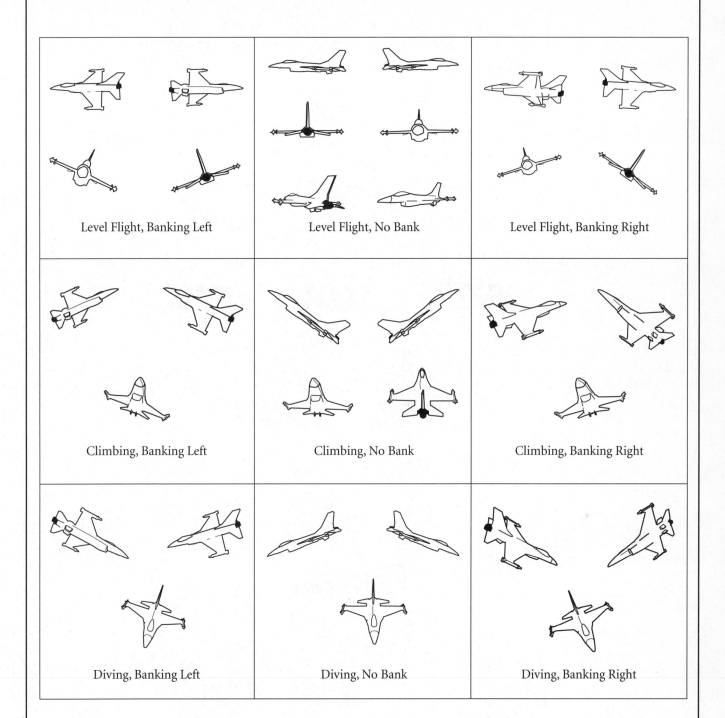

Level Flight, Banking Left

Level Flight, No Bank

Level Flight, Banking Right

Climbing, Banking Left

Climbing, No Bank

Climbing, Banking Right

Diving, Banking Left

Diving, No Bank

Diving, Banking Right

For each of the following questions, select the choice that most nearly represents the aircraft's position in relation to the position of the ship.

1.

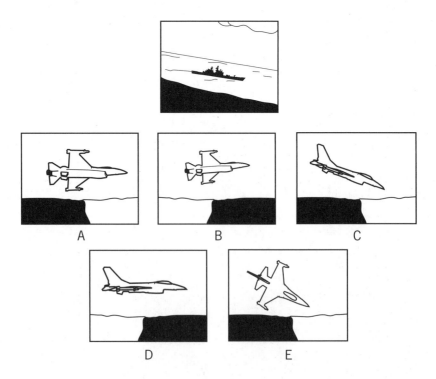

2.

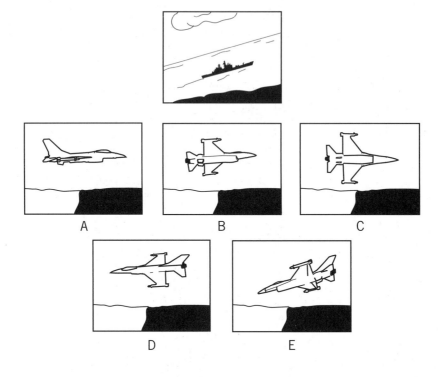

3

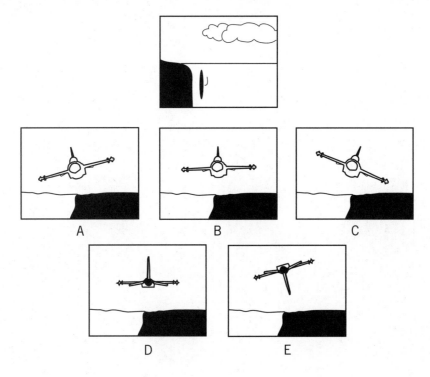

Section 18: Biographical Inventory

DIRECTIONS: This section consists of 76 questions concerning your background, hobbies, and academic interests. Because this section is mostly biographical, there are no right or wrong answers. The purpose is to provide the military with some information about your personal strengths, education, and experience.

Background and personality questions may include:

Background

What was the highest level of education you completed?

What was the highest level of education your mother completed?

Is anyone in your immediate family a pilot?

What size community do you prefer to live in?

Do you consider yourself mechanically inclined?

What do your parents think of your joining the Army?

Personality

Have you ever planted a garden?

Have you ever skydived?

Do you prefer long or short hair?

On your day off, do you get up early or sleep until noon?

Do you like to take charge or to follow orders?

5 ▶ Sample Military Flight Aptitude Test Answers

This chapter contains the answers for the sample military flight aptitude test you just took. Go over the answers carefully and see where you did best and where you may need some improvement.

Section 1: Verbal Analogies

1. c. The FLIGHT STATION is where the AIRPLANE is controlled from, just as BRIDGE is where a SHIP is controlled from.

2. a. A tractor is used on a field, as a racquet is used on a tennis court.

3. d. A rose is only one type of flower, just as a sweater is only one type of clothing.

4. d. A sail propels a ship, just as rowing propels a boat.

5. a. *Fly* and *drive* are both verbs, while *airplane* and *stake* are both nouns. The other phrase choices contain either both verbs or both nouns.

Section 2: Arithmetic Reasoning

1. b. The smaller field is one half the size of the larger field, making it 210 square yards. Since the area equals the length times the width, to get the width you must divide the area by the length. In this case, 210 divided by 15 equals 14 yards.

2. b. Since there are the same number of both types of plane, each pair of planes can carry a total of seven tons (two tons in the passenger plane and five tons in the cargo plane). Divide the total of 105 tons by seven tons per pair of aircraft to get 15 pairs. Two tons times the 15 passenger planes is a total of 30 tons.

3. d. The duration of sortie four is the total time flown, less the duration for each other sortie. One sortie was canceled, leaving only three sorties. First, solve for the total time flown: three sorties times the average of flight length of 93 minutes: $3 \times 93 = 279$ total minutes flown. Subtract 42 minutes each for sorties one and three: $279 - 42 - 42 = 195$ minutes.

4. e. If 40% were under 22 years of age, 60% would have been past their 22nd birthday. Multiply 450 by .6 (or 60%) to get 270 recruits.

5. d. To solve this distance problem, first convert to a common time base. Change seconds to minutes by dividing 1,800 seconds by 60 seconds per minute to get 30 minutes. Then, divide again by 60 minutes per hour to get .5 hours. To solve the distance, multiply 330 miles per hour by .5 hours to get 165 miles.

Section 3: Reading Skills

1. c. The other options are concerned with technology, specialization, and managerial structure, but the topic of the paragraph is harmony and cooperation between the various components of an organization.

2. d. Choices **a** and **c** are wrong because both are factors that PREVENT the production of toxin. Choice **e** is wrong because *Clostridium botulinum* is not rare, and exposing it to another bacterium is not a factor for toxin production. Choice **b** contradicts the implication in the paragraph that it takes a relatively long time for the toxin to develop.

3. c. The paragraph has just stated that the earth is a dynamic planet, so choice **a** is wrong. Temperature fluctuations are not caused by planetary interaction, so choice **d** is wrong, and choices **b** and **e** are only two of the many factors involved in causing the changes on the earth.

4. a. Choices **b** and **c** are not correct because they refer to species other than the two discussed in the paragraph. Choice **d** is wrong because *Mustela nigripes* is the scientific name for the black-footed ferret, and choice **e** is wrong because destruction of habitat by the European polecat has nothing to do with confusion between it and the ferret.

5. b. This is the only choice that relates to the similarity of art between Central America and Southeast Asia, which is where the paragraph begins. The other choices all refer to other parts of the world, and choice **a** is not explained by this theory.

Section 4: Word Knowledge

1. **c.** Crimson is a dark red color.
2. **d.** To *cease* means "to stop."
3. **a.** *Benign* means "harmless or to no visible effect."
4. **d.** When someone is sullen, he or she is angry or annoyed and may demonstrate it by scowling rather than speaking.
5. **a.** People using terse speech are often sharp or short in their speech, making their point without many words.

Section 5: Math Knowledge

1. **b.** When a number is marked off in groups of two digits each, starting at the decimal point, the square root of the largest square in the left-hand group, whether one or two digits, is the first digit of the square root of the number. In this case (5-90-43), 4 is the largest square in 5, and 2 is the square root of 4.
2. **c.** The circumference of a circle is two times the radius times pi. So, in this case, the distance is two times 35, times 22, divided by seven, or 220 miles.
3. **e.** The factorial of a positive integer is that integer times each of the integers between it and 1. In this case, 4 times 3 times 2 equals 24.
4. **a.** Divide both sides of the equation by $2x$. The result is x equals $\frac{1}{7}$.
5. **b.** The reciprocal of a number is that number divided into one. In this case that is $\frac{1}{5}$, or .2.

Section 6: Mechanical Comprehension

1. **a.** As shown in the diagram, gears R and S are not meshing, so gear S is not moving.
2. **b.** Water wheel S will turn for a longer time than R because the source is near the bottom of the tank, while the source for R is near the top.
3. **e.** Shaft C is at the low point on the cam to start with, so it will move up for the first half turn of S, and then it will move back down.
4. **c.** For B to move to the right, the clockwise torque must be increased. Choices **a** and **d** can be eliminated because they would increase the counterclockwise torque. To increase the clockwise torque, the initial tension toward B would have to be increased, or the small pulley would have to be decreased with respect to the larger one. (The torque is the tension times the pulley's radius.) With 30° angles, the initial tension at A is 50 pounds, and the tension at B is 12.5 pounds. The tension at B could be increased to 25 pounds ($\frac{1}{2}$ the tension at A) if the angle were increased to 90°. That means the larger pulley would have to be more than twice the size of the small pulley for the system to turn clockwise. From the diagram, that does not appear to be the case, so choice **b** can be eliminated. To increase the clockwise torque by reducing the smaller pulley, the smaller pulley would have to be less than one fourth the size of the larger pulley, because the tension at A is four times that at B. That eliminates choice **e**. Therefore, **c** is the answer.

5. b. In system A, all three springs have the same load. In system B, each spring carries $\frac{1}{3}$ of the load. Therefore, the tension of the springs in A is three times that of B.

Section 7: Instrument Comprehension

1. b. The ARTIFICIAL HORIZON shows a dive and bank right, and the COMPASS shows southeast.

2. d. The ARTIFICIAL HORIZON shows a shallow climb and bank right, and the COMPASS reads northeast.

3. c. The ARTIFICIAL HORIZON shows a steep climb and bank right and the COMPASS shows west.

4. a. the ARTIFICIAL HORIZON shows a shallow climb and bank right, and the COMPASS shows northeast. (Aircraft B is on a level plane.)

Section 8: Block Counting

1. d. Block 1 is touching block 2 (beside 1), blocks 3 and 4 (in front of 1), block 5 and another block (below1), and the block behind it.

2. b. Block 2 is touching block 1, two other blocks (beside 2), blocks 3 and 4 (in front of 2), and an unnumbered block (below 2).

3. a. Block 3 is touching blocks 1, 2, and an unnumbered block (behind 3), an unnumbered block (in front of 3), and block 4 (below 3).

4. e. Block 4 is touching blocks 1, 2, and an unnumbered block (behind 4), block 3 and an unnumbered block (on top of block 4), and block 5 and two unnumbered blocks (below 4).

5. e. Block 5 is touching block 1 and the unnumbered block behind 1, block 4 (above 5), three unnumbered blocks (on both sides of 5), and two unnumbered blocks (under block 5).

Section 9: Table Reading

1. b. The intersection of (X) 0 and (Y) 0 is 31.

2. a. The intersection of (X) –3 and (Y) +3 is 22.

3. c. The intersection of (X) +2 and (Y) –2 is 36.

4. e. The intersection of (X) 0 and (Y) +2 is 29.

5. d. The intersection of (X) –2 and (Y) +3 is 23.

Section 10: Aviation Information

1. a. At 0° angle of attack, a symmetrical airfoil will produce lift, but less than a positively cambered airfoil.

2. c. Airport runways are numbered according to the first two digits of compass heading, with the zero omitted for headings between 010 and 090.

3. b. Velocity will cause the greatest change in lift when doubled.

4. c. All changes in aircraft attitude occur about the center of gravity.

5. b. The port running lights are red; the starboard lights are green. Positional lights are white.

6. a. The pilot's true airspeed will equal indicated airspeed.

7. c. Transponder codes are as follows:

Loss of comms	7600
Emergency	7700
Hijacking	7500

8. a. The five major components of an aircraft are its wings, fuselage, empennage, landing gear, and engine.

9. c. Yaw is defined as the motion of the longitudinal axis about the vertical axis.

10. a. Vertigo is the sensation of spinning or whirling while the body remains stationary.

Section 11: Rotated Blocks

1. a.
2. b.
3. c.
4. b.
5. c.

Section 12: General Science

1. e. It is the moon that appears to cover the sun, and the moon's shadow that darkens the earth.

2. b. Catalysts initiate chemical reactions without undergoing change themselves.

3. d. Lack of iodine in one's diet can cause goiter.

4. b. The chief nutrient in lean meat is protein.

5. e. Adding salt to water creates a solution which needs a lower temperature to freeze.

Section 13: Hidden Figures

1. a. This one is fairly obvious; the rectangle A is in the lower-left portion of the drawing.

2. a. This one is somewhat deceptive. At first glance you may see either figure B or D in this drawing, but neither of those figures is complete. The rectangle A is located in the upper-right portion of the drawing. Remember that only one correct figure will be found in each drawing.

3. e. Figure E seems to appear twice in this drawing, but two arms of the upper figure are longer than shown in the example. The one centered at the bottom is more accurate than the figure above it.

4. d. Another deceptive drawing. At first glance you may see figure C in the lower-left corner, but it is not complete, and its stem is off-center. Figure D is located directly above the incomplete figure C.

5. c. The correct figure C is vertically centered and located near the right border. This drawing also appears to contain figure A, overlapping figure C and touching the left border, but its lower right side is not complete.

Section 14: Complex Movements

1. **c.** To center the dot in the circle, you must move a medium distance to the right and a short distance down.
2. **a.** To center the dot in the circle, you must move a long distance to the right and a long distance down.
3. **c.** To center the dot in the circle, you must move a short distance to the left and a short distance down.
4. **e.** To center the dot in the circle, you must move a short distance to the left and none up or down.

Section 15: Helicopter Knowledge

1. **b.** Pulling up the nose of the helicopter will initially increase its altitude.
2. **c.** Ng stabilizing below 50% and TOT rising slowly indicates a hung start.
3. **a.** True. A helicopter's anti-icing system cannot be used as a corrective measure if ice has already accumulated.
4. **b.** False. You must turn the BRIGHT-DIM switch to BRIGHT because of the difficulty of distinguishing amber-colored caution lights.
5. **c.** If your fuel pump caution light comes on and you have an indicated fuel pressure of zero, both boost pumps have failed.

Section 16: Cyclic Orientation

S1. The photos show the helicopter diving and banking to the left.

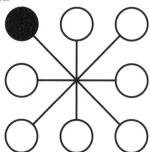

Section 17: Spatial Apperception

Question	Answer	Pitch	Roll	Direction
1.	e.	diving	banking right	flying out to sea
2.	a.	level flight	banking left	flying out to sea
3.	b.	level flight	no bank angle	coastline on left

Section 18: Biographical Inventory

There are no "right" or "wrong" answers for this section.

6 ▶ The LearningExpress Test Preparation System

Taking a military flight aptitude exam can be tough. It demands a lot of preparation if you want to achieve a top score. The LearningExpress Test Preparation System, developed exclusively for LearningExpress by leading test experts, gives you the discipline, attitude, and advantage you need to be a winner.

First, the bad news: Taking a military flight aptitude test is no picnic, and neither is getting ready for it. Your future career as a pilot or flight officer depends on getting a high score on the many parts of the test, but there are all sorts of pitfalls that can keep you from doing your best on this all-important exam. Here are some of the obstacles that can stand in the way of your success:

- Being unfamiliar with the format of the exam
- Being paralyzed by test anxiety
- Leaving your preparation to the last minute
- Not preparing at all!
- Not knowing vital test-taking skills, such as how to pace yourself through the exam, how to use the process of elimination, and when to guess
- Not being in tip-top mental and physical shape
- Working through the test on an empty stomach or shivering through the exam because the room is cold

What's the common denominator in all these test-taking pitfalls? One word: *control*. Who's in control, you or the exam?

Now the good news: The LearningExpress Test Preparation System puts you in control. In just nine easy-to-follow steps, you will learn everything you need to know to make sure that you are in charge of your preparation and your performance on the exam. Other test takers may let the test get the better of them; other test takers may be unprepared or out of shape, but not you. You will have taken all the steps you need to take to get a high score on any military flight aptitude exam.

Here's how the LearningExpress Test Preparation System works: Nine easy steps lead you through everything you need to know and do to get ready to master your exam. Each of the following steps involves some reading and activities that will help build confidence. It's important that you do the activities along with the reading, or else you won't be getting the full benefit of the system. Each step tells you approximately how much time that step will take you to complete.

Step 1. Get information	30 minutes
Step 2. Conquer test anxiety	20 minutes
Step 3. Make a plan	50 minutes
Step 4. Learn to manage your time	10 minutes
Step 5. Learn to use the process of elimination	20 minutes
Step 6. Know when to guess	20 minutes
Step 7. Reach your peak performance zone	10 minutes
Step 8. Get your act together	10 minutes
Step 9. Do it!	10 minutes
Total	**3 hours**

We estimate that working through the entire system will take you approximately three hours, although it's perfectly okay if you work faster or slower

than the time estimates assume. If you can take a whole afternoon or evening, you can work through the whole LearningExpress Test Preparation System in one sitting. Otherwise, you can break it up and do just one or two steps a day for the next several days. It's up to you—remember, you're in control.

Step 1: Get Information

Time to complete: 30 minutes
Activities: Read Chapter 3, "Test Maneuvers: Explanation of Military Flight Aptitude Tests," and Chapter 4, "Sample Military Flight Aptitude Test Questions."

Knowledge is power. The first step in the LearningExpress Test Preparation System is finding out everything you can about the military flight aptitude exam you will be taking. Once you have your information, the next steps in the LearningExpress Test Preparation System will show you what to do about it.

Straight Talk about Your Military Flight Aptitude Exam

A short history lesson: For all intents and purposes, the U.S. military invented and began general standardized testing around the time of World War I, and it was basically for recruits. With the advent of flight, potential pilots were required to take a standardized test as well. A military flight aptitude test is a test of specific aptitudes and abilities that an aviator needs. Some of these aptitudes, such as reading comprehension and math problem-solving skills, are important in most jobs; others, such as electronics, complex movements, and instrument comprehension, are quite specialized.

It's important for you to realize that your score on a military flight aptitude test does not determine what kind of person you are. There are all kinds of things a written exam like this can't test: whether you can follow orders, whether you can become part of a unit that works together cohesively, whether you will show courage under fire, and so on. Those kinds of things are hard to evaluate and aren't tested on this kind of exam.

What's on Most Military Flight Aptitude Exams

The skills that pilots or flight officers have to know are varied. Following are the most commonly tested subjects:

- Synonyms
- Verbal Analogies
- Reading Comprehension
- Arithmetic Reasoning
- Math Knowledge
- Data Interpretation
- Mechanical Comprehension
- Electrical Mazes
- Scale Reading
- Instrument Comprehension
- Block Counting
- Table Reading
- Aviation Information
- Nautical Information
- Rotated Blocks
- General Science
- Hidden Figures
- Complex Movements
- Cyclic Orientation
- Spatial Apperceptiion

If you haven't already done so, stop here and read Chapters 3 and 4 of this book for a complete overview of the military flight aptitude tests. Keep in mind that each branch of the military has its own qualifying tests. Then, move on to the next step and get rid of that test anxiety!

Step 2: Conquer Test Anxiety

Time to complete: 20 minutes
Activity: Take the Test Stress Test

Having complete information about the exam is the first step in getting control of the exam. Next, you have to overcome one of the biggest obstacles to test success: test anxiety. Test anxiety not only impairs your performance on the exam itself, but even keep you from preparing! In Step 2, you'll learn stress management techniques that will help you succeed on your exam. Learn these strategies now, and practice them as you work through the exams in this book, so they'll be second nature to you by exam day.

Combating Test Anxiety

The first thing you need to know is that a little test anxiety is a good thing. Everyone gets nervous before a big exam—and if that nervousness motivates you to prepare thoroughly, so much the better. It's said that Sir Laurence Olivier, one of the foremost British actors of the twentieth century, threw up before every performance. His stage fright didn't impair his performance; in fact, it probably gave him a little extra edge—just the kind of edge you need to do well, whether on a stage or in an exam room.

On page 79 is the Test Stress Test. Stop here and answer the questions on that page to find out whether your level of test anxiety is something you should worry about.

STRESS MANAGEMENT BEFORE THE TEST

If you feel your level of anxiety getting the best of you in the weeks before the test, here is what you need to do to bring the level down again:

- **Get prepared.** There's nothing like knowing what to expect. Being prepared will put you in control of test anxiety. That's why you are reading this book. Use it faithfully, and remind yourself that you're better prepared than most of the people taking the test.
- **Practice self-confidence.** A positive attitude is a great way to combat test anxiety. This is no time to be humble or shy. Stand in front of the mirror and say to your reflection, "I'm prepared. I'm full of self-confidence. I'm going to ace this test. I know I can do it." Say it into a recording device and play it back once a day. If you hear it often enough, you'll believe it.
- **Fight negative messages.** Every time someone starts telling you how hard the exam is or how it's almost impossible to get a high score, start telling them your self-confidence messages. If you are telling yourself that you don't do well on exams or that you just can't do this, don't listen. Just listen to your self-confidence messages instead.
- **Visualize.** Imagine yourself reporting for your first flight. Think of yourself developing flight plans, preflighting an airplane, or delivering cargo. Visualizing success can help make it happen—and it reminds you why you're preparing for the exam so diligently.
- **Exercise.** Physical activity helps calm your body down and focus your mind. Besides, being in good physical shape can actually help you do well on the exam. Go for a run, lift weights, go swimming—and do it regularly.

STRESS MANAGEMENT ON TEST DAY

There are several ways you can bring down your level of test anxiety on test day. To find a comfort level, practice these in the weeks before the test, and use the ones that work best for you:

- **Deep breathing.** Take a deep breath while you count to five. Hold it on the count of one, and then let it out on the count of five. Repeat several times.
- **Move your body.** Try rolling your head in a circle. Rotate your shoulders. Shake your hands from the wrist. Many people find these movements very relaxing.
- **Visualize again.** Think of the place where you are most relaxed: lying on the beach in the sun, walking through the park, or whatever. Now close your eyes and imagine you're actually there. If you practice in advance, you'll find that you only need a few seconds of this exercise to experience a significant increase in your sense of well-being.

When anxiety threatens to overwhelm you right there during the exam, there are still things you can do to manage the stress level:

- **Repeat your self-confidence messages.** You should have them memorized by now. Say them quietly to yourself, and believe them!
- **Visualize one more time.** This time, visualize yourself moving smoothly and quickly through the test answering every question right and finishing just before time is up. Like most visualization techniques, this one works best if you've practiced it ahead of time.
- **Find an easy question.** Skim over the test until you find an easy question, and answer it. Getting even one circle filled in gets you into the test-taking groove.

■ **Take a mental break.** Everyone loses concentration once in a while during a long test. It's normal, so you shouldn't worry about it. Instead, accept what has happened. Say to yourself, "Hey, I lost it there for a minute. My brain is taking a break." Put down your pencil, close your eyes, and do some deep breathing for a few seconds. Then you're ready to go back to work.

Try these techniques ahead of time, and see if they work for you!

Test Stress Test

You need to worry about test anxiety only if it is extreme enough to impair your performance. The following questionnaire will provide a diagnosis of your level of test anxiety. In the blank before each statement, write the number that most accurately describes your experience.

0 = Never   1 = Once or twice   2 = Sometimes   3 = Often

_____ I have gotten so nervous before an exam that I simply put down the books and didn't study for it.

_____ I have experienced disabling physical symptoms such as vomiting and severe headaches because I was nervous about an exam.

_____ I have simply not shown up for an exam because I was scared to take it.

_____ I have experienced dizziness and disorientation while taking an exam.

_____ I have had trouble filling in the little circles because my hands were shaking too hard.

_____ I have failed an exam because I was too nervous to complete it.

_____ **Total: Add up the numbers in the blanks above.**

Your Test Stress Score

Here are the steps you should take, depending on your score. If you scored:

■ **Below 3**, your level of test anxiety is nothing to worry about; it's probably just enough to give you the motivation to excel.

■ **Between 3 and 6**, your test anxiety may be enough to impair your performance, and you should practice the stress management techniques listed in this section to try to bring your test anxiety down to manageable levels.

■ **Above 6**, your level of test anxiety is a serious concern. In addition to practicing the stress management techniques listed in this section, you may want to seek additional, professional help. Call your local high school or community college and ask for the academic counselor. Tell the counselor that you have a level of test anxiety that sometimes keeps you from being able to take the exam. The counselor may be willing to help you or may suggest someone else you should talk to.

Step 3: Make a Plan

Time to complete: 50 minutes
Activity: Construct a study plan.

Maybe the most important thing you can do to get control of yourself and your exam is to make a study plan. Too many people fail to prepare simply because they fail to plan. Spending hours on the day before the exam poring over sample test questions not only raises your level of test anxiety, but also is simply no substitute for careful preparation and practice.

Don't fall into the cram trap. Take control of your preparation time by mapping out a study schedule. There are four sample schedules on the following pages, based on the amount of time you have before your military flight aptitude test. If you're the kind of person who needs deadlines and assignments to motivate you for a project, here they are. If you're the kind of person who doesn't like to follow other people's plans, you can use the suggested schedules here to construct your own.

Even more important than making a plan is making a commitment. You can't review everything you know about aviation in one night. You have to set aside some time every day for study and practice. Try for at least 20 minutes a day.

Even 10 minutes a day, with half an hour or more on weekends, can make a big difference in your score—and in your chances of making the grade you want!

Schedule A: The 30-Day Plan

If you have at least a month before you take your military flight aptitude test, you have plenty of time to prepare—as long as you don't waste it! If you have less than a month, turn to Schedule B.

Time	Preparation
Days 1–4	Skim over the written materials from your training program, particularly noting (1) areas you expect to be emphasized on the exam and (2) areas you don't remember well. On Day 4, concentrate on those areas.
Day 5	Take the practice exam.
Day 6	Score the exam, using the answer key at the end. Read the list of subsections on the sample test given in Chapter 4. Identify two areas that you will concentrate on before you take the practice exam a second time.
Days 7–10	Study the two areas you identified as your weak points. Don't worry about the other areas.
Day 11	Take the practice exam again.
Day 12	Score your practice exam. Identify one area to concentrate on before you repeat the process.
Days 13–18	Study the one area you identified for review. In addition, review both practice exams you've taken so far. Give special attention to the answer explanations and the length of time it took you to complete the exams.
Day 19	Take the practice exam for a third time.
Days 20–21	Study the one area you identified for review.

Days 22–25	Take an overview of all your training materials, consolidating your strengths and improving on your weaknesses.
Days 26–27	Review all the areas that have given you the most trouble in the three practice exams you've taken so far.
Day 28	Take the practice exam one final time. Note how much you've improved!
Day 29	Review one or two weak areas.
Day before the exam	Relax. Do something unrelated to the exam and go to bed at a reasonable hour.

Schedule B: The 10-Day Plan

If you have two weeks or less before you take the exam, you may have your work cut out for you. Use this 10-day schedule to help you make the most of your time.

Time	Preparation
Day 1	Take the practice exam and score it, using the answer key at the end. Skim through the list of subject areas on the exam in Chapter 4 to find out which areas need the most work—based on your exam score.
Day 2	Review one area that gave you trouble on the practice exam.
Day 3	Review another area that gave you trouble on the practice exam.
Day 4	Take the practice exam again and score it.
Day 5	If your second score on the practice exam doesn't show improvement on the two areas you studied, review them. If you did improve in those areas, choose a different trouble spot to study today.

Day 6	Take the practice exam a third time and score it.
Day 7	Choose your weakest area from your third practice exam to review.
Day 8	Review any areas that you have not yet reviewed.
Day 9	Take the practice exam a final time and score it.
Day 10	Use your last study day to brush up on any areas that are still giving you trouble.
Day before the exam	Relax. Do something unrelated to the exam and go to bed at a reasonable hour.

Step 4: Learn to Manage Your Time

Time to complete: 10 minutes to read, many hours of practice!

Activities: Practice these strategies as you take the sample tests in this book.

Steps 4, 5, and 6 of the LearningExpress Test Preparation System put you in charge of your exam by showing you test-taking strategies that work. Practice these strategies as you take the sample tests in this book, and then you'll be ready to use them on test day.

First, you'll take control of your time on the exam. Flight aptitude exams each have a time limit, which may give you more than enough time to complete all the questions—or may not. It's a terrible feeling to hear the examiner say "five minutes left" when you're only three-quarters of the way through the test. Here are some tips to keep that from happening to you.

■ **Follow directions**. If the directions are given orally, listen closely. If they're written on the exam booklet, read them carefully. Ask questions before the exam begins if there is anything you don't understand. If you're allowed to write in your exam booklet, write down the beginning time and the ending time of the exam.

■ **Pace yourself.** Glance at your watch every few minutes, and compare the time to how far you've gotten in the test. When one-quarter of the time has elapsed, you should be a quarter of the way through the section, and so on. If you're falling behind, pick up the pace a bit.

■ **Keep moving.** Don't waste time on one question. If you don't know the answer, skip the question and move on. Circle the number of the question in your test booklet in case you have time to come back to it later.

■ **Keep track of your place on the answer sheet.** If you skip a question, make sure you skip on the answer sheet, too. Check yourself every five to 10 questions to make sure the question number and the answer sheet number are still the same.

■ **Don't rush.** Although you should keep moving, rushing won't help. Try to keep calm and work methodically and quickly.

Step 5: Learn to Use the Process of Elimination

Time to complete: 20 minutes
Activity: Complete worksheet on Using the Process of Elimination.

After time management, your next most important tool for taking control of your exam is using the process of elimination wisely. It's standard test-taking wisdom that you should always read all the answer choices before choosing your answer. This helps you find the right answer by eliminating wrong answer choices. And, sure enough, that standard wisdom applies to your exam, too.

Let's say you're facing a general science question that goes like this:

13. "Biology uses a *binomial* system of classification." In this sentence, the word *binomial* most nearly means
   a. understanding the law.
   b. having two names.
   c. scientifically sound.
   d. having a double meaning.

If you happen to know what *binomial* means, of course, you don't need to use the process of elimination, but let's assume that, like most people, you don't. So you look at the answer choices. "Understanding the law" sure doesn't sound very likely for something having to do with biology. So you eliminate choice **a**—and now you have only three answer choices to deal with. Mark an X next to choice **a** so you don't read it again.

On to the other answer choices. If you know that the prefix *bi-* means "two," as in *bicycle*, you'll flag choice **b** as a possible answer. Mark a check mark beside it, meaning "good answer, I might use this one."

Choice **c**, "scientifically sound," is a possibility. At least it's about science, not law. It could work here, although, when you think about it, having a "scientifically sound" classification system in a scientific field is kind of redundant. You remember the *bi-* thing in *binomial* and probably continue to prefer choice **b**. But you're not sure, so you put a question mark next to choice **c**, meaning "well, maybe."

Now, choice **d**, "having a double meaning." You're still keeping in mind that *bi-* means "two," so this one looks possible at first. But then you look again at the sentence the word belongs in, and you think, "Why would biology want a system of classification that has two meanings? That wouldn't work very well!" If you're really taken with the idea that *bi-* means "two," you might put a question mark here. But if you're feeling a little more confident, you'll put an X. You've already got a better answer picked out.

Now your question looks like this:

13. "Biology uses a *binomial* system of classification." In this sentence, the word *binomial* most nearly means
    X a. understanding the law.
    √ b. having two names.
    ? c. scientifically sound.
    ? d. having a double meaning.

You've got just one check mark, for "good answer." If you're pressed for time, you should simply mark choice **b** on your answer sheet. If you've got the time to be extra careful, you could compare your check-mark answer to your question-mark answers to make sure that it's better. (The binomial system in biology is the one that gives a two-part genus and species name like *Homo sapiens*.)

It's good to have a system for marking good, bad, and maybe answers. We're recommending this one:

X = bad
√ = good
? = maybe

If you don't like these marks, devise your own system. Just make sure you do it long before test day—while you're working through the practice tests in this book—so you won't have to worry about it during the actual exam.

Even when you think you're absolutely clueless about a question, you can often use the process of elimination to get rid of one answer choice. If so, you're better prepared to make an educated guess, as you'll see in Step 6. More often, the process of elimination allows you to get down to only two possibly right answers. Then you're in a strong position to guess. And sometimes, even though you don't know the right answer, you find it simply by getting rid of the wrong ones, as you did in the example above.

Try using your powers of elimination on the questions in the worksheet "Using the Process of Elimination" now. The answer explanations there show one possible way you might use the process to arrive at the right answer.

The process of elimination is your tool for the next step, which is knowing when to guess.

Use the process of elimination to answer the following questions.

1. Ilsa is as old as Meghan will be in five years. The difference between Ed's age and Meghan's age is twice the difference between Ilsa's age and Meghan's age. Ed is 29. How old is Ilsa?
   a. 4
   b. 10
   c. 19
   d. 24

2. "All drivers of commercial vehicles must carry a valid commercial driver's license whenever operating a commercial vehicle." According to this sentence, which of the following people need NOT carry a commercial driver's license?
   a. a truck driver idling his engine while waiting to be directed to a loading dock
   b. a bus operator backing her bus out of the way of another bus in the bus lot
   c. a taxi driver driving his personal car to the grocery store
   d. a limousine driver taking the limousine to her home after dropping off her last passenger of the evening

3. Smoking tobacco has been linked to
   a. an increased risk of stroke and heart attack.
   b. all forms of respiratory disease.
   c. increasing mortality rates over the past 10 years.
   d. juvenile delinquency.

4. Which of the following words is spelled correctly?
   a. incorrigible
   b. outragous
   c. domestickated
   d. understandible

Here are the answers, as well as some suggestions as to how you might have used the process of elimination to find them.

1. d. You should have eliminated choice **a** immediately. Ilsa can't be four years old if Meghan is going to be Ilsa's age in five years. The best way to eliminate other answer choices is to try plugging them into the information given in the problem. For instance, for choice **b**, if Ilsa is 10, then Meghan must be five. The difference in their ages is five. The difference between Ed's age, 29, and Meghan's age, five, is 24. Is 24 two times five? No. Then choice **b** is wrong. You could eliminate choice **c** in the same way and be left with choice **d**.

2. c. Note the word *not* in the question, and go through the answers one by one. Is the truck driver in choice **a** "operating a commercial vehicle"? Yes, idling counts as operating, so he needs to have a commercial driver's license. Likewise, the bus operator in choice **b** is operating a commercial vehicle; the question doesn't say the operator has to be on the street. The limo driver in choice **d** is operating a commercial vehicle, even if it doesn't have a passenger in it. However, the cabbie in choice **c** is not operating a commercial vehicle, but his own private car.

3. a. You could eliminate choice **b** simply because of the presence of the word *all*. Such absolutes hardly ever appear in correct answer choices. Choice **c** looks attractive until you think a little about what you know—aren't fewer people smoking these days, rather than more? So how could smoking be responsible for a higher mortality rate? (If you didn't know that mortality rate means the rate at which people die, you might keep this choice as a possibility, but you'd still be able to eliminate two answers and have only two to choose from.) Choice **d** can't be proven, so you could eliminate that one, too. Now you're left with the correct choice, **a**.

4. a. How you used the process of elimination here depends on which words you recognized as being spelled incorrectly. If you knew that the correct spellings were *outrageous*, *domesticated*, and *understandable*, then you were home free. Surely you knew that at least one of those words was spelled wrong.

Step 6: Know When to Guess

Time to complete: 20 minutes
Activity: Complete the worksheet on "Your Guessing Ability."

Armed with the process of elimination, you're ready to take control of one of the big questions in test taking: Should I guess? The first and main answer is yes. Some exams have what's called a guessing penalty, in which a fraction of your wrong answers is subtracted from your right answers—but military flight aptitude exams don't tend to work like that. The number of questions you answer correctly yields your raw score. So you have nothing to lose and everything to gain by guessing.

The more complicated answer to the question, "Should I guess?" depends on you, your personality, and your guessing intutition. There are two things you need to know about yourself before you go into the exam:

- Are you a risk taker?
- Are you a good guesser?

You'll have to decide about your risk-taking quotient on your own. To find out if you're a good guesser, complete the worksheet "Your Guessing Ability" that follows. Frankly, even if you're a play-it-safe person with terrible intuition, you're still safe in guessing every time. The best thing would be if you could overcome your anxieties and go ahead and mark an answer. But you may want to have a sense of how good your intuition is before you go into the exam.

Your Guessing Ability

Following are 10 really hard questions. You're not supposed to know the answers. Rather, this is an assessment of your ability to guess when you don't have a clue. Read each question carefully, just as if you did expect to answer it. If you have any knowledge at all of the subject of the question, use that knowledge to help you eliminate wrong answer choices. Use the following answer grid to fill in your answers to the questions.

1. ⓐ ⓑ ⓒ ⓓ   7. ⓐ ⓑ ⓒ ⓓ
2. ⓐ ⓑ ⓒ ⓓ   8. ⓐ ⓑ ⓒ ⓓ
3. ⓐ ⓑ ⓒ ⓓ   9. ⓐ ⓑ ⓒ ⓓ
4. ⓐ ⓑ ⓒ ⓓ   10. ⓐ ⓑ ⓒ ⓓ
5. ⓐ ⓑ ⓒ ⓓ
6. ⓐ ⓑ ⓒ ⓓ

1. September 7 is Independence Day in
   a. India.
   b. Costa Rica.
   c. Brazil.
   d. Australia.

2. Which of the following is the formula for determining the momentum of an object?
   a. $p = mv$
   b. $F = ma$
   c. $P = IV$
   d. $E = mc^2$

3. Because of the expansion of the universe, the stars and other celestial bodies are all moving away from each other. This phenomenon is known as
   a. Newton's first law.
   b. the big bang.
   c. gravitational collapse.
   d. Hubble flow.

4. American author Gertrude Stein was born in
   a. 1713.
   b. 1830.
   c. 1874.
   d. 1901.

5. Which of the following is NOT one of the Five Classics attributed to Confucius?
   a. the I Ching
   b. the Book of Holiness
   c. the Spring and Autumn Annals
   d. the Book of History

6. The religious and philosophical doctrine that holds that the universe is constantly in a struggle between good and evil is known as
   a. Pelagianism.
   b. Manichaeanism.
   c. neo-Hegelianism.
   d. Epicureanism.

7. The third Chief Justice of the U.S. Supreme Court was
   a. John Blair.
   b. William Cushing.
   c. James Wilson.
   d. John Jay.

8. Which of the following is the poisonous portion of a daffodil?
   a. the bulb
   b. the leaves
   c. the stem
   d. the flowers

9. The winner of the Masters golf tournament in 1953 was
   a. Sam Snead.
   b. Cary Middlecoff.
   c. Arnold Palmer.
   d. Ben Hogan.

10. The state with the highest per capita personal income in 1980 was
   a. Alaska.
   b. Connecticut.
   c. New York.
   d. Texas.

Answers

Check your answers against the following correct answers.

1. c.
2. a.
3. d.
4. c.
5. b.
6. b.
7. b.
8. a.
9. d.
10. a.

You may have simply gotten lucky or actually known the answer to one or two questions. In addition, your guessing was more successful if you were able to use the process of elimination on any of the questions. Maybe you didn't know who the third Chief Justice was (question 7), but you knew that John Jay was the first. In that case, you would have eliminated choice **d** and therefore improved your odds of guessing right from one in four to one in three.

According to probability, you should get $2\frac{1}{2}$ answers correct, so getting either two or three right would be average. If you got four or more right, you may be a really terrific guesser. If you got one or none right, you may not guess well.

Keep in mind, though, that this is only a small sample. You should continue to keep track of your guessing ability as you work through the sample questions in this book. Circle the numbers of questions where you guess; or, if you don't have time during the practice tests, go back afterward and try to remember which answers you guessed. Remember, on a test with four answer choices, your chances of getting a right answer is one in four. So keep a separate guessing score for each exam. How many answers did you guess? How many did you get right? If the number you got right is at least one-fourth of the number of answers you guessed, you are at least an average guesser, maybe better—and you should always go ahead and guess on the real exam. If the number you got right is significantly lower than one-fourth of the number you guessed, you should not guess on exams where there is a guessing penalty unless you can eliminate a wrong answer. If there's no guessing penalty, you would, frankly, be safe in guessing anyway, but maybe you'd feel more comfortable if you guessed only selectively, when you can eliminate a wrong answer or at least have a good feeling about one of the answer choices.

Step 7: Reach Your Peak Performance Zone

Time to complete: 10 minutes to read; weeks to complete!

Activity: Complete the Physical Preparation Checklist.

To get ready for a challenge like a big exam, you have to take control of your physical, as well as your mental state. Exercise, proper diet, and rest will ensure that your body works with, rather than against, your mind on test day, as well as during your preparation.

Exercise

If you don't already have a regular exercise program going, the time during which you're preparing for an exam is actually an excellent time to start one. You'll have to be pretty fit to pass your physical ability test anyway. And if you are already keeping fit—or trying to get that way—don't let the pressure of preparing for an exam fool you into quitting now. Exercise helps reduce stress by pumping wonderful good-feeling hormones called endorphins into your system. It also increases the oxygen supply throughout your body and your brain, so you'll be at peak performance on test day.

A half hour of vigorous activity—enough to raise a sweat—every day should be your aim. If you are really pressed for time, every other day is okay. Choose an activity you like and get out there and do it. Jogging with a friend always makes the time go faster, as does listening to music.

But don't overdo it. You don't want to exhaust yourself. Moderation is the key.

Diet

First of all, cut out the junk. Go easy on caffeine and nicotine, and eliminate alcohol and any other drugs from your system at least two weeks before the exam. Promise to treat yourself the night after the exam, if need be.

What your body needs for peak performance is simply a balanced diet. Eat plenty of fruits and vegetables, along with protein and carbohydrates. Foods that are high in lecithin (an amino acid), such as fish and beans, are especially good brain foods.

Rest

You probably know how much sleep you need every night to be at your best, even if you don't always get it. Make sure you do get that much sleep, though, for at least a week before the exam. Moderation is important here, too. Extra sleep will just make you groggy.

If you are not a morning person and your exam will be given in the morning, you should reset your internal clock so that your body doesn't think you are taking an exam at 3 A.M. You have to start this process well before the exam. The way it works is to get up half an hour earlier each morning, and then go to bed half an hour earlier that night. Don't try it the other way around; you will just toss and turn if you go to bed early without getting up early. The next morning, get up another half an hour earlier, and so on. How long you will have to do this depends on how late you are used to getting up. Use the following "Physical Preparation Checklist" to make sure you are in tip-top form.

Physical Preparation Checklist

For the week before the test, write down 1) what physical exercise you engaged in and for how long and 2) what you ate for each meal. Remember, you're trying for at least half an hour of exercise every other day (preferably every day) and a balanced diet that's light on junk food.

Exam minus 7 days

    Exercise: _____ for _____ minutes

    Breakfast: _____

    Lunch: _____

    Dinner: _____

    Snacks: _____

Exam minus 6 days

    Exercise: _____ for _____ minutes

    Breakfast: _____

    Lunch: _____

    Dinner: _____

    Snacks: _____

Exam minus 5 days

    Exercise: _____ for _____ minutes

    Breakfast: _____

    Lunch: _____

    Dinner: _____

    Snacks: _____

Exam minus 4 days

    Exercise: _____ for _____ minutes

    Breakfast: _____

    Lunch: _____

    Dinner: _____

    Snacks: _____

Exam minus 3 days

    Exercise: _____ for _____ minutes

    Breakfast: _____

    Lunch: _____

    Dinner: _____

    Snacks: _____

Exam minus 2 days

    Exercise: _____ for _____ minutes

    Breakfast: _____

    Lunch: _____

    Dinner: _____

    Snacks: _____

Exam minus 1 day

    Exercise: _____ for _____ minutes

    Breakfast: _____

    Lunch: _____

    Dinner: _____

    Snacks: _____

Step 8: Get Your Act Together

Time to complete: 10 minutes to read; time to complete will vary.
Activity: Complete the "Final Preparations" worksheet.

Once you feel in control of your mind and body, you are in charge of test anxiety, test preparation, and test-taking strategies. Now it's time to make charts and gather the materials you'll need to take to the exam.

Gather Your Materials

The night before the exam, lay out the clothes you will wear and the materials you have to bring with you to the exam. Plan on dressing in layers, because you won't have any control over the temperature of the exam room. Have a sweater or jacket you can take off if it's warm. Use the checklist on the following worksheet, "Final Preparations," to help you pull together what you will need.

Final Preparations

Final Preparations

Getting to the exam site

Location of exam:_____

Date of exam:_____

Time of exam:_____

Do I know how to get to the exam site? Yes _____ No _____

    If no, make a trial run.

Time it will take to get to the exam site:_____

Things to lay out the night before

Clothes I will wear_____

Sweater/jacket_____

Watch_____

Photo ID_____

Admission card_____

4 No. 2 pencils_____

_____

_____

_____

Don't Skip Breakfast

Even if you don't usually eat breakfast, do so on exam morning. A cup of coffee doesn't count. Don't eat doughnuts or other sweet foods, either. A sugar high will leave you with a sugar low in the middle of the exam. A mix of protein and carbohydrates is best: cereal with milk and just a little sugar or eggs with toast will do your body a world of good.

Step 9: Do It!

Time to complete: 10 minutes, plus test-taking time
Activity: Ace the Military Flight Aptitude Test!

Fast forward to exam day. You are ready. You made a study plan and followed through. You practiced your test-taking strategies while working through this book.

You are in control of your physical, mental, and emotional state. You know when and where to show up and what to bring with you. In other words, you're better prepared than most of the other people taking the military flight aptitude test with you. You are psyched!

Just one more thing. When you're done with the exam, you will have earned a reward. Plan a celebration. Call your friends and plan a party, or have a nice dinner for two—whatever your heart desires. Give yourself something to look forward to.

And then do it. Go into the exam, full of confidence, armed with test-taking strategies you have practiced until they are second nature. You are in control of yourself, your environment, and your performance on exam day. You are ready to succeed. So do it. Go in there and ace the exam! And, then, look forward to your future career as a pilot or flight officer.

7 ▶ Air Force Officer Qualifying Test (AFOQT)

This sample Air Force Officer Qualifying Test (AFOQT) tests you on some of the skills—verbal analogies, arithmetic reasoning, word knowledge, math knowledge, instrument comprehension, block counting, table reading, aviation information, general science, rotated blocks, and finding hidden figures—you will need in order to become a successful Air Force aviator.

SECTION 1: VERBAL ANALOGIES

1.	ⓐ ⓑ ⓒ ⓓ ⓔ	10.	ⓐ ⓑ ⓒ ⓓ ⓔ	19.	ⓐ ⓑ ⓒ ⓓ ⓔ
2.	ⓐ ⓑ ⓒ ⓓ ⓔ	11.	ⓐ ⓑ ⓒ ⓓ ⓔ	20.	ⓐ ⓑ ⓒ ⓓ ⓔ
3.	ⓐ ⓑ ⓒ ⓓ ⓔ	12.	ⓐ ⓑ ⓒ ⓓ ⓔ	21.	ⓐ ⓑ ⓒ ⓓ ⓔ
4.	ⓐ ⓑ ⓒ ⓓ ⓔ	13.	ⓐ ⓑ ⓒ ⓓ ⓔ	22.	ⓐ ⓑ ⓒ ⓓ ⓔ
5.	ⓐ ⓑ ⓒ ⓓ ⓔ	14.	ⓐ ⓑ ⓒ ⓓ ⓔ	23.	ⓐ ⓑ ⓒ ⓓ ⓔ
6.	ⓐ ⓑ ⓒ ⓓ ⓔ	15.	ⓐ ⓑ ⓒ ⓓ ⓔ	24.	ⓐ ⓑ ⓒ ⓓ ⓔ
7.	ⓐ ⓑ ⓒ ⓓ ⓔ	16.	ⓐ ⓑ ⓒ ⓓ ⓔ	25.	ⓐ ⓑ ⓒ ⓓ ⓔ
8.	ⓐ ⓑ ⓒ ⓓ ⓔ	17.	ⓐ ⓑ ⓒ ⓓ ⓔ		
9.	ⓐ ⓑ ⓒ ⓓ ⓔ	18.	ⓐ ⓑ ⓒ ⓓ ⓔ		

SECTION 2: ARITHMETIC REASONING

1.	ⓐ ⓑ ⓒ ⓓ ⓔ	10.	ⓐ ⓑ ⓒ ⓓ ⓔ	19.	ⓐ ⓑ ⓒ ⓓ ⓔ
2.	ⓐ ⓑ ⓒ ⓓ ⓔ	11.	ⓐ ⓑ ⓒ ⓓ ⓔ	20.	ⓐ ⓑ ⓒ ⓓ ⓔ
3.	ⓐ ⓑ ⓒ ⓓ ⓔ	12.	ⓐ ⓑ ⓒ ⓓ ⓔ	21.	ⓐ ⓑ ⓒ ⓓ ⓔ
4.	ⓐ ⓑ ⓒ ⓓ ⓔ	13.	ⓐ ⓑ ⓒ ⓓ ⓔ	22.	ⓐ ⓑ ⓒ ⓓ ⓔ
5.	ⓐ ⓑ ⓒ ⓓ ⓔ	14.	ⓐ ⓑ ⓒ ⓓ ⓔ	23.	ⓐ ⓑ ⓒ ⓓ ⓔ
6.	ⓐ ⓑ ⓒ ⓓ ⓔ	15.	ⓐ ⓑ ⓒ ⓓ ⓔ	24.	ⓐ ⓑ ⓒ ⓓ ⓔ
7.	ⓐ ⓑ ⓒ ⓓ ⓔ	16.	ⓐ ⓑ ⓒ ⓓ ⓔ	25.	ⓐ ⓑ ⓒ ⓓ ⓔ
8.	ⓐ ⓑ ⓒ ⓓ ⓔ	17.	ⓐ ⓑ ⓒ ⓓ ⓔ		
9.	ⓐ ⓑ ⓒ ⓓ ⓔ	18.	ⓐ ⓑ ⓒ ⓓ ⓔ		

SECTION 3: INSTRUMENT COMPREHENSION

1.	ⓐ ⓑ ⓒ ⓓ	8.	ⓐ ⓑ ⓒ ⓓ	15.	ⓐ ⓑ ⓒ ⓓ
2.	ⓐ ⓑ ⓒ ⓓ	9.	ⓐ ⓑ ⓒ ⓓ	16.	ⓐ ⓑ ⓒ ⓓ
3.	ⓐ ⓑ ⓒ ⓓ	10.	ⓐ ⓑ ⓒ ⓓ	17.	ⓐ ⓑ ⓒ ⓓ
4.	ⓐ ⓑ ⓒ ⓓ	11.	ⓐ ⓑ ⓒ ⓓ	18.	ⓐ ⓑ ⓒ ⓓ
5.	ⓐ ⓑ ⓒ ⓓ	12.	ⓐ ⓑ ⓒ ⓓ	19.	ⓐ ⓑ ⓒ ⓓ
6.	ⓐ ⓑ ⓒ ⓓ	13.	ⓐ ⓑ ⓒ ⓓ	20.	ⓐ ⓑ ⓒ ⓓ
7.	ⓐ ⓑ ⓒ ⓓ	14.	ⓐ ⓑ ⓒ ⓓ		

SECTION 4: BLOCK COUNTING

1.	ⓐ ⓑ ⓒ ⓓ ⓔ	8.	ⓐ ⓑ ⓒ ⓓ ⓔ	15.	ⓐ ⓑ ⓒ ⓓ ⓔ
2.	ⓐ ⓑ ⓒ ⓓ ⓔ	9.	ⓐ ⓑ ⓒ ⓓ ⓔ	16.	ⓐ ⓑ ⓒ ⓓ ⓔ
3.	ⓐ ⓑ ⓒ ⓓ ⓔ	10.	ⓐ ⓑ ⓒ ⓓ ⓔ	17.	ⓐ ⓑ ⓒ ⓓ ⓔ
4.	ⓐ ⓑ ⓒ ⓓ ⓔ	11.	ⓐ ⓑ ⓒ ⓓ ⓔ	18.	ⓐ ⓑ ⓒ ⓓ ⓔ
5.	ⓐ ⓑ ⓒ ⓓ ⓔ	12.	ⓐ ⓑ ⓒ ⓓ ⓔ	19.	ⓐ ⓑ ⓒ ⓓ ⓔ
6.	ⓐ ⓑ ⓒ ⓓ ⓔ	13.	ⓐ ⓑ ⓒ ⓓ ⓔ	20.	ⓐ ⓑ ⓒ ⓓ ⓔ
7.	ⓐ ⓑ ⓒ ⓓ ⓔ	14.	ⓐ ⓑ ⓒ ⓓ ⓔ		

SECTION 5: WORD KNOWLEDGE

1. ⓐ ⓑ ⓒ ⓓ ⓔ
2. ⓐ ⓑ ⓒ ⓓ ⓔ
3. ⓐ ⓑ ⓒ ⓓ ⓔ
4. ⓐ ⓑ ⓒ ⓓ ⓔ
5. ⓐ ⓑ ⓒ ⓓ ⓔ
6. ⓐ ⓑ ⓒ ⓓ ⓔ
7. ⓐ ⓑ ⓒ ⓓ ⓔ
8. ⓐ ⓑ ⓒ ⓓ ⓔ
9. ⓐ ⓑ ⓒ ⓓ ⓔ

10. ⓐ ⓑ ⓒ ⓓ ⓔ
11. ⓐ ⓑ ⓒ ⓓ ⓔ
12. ⓐ ⓑ ⓒ ⓓ ⓔ
13. ⓐ ⓑ ⓒ ⓓ ⓔ
14. ⓐ ⓑ ⓒ ⓓ ⓔ
15. ⓐ ⓑ ⓒ ⓓ ⓔ
16. ⓐ ⓑ ⓒ ⓓ ⓔ
17. ⓐ ⓑ ⓒ ⓓ ⓔ
18. ⓐ ⓑ ⓒ ⓓ ⓔ

19. ⓐ ⓑ ⓒ ⓓ ⓔ
20. ⓐ ⓑ ⓒ ⓓ ⓔ
21. ⓐ ⓑ ⓒ ⓓ ⓔ
22. ⓐ ⓑ ⓒ ⓓ ⓔ
23. ⓐ ⓑ ⓒ ⓓ ⓔ
24. ⓐ ⓑ ⓒ ⓓ ⓔ
25. ⓐ ⓑ ⓒ ⓓ ⓔ

SECTION 6: TABLE READING

1. ⓐ ⓑ ⓒ ⓓ ⓔ
2. ⓐ ⓑ ⓒ ⓓ ⓔ
3. ⓐ ⓑ ⓒ ⓓ ⓔ
4. ⓐ ⓑ ⓒ ⓓ ⓔ
5. ⓐ ⓑ ⓒ ⓓ ⓔ
6. ⓐ ⓑ ⓒ ⓓ ⓔ
7. ⓐ ⓑ ⓒ ⓓ ⓔ
8. ⓐ ⓑ ⓒ ⓓ ⓔ
9. ⓐ ⓑ ⓒ ⓓ ⓔ
10. ⓐ ⓑ ⓒ ⓓ ⓔ
11. ⓐ ⓑ ⓒ ⓓ ⓔ
12. ⓐ ⓑ ⓒ ⓓ ⓔ
13. ⓐ ⓑ ⓒ ⓓ ⓔ
14. ⓐ ⓑ ⓒ ⓓ ⓔ

15. ⓐ ⓑ ⓒ ⓓ ⓔ
16. ⓐ ⓑ ⓒ ⓓ ⓔ
17. ⓐ ⓑ ⓒ ⓓ ⓔ
18. ⓐ ⓑ ⓒ ⓓ ⓔ
19. ⓐ ⓑ ⓒ ⓓ ⓔ
20. ⓐ ⓑ ⓒ ⓓ ⓔ
21. ⓐ ⓑ ⓒ ⓓ ⓔ
22. ⓐ ⓑ ⓒ ⓓ ⓔ
23. ⓐ ⓑ ⓒ ⓓ ⓔ
24. ⓐ ⓑ ⓒ ⓓ ⓔ
25. ⓐ ⓑ ⓒ ⓓ ⓔ
26. ⓐ ⓑ ⓒ ⓓ ⓔ
27. ⓐ ⓑ ⓒ ⓓ ⓔ
28. ⓐ ⓑ ⓒ ⓓ ⓔ

29. ⓐ ⓑ ⓒ ⓓ ⓔ
30. ⓐ ⓑ ⓒ ⓓ ⓔ
31. ⓐ ⓑ ⓒ ⓓ ⓔ
32. ⓐ ⓑ ⓒ ⓓ ⓔ
33. ⓐ ⓑ ⓒ ⓓ ⓔ
34. ⓐ ⓑ ⓒ ⓓ ⓔ
35. ⓐ ⓑ ⓒ ⓓ ⓔ
36. ⓐ ⓑ ⓒ ⓓ ⓔ
37. ⓐ ⓑ ⓒ ⓓ ⓔ
38. ⓐ ⓑ ⓒ ⓓ ⓔ
39. ⓐ ⓑ ⓒ ⓓ ⓔ
40. ⓐ ⓑ ⓒ ⓓ ⓔ

SECTION 7: MATH KNOWLEDGE

1. ⓐ ⓑ ⓒ ⓓ
2. ⓐ ⓑ ⓒ ⓓ
3. ⓐ ⓑ ⓒ ⓓ
4. ⓐ ⓑ ⓒ ⓓ
5. ⓐ ⓑ ⓒ ⓓ
6. ⓐ ⓑ ⓒ ⓓ
7. ⓐ ⓑ ⓒ ⓓ
8. ⓐ ⓑ ⓒ ⓓ
9. ⓐ ⓑ ⓒ ⓓ

10. ⓐ ⓑ ⓒ ⓓ
11. ⓐ ⓑ ⓒ ⓓ
12. ⓐ ⓑ ⓒ ⓓ
13. ⓐ ⓑ ⓒ ⓓ
14. ⓐ ⓑ ⓒ ⓓ
15. ⓐ ⓑ ⓒ ⓓ
16. ⓐ ⓑ ⓒ ⓓ
17. ⓐ ⓑ ⓒ ⓓ
18. ⓐ ⓑ ⓒ ⓓ

19. ⓐ ⓑ ⓒ ⓓ
20. ⓐ ⓑ ⓒ ⓓ
21. ⓐ ⓑ ⓒ ⓓ
22. ⓐ ⓑ ⓒ ⓓ
23. ⓐ ⓑ ⓒ ⓓ
24. ⓐ ⓑ ⓒ ⓓ
25. ⓐ ⓑ ⓒ ⓓ

SECTION 8: AVIATION INFORMATION

1. (a) (b) (c) (d) (e)
2. (a) (b) (c) (d) (e)
3. (a) (b) (c) (d) (e)
4. (a) (b) (c) (d) (e)
5. (a) (b) (c) (d) (e)
6. (a) (b) (c) (d) (e)
7. (a) (b) (c) (d) (e)

8. (a) (b) (c) (d) (e)
9. (a) (b) (c) (d) (e)
10. (a) (b) (c) (d) (e)
11. (a) (b) (c) (d) (e)
12. (a) (b) (c) (d) (e)
13. (a) (b) (c) (d) (e)
14. (a) (b) (c) (d) (e)

15. (a) (b) (c) (d) (e)
16. (a) (b) (c) (d) (e)
17. (a) (b) (c) (d) (e)
18. (a) (b) (c) (d) (e)
19. (a) (b) (c) (d) (e)
20. (a) (b) (c) (d) (e)

SECTION 9: ROTATED BLOCKS

1. (a) (b) (c) (d) (e)
2. (a) (b) (c) (d) (e)
3. (a) (b) (c) (d) (e)
4. (a) (b) (c) (d) (e)
5. (a) (b) (c) (d) (e)

6. (a) (b) (c) (d) (e)
7. (a) (b) (c) (d) (e)
8. (a) (b) (c) (d) (e)
9. (a) (b) (c) (d) (e)
10. (a) (b) (c) (d) (e)

11. (a) (b) (c) (d) (e)
12. (a) (b) (c) (d) (e)
13. (a) (b) (c) (d) (e)
14. (a) (b) (c) (d) (e)
15. (a) (b) (c) (d) (e)

SECTION 10: GENERAL SCIENCE

1. (a) (b) (c) (d) (e)
2. (a) (b) (c) (d) (e)
3. (a) (b) (c) (d) (e)
4. (a) (b) (c) (d) (e)
5. (a) (b) (c) (d) (e)
6. (a) (b) (c) (d) (e)
7. (a) (b) (c) (d) (e)

8. (a) (b) (c) (d) (e)
9. (a) (b) (c) (d) (e)
10. (a) (b) (c) (d) (e)
11. (a) (b) (c) (d) (e)
12. (a) (b) (c) (d) (e)
13. (a) (b) (c) (d) (e)
14. (a) (b) (c) (d) (e)

15. (a) (b) (c) (d) (e)
16. (a) (b) (c) (d) (e)
17. (a) (b) (c) (d) (e)
18. (a) (b) (c) (d) (e)
19. (a) (b) (c) (d) (e)
20. (a) (b) (c) (d) (e)

SECTION 11: HIDDEN FIGURES

1. (a) (b) (c) (d) (e)
2. (a) (b) (c) (d) (e)
3. (a) (b) (c) (d) (e)
4. (a) (b) (c) (d) (e)
5. (a) (b) (c) (d) (e)

6. (a) (b) (c) (d) (e)
7. (a) (b) (c) (d) (e)
8. (a) (b) (c) (d) (e)
9. (a) (b) (c) (d) (e)
10. (a) (b) (c) (d) (e)

11. (a) (b) (c) (d) (e)
12. (a) (b) (c) (d) (e)
13. (a) (b) (c) (d) (e)
14. (a) (b) (c) (d) (e)
15. (a) (b) (c) (d) (e)

Section 1: Verbal Analogies

DIRECTIONS: This part of the test measures your ability to reason and see relationships between words. You are to choose the answer that best completes the analogy developed at the beginning of each question. The best way to approach this type of test is to look for patterns or comparisons between the first phrase and the choices available to you. You will have eight (8) minutes to complete this section of the test.

Questions: 25
Time: 8 minutes

For sample Verbal Analogies questions, see page 41.

1. CUP is to COFFEE as BOWL is to
   a. dish
   b. soup
   c. spoon
   d. food
   e. saucer

2. BICYCLE is to PEDAL as CANOE is to
   a. water
   b. kayak
   c. oar
   d. fleet
   e. lake

3. WINDOW is to PANE as BOOK is to
   a. novel
   b. glass
   c. cover
   d. page
   e. index

4. PLAY is to ACTOR as CONCERT is to
   a. symphony
   b. musician
   c. piano
   d. percussion
   e. violin

5. PRIDE is to LION as SCHOOL is to
   a. teacher
   b. student
   c. self-respect
   d. learning
   e. fish

6. ELATED is to DESPONDENT as ENLIGHTENED is to
   a. aware
   b. ignorant
   c. miserable
   d. tolerant
   e. humble

7. EMBARRASSED is to HUMILIATED as FRIGHTENED is to
   a. terrified
   b. agitated
   c. courageous
   d. reckless
   e. timid

8. ODOMETER is to MILEAGE as COMPASS is to
   a. speed
   b. hiking
   c. needle
   d. direction
   e. humidity

9. FRAY is to RAVEL as
   a. tremble is to roll
   b. hungry is to eat
   c. jolt is to shake
   d. stroll is to run
   e. stitch is to tear

10. ELEPHANT is to PACHYDERM as
   a. mantis is to rodent
   b. poodle is to feline
   c. kangaroo is to marsupial
   d. zebra is to horse
   e. tuna is to mollusk

11. PSYCHOLOGIST is to NEUROSIS as
   a. ophthalmologist is to cataract
   b. dermatologist is to fracture
   c. infant is to pediatrician
   d. rash is to orthopedist
   e. oncologist is to measles

12. COTTON is to BALE as
   a. butter is to churn
   b. wine is to ferment
   c. grain is to shock
   d. curd is to cheese
   e. beef is to steak

13. DIVISION is to SECTION as
   a. layer is to tier
   b. tether is to bundle
   c. chapter is to verse
   d. riser is to stage
   e. dais is to speaker

14. MECHANIC is to GARAGE as
   a. teacher is to recess
   b. actor is to role
   c. jockey is to horse
   d. surgeon is to hospital
   e. author is to book

15. CHICKADEE is to BIRD as
   a. crocodile is to alligator
   b. giraffe is to reptile
   c. Siamese is to cat
   d. shepherd is to marsupial
   e. grasshopper is to ant

16. WALK is to SAUNTER as
   a. trot is to race
   b. swim is to dive
   c. hop is to shuffle
   d. juggle is to bounce
   e. rain is to drizzle

17. TAILOR is to SUIT as
   a. scheme is to agent
   b. edit is to manuscript
   c. revise is to writer
   d. mention is to opinion
   e. implode is to building

18. JAUNDICE is to LIVER as
   a. rash is to skin
   b. dialysis is to kidney
   c. smog is to lung
   d. valentine is to heart
   e. imagination is to brain

19. INTEREST is to OBSESSION as
   a. mood is to feeling
   b. weeping is to sadness
   c. dream is to fantasy
   d. plan is to negation
   e. highlight is to indication

20. SLAPSTICK is to LAUGHTER as
   a. fallacy is to dismay
   b. genre is to mystery
   c. satire is to anger
   d. mimicry is to tears
   e. horror is to fear

21. VERVE is to ENTHUSIASM as
    a. loyalty is to duplicity
    b. devotion is to reverence
    c. intensity is to color
    d. eminence is to anonymity
    e. generosity is to elation

22. CONVICTION is to INCARCERATION as
    a. reduction is to diminution
    b. induction is to amelioration
    c. radicalization is to estimation
    d. marginalization is to intimidation
    e. proliferation is to alliteration

23. PROFESSOR is to ERUDITE as
    a. aviator is to licensed
    b. inventor is to imaginative
    c. procrastinator is to conscientious
    d. overseer is to wealthy
    e. moderator is to vicious

24. DEPENDABLE is to CAPRICIOUS as
    a. fallible is to cantankerous
    b. erasable is to obtuse
    c. malleable is to limpid
    d. capable is to inept
    e. incorrigible is to guilty

25. DOMINANCE is to HEGEMONY as
    a. romance is to sympathy
    b. furtherance is to melancholy
    c. independence is to autonomy
    d. tolerance is to philanthropy
    e. recompense is to hilarity

Section 2: Arithmetic Reasoning

Directions: This section of the test measures mathematical reasoning and problem solving. Each problem is followed by five possible answers. Decide which one of the five answers is most nearly correct. A method for attacking each of these questions is given in the answer block at the end of this chapter. You will have twenty-nine (29) minutes to complete this section of the test.

Questions: 25
Time: 29 minutes

For sample Arithmetic Reasoning questions, see page 42.

1. What is the estimated product when 157 and 817 are rounded to the nearest hundred and multiplied?
   a. 16,000
   b. 80,000
   c. 160,000
   d. 180,000
   e. 1,600,000

2. Mr. James Rossen is just beginning a computer consulting firm and has purchased the following equipment:

    3 telephone sets, each costing $125
    2 computers, each costing $1,300
    2 computer monitors, each costing $950
    1 printer, costing $600
    1 answering machine, costing $50

    Mr. Rossen is reviewing his finances. What should he write as the total value of the equipment he has purchased so far?
    a. $3,025
    b. $4,025
    c. $5,400
    d. $5,525
    e. $6,525

3. One lap on a particular outdoor track measures a quarter of a mile around. To run a total of three-and-a-half miles, how many laps must a person complete?

- **a.** 7
- **b.** 9
- **c.** 10
- **d.** 13
- **e.** 14

4. $2\frac{1}{4} + \frac{1}{2} =$

- **a.** $6\frac{3}{4}$
- **b.** $6\frac{7}{8}$
- **c.** $7\frac{1}{4}$
- **d.** $7\frac{3}{8}$
- **e.** $7\frac{3}{4}$

5. Newly hired nurses have to buy duty shoes at the full price of $84.50, but nurses who have served at least a year get a 15% discount. Nurses who have served at least three years get an additional 10% off the discounted price. How much does a nurse who has served at least three years have to pay for shoes?

- **a.** $63.78
- **b.** $64.65
- **c.** $67.49
- **d.** $71.83
- **e.** $72.05

6. The basal metabolic rate (BMR) is the rate at which our bodies use calories. The BMR for a man in his twenties is about 1,700 calories per day. If 204 of those calories should come from protein, about what percentage of this man's diet should be protein?

- **a.** 1.2%
- **b.** 8.3%
- **c.** 12%
- **d.** 16%
- **e.** 18%

7. How much water must be added to one liter of a 5% saline solution to get a 2% saline solution?

- **a.** .5 liter
- **b.** 1 liter
- **c.** 1.5 liters
- **d.** 2 liters
- **e.** 2.5 liters

8. All of the rooms in a building are rectangular, with eight-foot ceilings. One room is nine feet wide by 11 feet long. What is the combined area of the four walls, including doors and windows?

- **a.** 90 square feet
- **b.** 180 square feet
- **c.** 280 square feet
- **d.** 460 square feet
- **e.** 580 square feet

9. A child has a temperature of 40° C. What is the child's temperature in degrees Fahrenheit? $(F = \frac{9}{5}C + 32)$

- **a.** 100° F
- **b.** 101° F
- **c.** 102° F
- **d.** 103° F
- **e.** 104° F

10. A woman drives west at 45 miles per hour. After half an hour, a man starts to follow her. How fast must he drive to catch up to her three hours after he starts?

- **a.** 52.5 miles per hour
- **b.** 55 miles per hour
- **c.** 60 miles per hour
- **d.** 65 miles per hour
- **e.** 67.5 miles per hour

11. Jason is six times as old as Kate. In two years, Jason will be twice as old as Kate is then. How old is Jason now?

    a. 3 years old

    b. 6 years old

    c. 9 years old

    d. 12 years old

    e. 15 years old

12. A flash drive shows 827,036 bytes free. If you delete a file of size 542,159 bytes and create a new file of size 489,986 bytes, how many free bytes will the flash drive have?

    a. 489,986 free bytes

    b. 577,179 free bytes

    c. 681,525 free bytes

    d. 774,863 free bytes

    e. 879,209 free bytes

13. On the cardiac ward, there are seven nursing assistants. NA Basil has eight patients; NA Hobbes has five patients; NA McGuire has nine patients; NA Hicks has 10 patients; NA Garcia has 10 patients; NA James has 14 patients; and NA Davis has seven patients. What is the average number of patients per nursing assistant?

    a. 6

    b. 7

    c. 8

    d. 9

    e. 10

14. A patient's hospice stay cost one-fourth as much as his visit to the emergency room. His home nursing cost twice as much as his hospice stay. If his total health care bill was $140,000, how much did his home nursing cost?

    a. 10,000

    b. 20,000

    c. 40,000

    d. 60,000

    e. 80,000

15. At a certain school, half the students are female and one-twelfth of the students are from outside the state. What proportion of the students would you expect to be females from outside the state?

    a. $\frac{1}{12}$

    b. $\frac{1}{24}$

    c. $\frac{1}{8}$

    d. $\frac{1}{6}$

    e. $\frac{1}{3}$

16. Based on the following information, estimate the weight of a person who is 5'5" tall.

Height	Weight
5'	110 lbs.
6'	170 lbs.

    a. 125

    b. 130

    c. 135

    d. 140

    e. 145

17. During exercise, a person's heart rate should be between 60% and 90% of the difference between 220 and the person's age. According to this guideline, what should a 30-year-old person's maximum heart rate be during exercise?

    a. 114

    b. 132

    c. 156

    d. 171

    e. 198

18. A certain water pollutant is unsafe at a level of 20 ppm (parts per million). A city's water supply now contains 50 ppm of this pollutant. What percentage of improvement will make the water safe?

   a. 20%
   b. 30%
   c. 40%
   d. 50%
   e. 60%

19. A study shows that 600,000 women die each year in pregnancy and childbirth, one-fifth more than scientists previously estimated. How many such deaths did the scientists previously estimate?

   a. 120,000
   b. 240,000
   c. 300,000
   d. 480,000
   e. 500,000

20. What is 250 mg in terms of grams?

   a. 0.0250 g
   b. 0.250 g
   c. 2.50 g
   d. 25 g
   e. 250,000 g

21. An Army food supply truck can carry three tons. A breakfast ration weighs 12 ounces, and the other two daily meals weigh 18 ounces each. Assuming each soldier gets three meals per day, on a 10-day trip, how many soldiers can be supplied by one truck?

   a. 100 soldiers
   b. 150 soldiers
   c. 200 soldiers
   d. 320 soldiers
   e. 270 soldiers

22. If you take recyclables to whichever recycler will pay the most, what is the greatest amount of money you could get for 2,200 lbs. of aluminum, 1,400 lbs. of cardboard, 3,100 lbs. of glass, and 900 lbs. of plastic?

	Aluminum	Cardboard	Glass	Plastic
Recycler X	6 cents/pound	3 cents/pound	8 cents/pound	2 cents/pound
Recycler Y	7 cents/pound	4 cents/pound	7 cents/pound	3 cents/pound

   a. $440
   b. $447
   c. $454
   d. $469
   e. $485

23. A train must travel 3,450 miles in six days. How many miles must it travel each day?

   a. 525
   b. 550
   c. 600
   d. 575
   e. 625

24. A dormitory now houses 30 men and allows 42 square feet of space per man. If five more men are put into this dormitory, how much less space will each man have?

   a. 5 square feet
   b. 6 square feet
   c. 7 square feet
   d. 8 square feet
   e. 9 square feet

25. Ron is half as old as Sam, who is three times as old as Ted. The sum of their ages is 55. How old is Ron?

   a. 5 years old
   b. 10 years old
   c. 15 years old
   d. 20 years old
   e. 30 years old

Section 3:
Instrument Comprehension

Directions: This test measures your ability to determine the position of an aircraft in flight by reading instruments showing its compass heading, its amount of climb or dive, and its degree of bank to right or left. In each test item, the left-hand dial is labeled ARTIFICIAL HORIZON. The small aircraft silhouette remains stationary on the face of this dial, while the positions of the heavy black line and black pointer vary with the changes in the position of the aircraft in which the instrument is located.

The heavy black line represents the HORIZON LINE, and the black pointer shows the degree of BANK to right or left. If the aircraft is neither climbing nor diving, the horizon line is directly on the silhouette's fuselage. If the aircraft has no bank, the black pointer will point to zero (Dial 1).

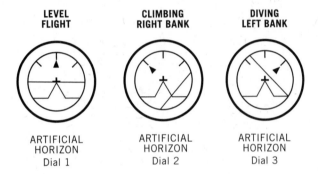

If the aircraft is climbing, the fuselage silhouette is seen between the horizon line and the pointer. The greater the amount of climb, the greater the distance between the horizon line and the fuselage silhouette. If the aircraft is banked to the pilot's right, the pointer will point to the left of zero (Dial 2).

If the aircraft is diving, the horizon line is between the fuselage silhouette and the pointer. The greater the amount of dive, the greater the distance between the horizon line and the fuselage silhouette. If the aircraft is banked to the pilot's left, the pointer will point to the right of zero (Dial 3).

The HORIZON LINE tilts as the aircraft is banked. It is always at a right angles to the pointer.

In each test item, the right-hand dial is the COMPASS. This dial shows the direction in which the aircraft is headed. Dial 4 shows north, Dial 5 is west, and Dial 6 is northwest.

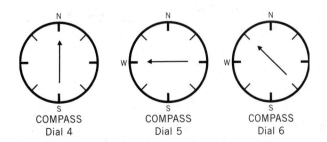

Each item in this test consists of two dials and four silhouettes of aircraft in flight. Your task is to determine which of the four aircraft is closest to the position indicated by the two dials. Remember, you are always looking NORTH at the same altitude as each plane. East is always to the RIGHT as you look at the page. (NOTE: C in Question 2 is the rear view of the aircraft, and B is the front view.)

You will have nine (9) minutes to complete this portion of the test.

Questions: 20
Time: 9 minutes

For sample Instrument Comprehension questions, see page 47.

1.

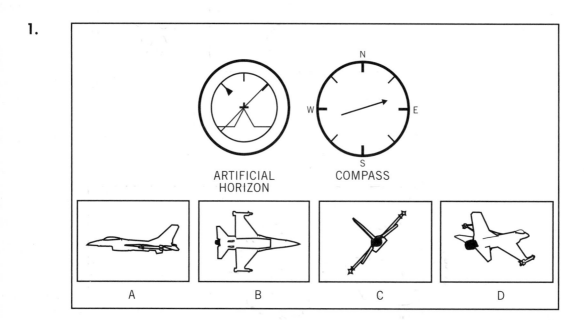

2.

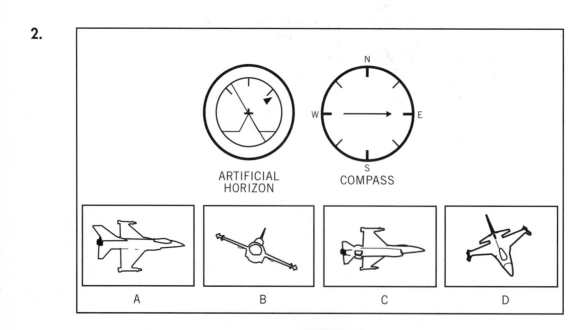

3.

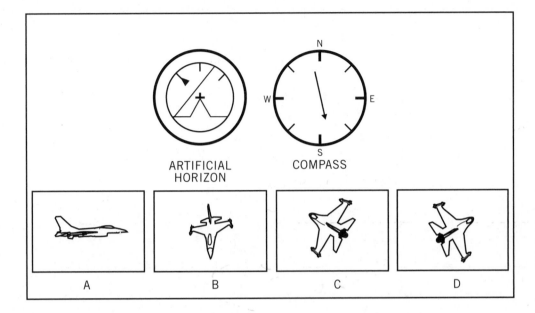

4.

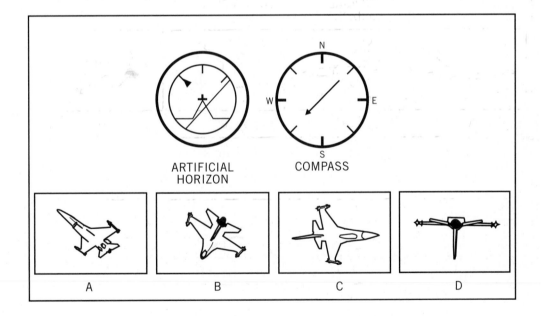

5.

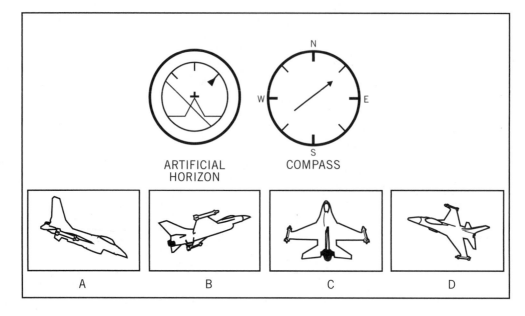

6.

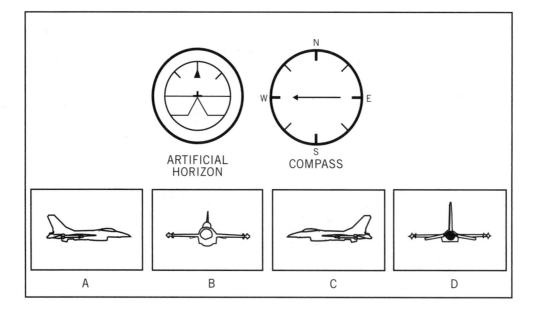

7.

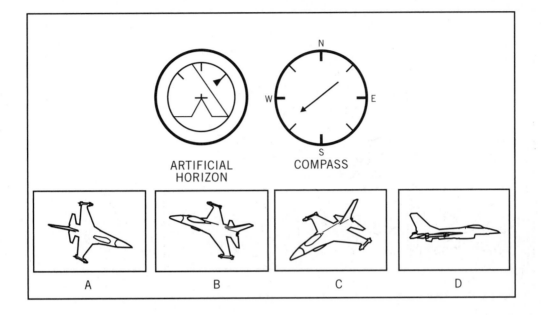

8.

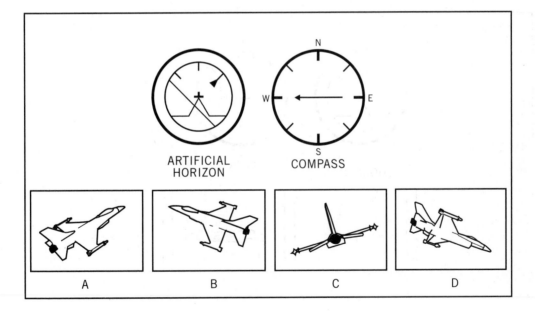

9.

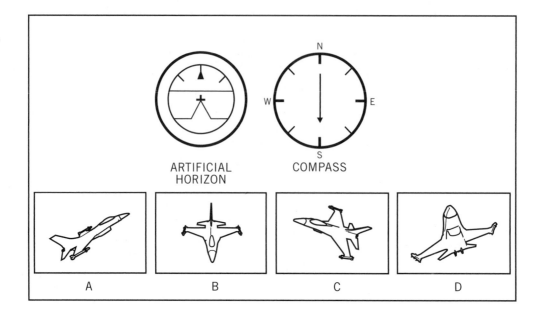

10.

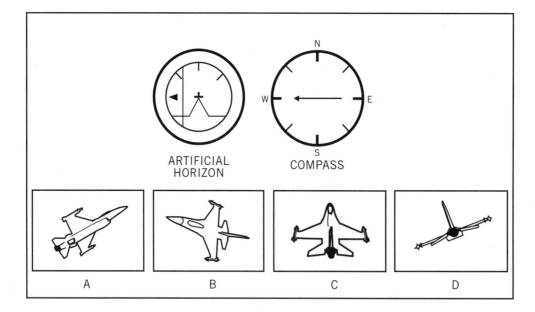

11.

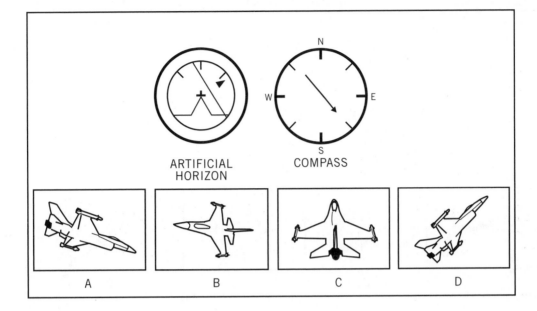

ARTIFICIAL HORIZON   COMPASS

A   B   C   D

12.

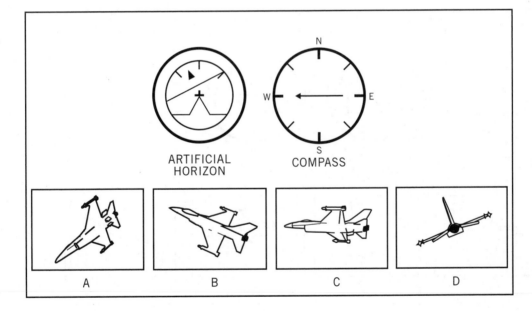

ARTIFICIAL HORIZON   COMPASS

A   B   C   D

13.

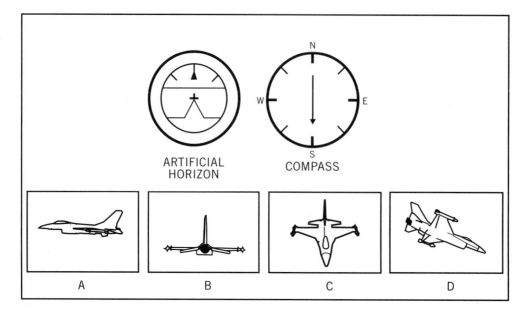

14.

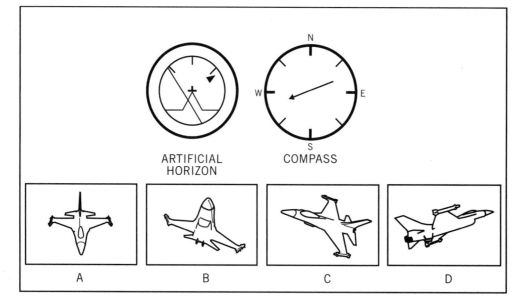

15.

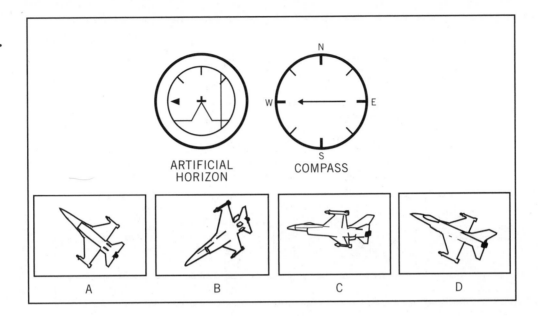

16.

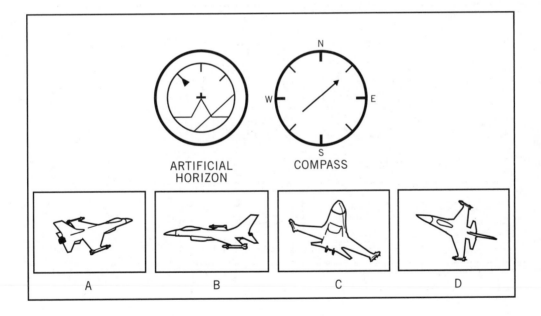

17.

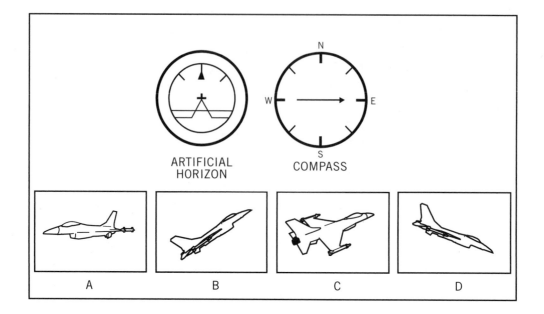

18.

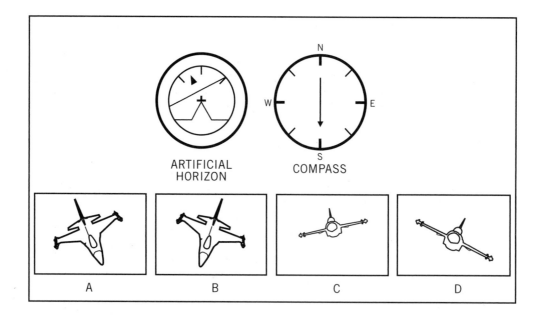

19.

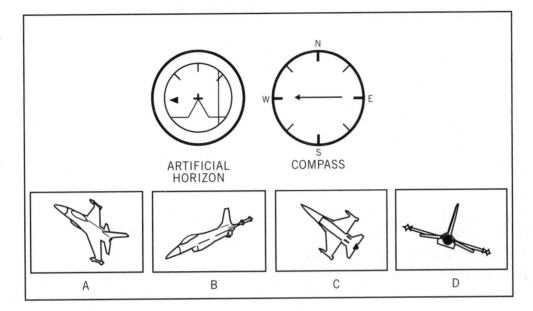

20.

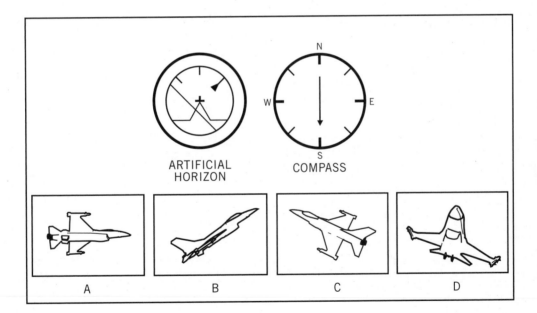

Section 4: Block Counting

Directions: This is a test of your ability to see into a three-dimensional stack of blocks to determine how many pieces are touched by the numbered blocks. It is also a test of your abilities to observe and deduce what you cannot specifically see. Closely study the way in which the blocks are stacked. You may find it helpful to remember that all of the blocks in a pile are the same size and shape. Each stack of blocks is followed by five questions pertaining only to that stack. You will have three (3) minutes to complete this section of the test.

Questions: 20
Time: 3 minutes

For sample Block Counting questions, see page 50.

For questions 1–5, refer to Figure I-1.

Figure I-1

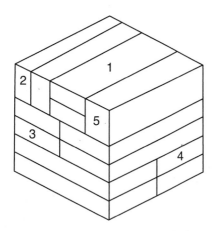

1. Block 1 is touched by _____ other blocks.
   - **a.** 2
   - **b.** 3
   - **c.** 4
   - **d.** 5
   - **e.** 6

2. Block 2 is touched by _____ other blocks.
   - **a.** 2
   - **b.** 3
   - **c.** 4
   - **d.** 5
   - **e.** 6

3. Block 3 is touched by _____ other blocks.
   - **a.** 2
   - **b.** 3
   - **c.** 4
   - **d.** 5
   - **e.** 6

4. Block 4 is touched by _____ other blocks.
   - **a.** 2
   - **b.** 3
   - **c.** 4
   - **d.** 5
   - **e.** 6

5. Block 5 is touched by _____ other blocks.
   - **a.** 2
   - **b.** 3
   - **c.** 4
   - **d.** 5
   - **e.** 6

For questions 6–10, refer to Figure I-2.

Figure I-2

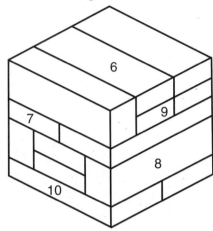

6. Block 6 is touched by _____ other blocks.
   a. 2
   b. 3
   c. 4
   d. 5
   e. 6

7. Block 7 is touched by _____ other blocks.
   a. 2
   b. 3
   c. 4
   d. 5
   e. 6

8. Block 8 is touched by _____ other blocks.
   a. 2
   b. 3
   c. 4
   d. 5
   e. 6

9. Block 9 is touched by _____ other blocks.
   a. 2
   b. 3
   c. 4
   d. 5
   e. 6

10. Block 10 is touched by _____ other blocks.
   a. 2
   b. 3
   c. 4
   d. 5
   e. 6

For questions 11–15, refer to Figure I-3.

Figure I-3

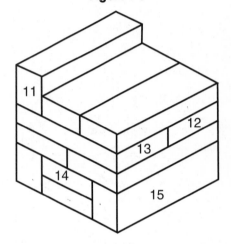

11. Block 11 is touched by _____ other blocks.
   a. 2
   b. 3
   c. 4
   d. 5
   e. 6

12. Block 12 is touched by _____ other blocks.
   a. 2
   b. 3
   c. 4
   d. 5
   e. 6

13. Block 13 is touched by _____ other blocks.
   a. 2
   b. 3
   c. 4
   d. 5
   e. 6

14. Block 14 is touched by _____ other blocks.
- **a.** 2
- **b.** 3
- **c.** 4
- **d.** 5
- **e.** 6

15. Block 15 is touched by _____ other blocks.
- **a.** 2
- **b.** 3
- **c.** 4
- **d.** 5
- **e.** 6

For questions 16–20, refer to Figure I-4.

Figure I-4

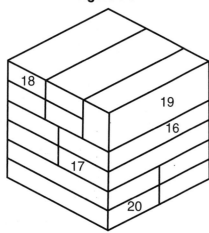

16. Block 16 is touched by _____ other blocks.
- **a.** 2
- **b.** 3
- **c.** 4
- **d.** 5
- **e.** 6

17. Block 17 is touched by _____ other blocks.
- **a.** 2
- **b.** 3
- **c.** 4
- **d.** 5
- **e.** 6

18. Block 18 is touched by _____ other blocks.
- **a.** 2
- **b.** 3
- **c.** 4
- **d.** 5
- **e.** 6

19. Block 19 is touched by _____ other blocks.
- **a.** 2
- **b.** 3
- **c.** 4
- **d.** 5
- **e.** 6

20. Block 20 is touched by _____ other blocks.
- **a.** 2
- **b.** 3
- **c.** 4
- **d.** 5
- **e.** 6

Section 5: Word Knowledge

Directions: This part of the test measures your vocabulary comprehension. For each question you are to choose the answer that most closely means the same as the capitalized word. If you are somewhat familiar with the capitalized word, you can quickly eliminate the options that you know are incorrect. You will have five (5) minutes to complete this section of the test.

Questions: 25
Time: 5 minutes

For sample Word Knowledge questions, see page 44.

1. GAUCHE
   a. awkward
   b. tactful
   c. graceful
   d. experienced
   e. expert

2. ENUMERATE
   a. pronounce
   b. count
   c. explain
   d. plead
   e. exhaust

3. TRIUMPHANT
   a. defeated
   b. vanquished
   c. victorious
   d. musical
   e. beaten

4. MAGNANIMOUS
   a. enormous
   b. scholarly
   c. generous
   d. dignified
   e. wealthy

5. AVERSION
   a. harmony
   b. greed
   c. weariness
   d. dislike
   e. outrage

6. POIGNANT
   a. varied
   b. exclusive
   c. singular
   d. pungent
   e. comprehensive

7. ANTAGONIST
   a. comrade
   b. leader
   c. master
   d. perfectionist
   e. opponent

8. PERSEVERANCE
   a. unhappiness
   b. fame
   c. persistence
   d. humility
   e. efficiency

9. HOMOGENEOUS
   a. alike
   b. plain
   c. native
   d. dissimilar
   e. ordinary

10. CONSPICUOUS
    a. unknown
    b. excel
    c. obvious
    d. forgotten
    e. stellar

11. RECLUSE
   a. prophet
   b. fool
   c. intellectual
   d. hermit
   e. perfectionist

12. TOTE
   a. acquire
   b. complete
   c. tremble
   d. abandon
   e. carry

13. PREEMINENT
   a. basic
   b. final
   c. observed
   d. responsible
   e. outstanding

14. GROTESQUE
   a. extreme
   b. frenzied
   c. bizarre
   d. typical
   e. majestic

15. OUTMODED
   a. worthless
   b. unusable
   c. obsolete
   d. unnecessary
   e. pretentious

16. GARBLED
   a. lucid
   b. unintelligible
   c. devoured
   d. outrageous
   e. invalid

17. FRAIL
   a. vivid
   b. delicate
   c. robust
   d. adaptable
   e. scarce

18. VINDICTIVE
   a. disorderly
   b. outrageous
   c. insulting
   d. offensive
   e. spiteful

19. ORATION
   a. nuisance
   b. independence
   c. address
   d. length
   e. elaboration

20. GLIB
   a. angry
   b. superficial
   c. insulting
   d. dishonest
   e. descriptive

21. ECCENTRIC
   a. normal
   b. frugal
   c. wild
   d. selective
   e. peculiar

22. PANACEA
   a. cure
   b. result
   c. cause
   d. necessity
   e. problem

23. DETRIMENTAL

    a. harmful

    b. beneficial

    c. cumulative

    d. angered

    e. outstanding

24. OSTENTATIOUS

    a. hilarious

    b. pretentious

    c. outrageous

    d. obnoxious

    e. obsequious

25. NEGLIGIBLE

    a. insignificant

    b. delicate

    c. meaningful

    d. illegible

    e. nonchalant

Section 6: Table Reading

Directions: This is a test of your ability to read tables quickly and accurately. Notice that the X values in each table are shown at the top of the table and the Y values are shown on the left of the table. In this test, you are to find the entry that occurs at the intersection of the row and the column corresponding to the values given. On your answer sheet, fill in the letter that corresponds with the number at the intersection of the X and Y values. Accuracy is important. You will have seven (7) minutes to complete this section of the test.

Questions: 40

Time: 7 minutes

For sample Table Reading questions, see page 51.

Using Figure B-1 for questions 1 through 5, determine the correct value for the X and Y values in each question given.

FIGURE B-1

		X VALUE						
		−3	−2	−1	0	1	2	3
Y VALUE	−3	45	23	77	93	52	54	92
	−2	82	12	71	55	25	48	30
	−1	13	65	33	14	50	38	19
	0	40	84	85	53	66	73	88
	1	55	43	22	70	20	99	32
	2	23	10	62	62	15	42	63
	3	32	44	55	72	83	11	60

1. −3, 2

    a. 82

    b. 54

    c. 23

    d. 44

    e. 36

2. 2, –2
   a. 12
   b. 10
   c. 48
   d. 42
   e. 38

3. –2, 3
   a. 44
   b. 82
   c. 30
   d. 23
   e. 32

4. 0, –0
   a. 85
   b. 33
   c. 53
   d. 70
   e. 14

5. 3, 1
   a. 13
   b. 55
   c. 32
   d. 83
   e. 44

Using Figure B-2 for questions 6 through 10, determine the correct value for the given X and Y values.

FIGURE B-2

X VALUE

Y VALUE	–3	–2	–1	0	1	2	3
–3	32	64	12	98	25	74	15
–2	35	57	97	66	43	52	44
–1	76	49	84	12	68	14	68
0	45	29	79	61	37	82	11
1	92	28	63	24	77	29	65
2	74	26	99	54	55	16	62
3	97	58	46	81	22	34	53

6. 2, –1
   a. 99
   b. 88
   c. 55
   d. 43
   e. 14

7. 0, 0
   a. 11
   b. 45
   c. 0
   d. 61
   e. 76

8. –2, –1
   a. 25
   b. 33
   c. 39
   d. 45
   e. 49

9. −1, 2
   a. 24
   b. 14
   c. 29
   d. 55
   e. 99

10. 3, 3
   a. 32
   b. 53
   c. 61
   d. 82
   e. 62

Using Figure B-3 for questions 11 through 15, determine the correct value for the given X and Y values.

FIGURE B-3

		X VALUE					
		−3	−2	−1	0	1	2	3
Y VALUE	−3	45	89	79	77	29	68	58
	−2	86	27	48	38	97	66	96
	−1	39	37	43	36	45	56	78
	0	18	17	55	98	44	87	34
	1	88	49	31	59	28	69	67
	2	37	76	47	22	16	45	33
	3	46	19	99	54	57	18	26

11. −1, −1
   a. 28
   b. 43
   c. 41
   d. 45
   e. 26

12. −2, 1
   a. 49
   b. 56
   c. 86
   d. 93
   e. 99

13. −3, 0
   a. 18
   b. 77
   c. 54
   d. 34
   e. 26

14. 1, 3
   a. 29
   b. 34
   c. 41
   d. 52
   e. 57

15. −3, −2
   a. 96
   b. 86
   c. 33
   d. 18
   e. 89

Using Figure B-4 for questions 16 through 20, determine the correct value for the given X and Y values.

FIGURE B-4

X VALUE

Y VALUE		-3	-2	-1	0	1	2	3
	-3	24	17	72	55	23	95	35
	-2	12	53	93	97	66	32	13
	-1	56	65	34	22	44	87	43
	0	75	52	43	48	92	45	85
	1	84	87	36	16	76	54	82
	2	46	15	86	64	83	14	26
	3	73	74	62	33	225	63	42

16. −3, −3
  a. 24
  b. 35
  c. 42
  d. 73
  e. 82

17. 2, 2
  a. 14
  b. 53
  c. 34
  d. 23
  e. 13

18. −2, 3
  a. 12
  b. 17
  c. 35
  d. 74
  e. 76

19. −1, 0
  a. 22
  b. 48
  c. 34
  d. 52
  e. 43

20. 0, 2
  a. 12
  b. 45
  c. 64
  d. 93
  e. 97

Using Figure B-5 for questions 21 through 25, determine the correct value for the given X and Y values.

FIGURE B-5

X VALUE

Y VALUE		-3	-2	-1	0	1	2	3
	-3	12	92	69	63	29	43	13
	-2	99	31	72	42	91	82	41
	-1	33	97	39	28	18	42	53
	0	49	52	23	21	51	32	23
	1	81	73	58	93	68	59	38
	2	78	89	61	79	98	22	19
	3	83	71	88	48	62	11	34

21. 2, −3
  a. 82
  b. 43
  c. 11
  d. 92
  e. 71

22. −1, 3
  a. 69
  b. 88
  c. 29
  d. 62
  e. 53

23. 2, 2
  a. 13
  b. 22
  c. 82
  d. 89
  e. 91

24. −3, 1
a. 53
b. 69
c. 81
d. 88
e. 93

25. 2, 3
a. 19
b. 92
c. 71
d. 11
e. 99

Using Figure B-6 for questions 26 through 40, determine the correct value for the given X and Y values.

FIGURE B-6

X VALUE

Y VALUE	−9	−8	−7	−6	−5	−4	−3	−2	−1	0	1	2	3	4	5	6	7	8	9
−9	48	57	52	13	86	91	54	82	52	87	46	68	92	47	53	38	52	45	78
−8	78	58	26	90	54	77	50	41	24	18	12	32	54	16	39	28	59	83	57
−7	54	43	77	23	49	54	45	81	64	21	54	87	56	10	15	50	35	68	99
−6	52	56	21	42	25	62	70	88	28	55	15	48	56	15	85	52	87	74	62
−5	19	23	58	98	38	58	47	56	74	21	99	84	28	48	24	56	65	11	56
−4	25	82	54	12	33	76	25	43	93	53	31	10	20	34	76	92	28	33	52
−3	43	65	21	45	21	58	86	96	35	71	70	80	45	85	43	23	51	52	14
−2	58	87	26	65	52	55	43	76	55	26	29	96	54	19	14	87	74	55	92
−1	82	73	34	52	95	42	26	74	49	83	75	96	28	21	31	78	46	39	76
0	21	85	58	43	74	38	72	81	11	18	84	73	52	66	62	81	12	43	17
1	50	26	54	45	25	84	95	31	18	45	76	61	41	30	24	46	66	83	73
2	86	52	64	25	21	17	64	23	71	13	90	56	44	70	12	27	48	87	33
3	74	13	75	17	85	56	50	43	68	10	37	85	71	16	52	49	18	66	95
4	32	69	78	68	73	54	15	61	42	78	91	28	93	85	34	70	59	46	35
5	15	55	90	33	91	12	99	23	53	62	79	81	64	40	38	26	69	73	13
6	64	38	62	54	18	22	36	28	93	38	61	98	14	30	49	63	88	12	41
7	84	56	53	56	76	45	64	11	83	47	23	74	31	89	57	38	32	78	19
8	56	84	21	86	21	18	29	31	12	25	59	40	72	98	53	22	45	88	74
9	46	19	64	47	54	53	75	82	69	45	80	13	22	15	70	18	49	59	16

26. 9, −4
a. 14
b. 35
c. 52
d. 25
e. 32

27. −5, 9
a. 54
b. 90
c. 32
d. 53
e. 56

28. −1, −4
a. 14
b. 93
c. 28
d. 91
e. 42

29. −3, 8
a. 29
b. 75
c. 50
d. 72
e. 52

30. 5, −3
a. 99
b. 64
c. 47
d. 28
e. 43

31. 0, −7
a. 74
b. 47
c. 58
d. 12
e. 21

32. 4, −4
a. 85
b. 48
c. 20
d. 76
e. 34

33. 7, −3
a. 32
b. 21
c. 52
d. 31
e. 51

34. −9, 3
a. 43
b. 74
c. 54
d. 92
e. 47

35. 1, −8
a. 34
b. 74
c. 24
d. 12
e. 73

36. 0, 0
a. 84
b. 11
c. 18
d. 87
e. 80

37. −5, 0
a. 62
b. 74
c. 21
d. 26
e. 58

38. −2, 7
a. 81
b. 87
c. 11
d. 74
e. 14

39. −8, 5
a. 55
b. 23
c. 39
d. 54
e. 83

40. −6, 4
   a. 26
   b. 68
   c. 23
   d. 74
   e. 92

Section 7: Math Knowledge

Directions: This part of the test measures your ability to use learned mathematical relationships. Each problem is followed by four possible answers. You must decide which one of the four answers is correct. The best method for attacking each of these questions is given in the answer block at the end of this chapter. When you take the actual test, scratch paper will be provided for working out the problems. You will have twenty-two (22) minutes to finish this section of the test.

Questions: 25
Time: 22 minutes

For sample Math Knowledge questions, see page 45.

1. The first digit of the square root of 112,092 is
   a. 1
   b. 2
   c. 3
   d. 4
   e. 5

2. Roberta draws two similar pentagons. The perimeter of the larger pentagon is 93 feet; one of its sides measures 24 feet If the perimeter of the smaller pentagon equals 31 feet, then the corresponding side of the smaller pentagon measures
   a. $5s = 31$
   b. $93s = 24 \times 31$
   c. $93 \times 24 = 31s$
   d. $5 \times 31 = s$
   e. $31 \times 24 = s$

3. Which measurement uses the largest increment?
   a. perimeter
   b. area
   c. surface area
   d. volume
   e. They all use the same size increment.

4. What is the distance, in miles, around a circular course with a radius of 49 miles (use $\text{pi} = \frac{22}{7}$)?
   a. 154 miles
   b. 308 miles
   c. 462 miles
   d. 539 miles
   e. 616 miles

5. Examine (A), (B), and (C) and choose the best answer.
   (A) 0.5
   (B) 5%
   (C) $\frac{1}{5}$
   a. (A) is greater than (B).
   b. (B) is greater than (A).
   c. (C) is greater than (A).
   d. (A) and (B) are equal.
   e. (B) times (A) is equal to (C).

6. Examine (A), (B), and (C) and choose the best answer.
   (A) $n \times n$
   (B) n^2
   (C) $n(n)$
   a. (A) plus (C) equals (B).
   b. (B) is greater than (C) but less than (A).
   c. (A) is less than (C).
   d. (A), (B), and (C) are all equal.
   e. (B) times (A) is equal to (C).

7. Find the circumference of a circle with a diameter of 10 centimeters.

   a. 3.14 cm

   b. 31.4 cm

   c. 62.8 cm

   d. 6.28 cm

   e. none of the above

8. Which of the measures represents an obtuse angle?

   a. $45°$

   b. $60°$

   c. $85°$

   d. $90°$

   e. $105°$

9. $\frac{n^2}{n^2} =$

   a. n^7

   b. n^2

   c. n^3

   d. $2n^3$

   e. $7n$

10. Simplify the following radical expression: $\sqrt{3n^2}$

   a. $n\sqrt{3}$

   b. $9n$

   c. $n\sqrt{9}$

   d. $\sqrt{9}$

   e. $3\sqrt{n}$

11. Look at this series: $\frac{1}{6}, \frac{1}{6}, \frac{1}{2}, \frac{2}{3}, \ldots$ What number should come next?

   a. 1

   b. $\frac{4}{6}$

   c. $\frac{5}{6}$

   d. $\frac{8}{9}$

   e. $\frac{7}{12}$

12. Find the volume of a pyramid with four congruent base sides. The length of each base side and the prism's height measure 2.4 feet.

   a. 46 cubic feet

   b. 4.6 cubic feet

   c. 4.8 cubic feet

   d. 48 cubic feet

   e. 1.2 cubic feet

13. What number is 42 less than $\frac{1}{5}$ of 820?

   a. 98

   b. 112

   c. 122

   d. 210

   e. 222

14. Simplify the following radical expression: $2\sqrt{7} - 3\sqrt{28}$

   a. $-6\sqrt{7}$

   b. $5\sqrt{196}$

   c. $-5\sqrt{196}$

   d. $4\sqrt{7}$

   e. $-4\sqrt{7}$

15. $\frac{8xy^2}{2xy} =$

   a. $2xy$

   b. $4x^2$

   c. $16y$

   d. $4y$

   e. $4y^2$

16. What number is 6 less than $\frac{2}{5}$ of 25?

   a. -4

   b. 1

   c. 4

   d. 9

   e. 12

17. What number is 3 times 4% of 20?

   a. 2.4
   b. 5.4
   c. 24
   d. 27
   e. 32

18. Examine (A), (B), and (C) and choose the best answer.

   (A) 7^2
   (B) 4^3
   (C) $3^2 + 6$

   a. (A) and (B) are equal.
   b. (A) is greater than (B).
   c. (B) minus (A) is equal to (C).
   d. (B) and (C) are equal to (A).
   e. (B) times (A) is equal to (C).

19. The expression *5 factorial* equals

   a. $\frac{1}{4}$
   b. 16
   c. 50
   d. 120
   e. 500

20. What number added to 15% of 30 equals 20?

   a. −25
   b. 4.5
   c. 12
   d. 15.5
   e. 25.5

21. The reciprocal of 10 is

   a. 0.1
   b. 0.2
   c. 0.5
   d. 1.0
   e. 2.0

22. What number plus 2 times the same number equals 99?

   a. 16
   b. 33
   c. 66
   d. 297
   e. 365

23. Examine (A), (B), and (C) and choose the best answer.

   (A) $\frac{2}{5}$ of 100
   (B) $\frac{1}{2}$ of 80
   (C) $\frac{1}{8}$ of 160

   a. (A) is less than (B) or (C).
   b. (A) and (B) are equal.
   c. (B) and (C) are equal.
   d. (B) is greater than (A) but less than (C).
   e. (B) times (A) is equal to (C).

24. Isadora wants to know the perimeter of the face of a building; however, she does not have a ladder. She knows that the building's rectangular facade casts a 36-foot shadow at noon, while a nearby mailbox casts a 12-foot shadow at noon. The mailbox is 4.5-feet tall. If the length of the façade is 54 feet, what is the measure of the façade's perimeter?

   a. $p = 13.5 \times 4$
   b. $p = 54 \times 4$
   c. $p = 4.5(2) + 12(2)$
   d. $p = 13.5(2) + 54(2)$
   e. $p = 13.5 + 4$

25. Find the circumference, in meters, of a circle with a radius of 25 centimeters.

   a. 1.57 m
   b. 157 m
   c. 15.7 cm
   d. 78.5 m
   e. 7.85 m

Section 8: Aviation Information

Directions: This part of the test measures your knowledge of aviation. This portion is common to all three service selection tests, although the number of questions varies from one service to another. Each of the questions or incomplete statements is followed by several choices. You must decide which one of the choices best completes the statement or answers the question. Eliminating any obviously incorrect choices first will increase your chances of selecting the correct answer. You will have eight (8) minutes to complete these questions.

Questions: 20
Time: 8 minutes

For sample Aviation Information questions, see page 52.

1. If the rudder of an aircraft is deflected, the aircraft will move about the _____ axis.
   a. centroid
   b. pitch
   c. roll
   d. yaw
   e. none of the above

2. If the elevator is deflected, the aircraft will move about the _____ axis.
   a. centroid
   b. pitch
   c. roll
   d. yaw
   e. none of the above

3. If the aileron is deflected, the aircraft will move about the _____ axis.
   a. centroid
   b. pitch
   c. roll
   d. yaw
   e. none of the above

4. Pushing the right rudder pedal in causes the rudder to deflect to the right of center, causing which movement of the aircraft?
   a. Pushes the tail of the aircraft right, and the nose of the aircraft left.
   b. Pushes the tail of the aircraft left, and the nose of the aircraft right.
   c. Pushes the tail of the aircraft left, and the nose of the aircraft left.
   d. Pushes the tail of the aircraft right and the nose of the aircraft right.
   e. none of the above

5. What is the "angle of attack"?
   a. the angle between the airfoil chord and relative direction of motion
   b. the angle between blade center and angle of incidence
   c. the angle between airfoil chord and angle of incidence
   d. the angle between the induced air flow and relative direction of motion
   e. none of the above

6. What do we call the force acting rearward on an aircraft caused by air friction and lift?
   a. lift
   b. thrust
   c. drag
   d. weight
   e. none of the above

7. The shape of a wing's cross-section, which causes lift, is described using what term?

    a. camber

    b. delta

    c. swept

    d. straight

    e. none of the above

8. Pulling back on the aircraft controls will deflect which control surface on the aircraft?

    a. rudder

    b. trim tabs

    c. ailerons

    d. flaps

    e. elevators

9. Increasing which parameter will eventually cause a stall of the aircraft?

    a. air density

    b. angle of attack

    c. airspeed

    d. pitch angle

    e. none of the above

10. Aviation speeds are generally measured in nautical miles per hour (knots). Which statement is true about knots?

    a. 100 knots is identical 100 miles per hour (mph).

    b. 100 knots is faster than 100 mph.

    c. 100 knots is slower than 100 mph.

    d. 100 knots has no relationship to mph.

    e. none of the above

11. The transponder codes for loss of communication and for emergency, respectively, are?

    a. 7600 and 7500

    b. 7700 and 7600

    c. 7600 and 7700

    d. 7500 and 7600

    e. 7500 and 7700

12. Used in aviation, *Zulu time* refers to what?

    a. Eastern Standard Time

    b. Eastern Daylight Saving Time

    c. Time at International Date Line

    d. Greenwich Mean Time

    e. Pacific Standard Time

13. What does the Pitot Static system in an aircraft measure?

    a. airspeed and altitude

    b. fuel quantity and fuel weight

    c. manifold pressure and air pressure

    d. cabin pressure and manifold pressure

    e. none of the above

14. Pitch angle is the angle between the fuselage of the aircraft and what?

    a. relative wind

    b. horizon

    c. runway threshold

    d. propeller

    e. none of the above

15. In general, which statement is true when an aircraft fully extends its flaps and does not change other parameters?

    a. Wing produces more lift and more drag.

    b. Wing produces more lift, but less drag.

    c. Wing produces same amount of lift, but more drag.

    d. Wing produces less lift and less drag.

    e. Wing produces less lift, but more drag.

16. In relation to the air flowing beneath the wing, how does the air flowing over the top of a wing, producing lift, move?

    a. same speed

    b. slower

    c. stops

    d. faster

    e. none of the above

17. Airport runways are numbered according to?
  a. length and width
  b. wind direction
  c. by first two digits of compass direction
  d. order of construction
  e. aircraft type

18. What causes wake turbulence?
  a. wind from thunderstorms blowing across runways
  b. microburst
  c. vortices off wings of aircraft caused by generating lift
  d. dust devils
  e. solar bursts

19. What are the colors of the port and starboard running lights?
  a. white/white
  b. red/red
  c. green/red
  d. red/white
  e. green/white

20. Mach 1 refers to what in aviation?
  a. speed of light
  b. speed of sound
  c. speed of heat
  d. speed of any jet
  e. none of the above

Section 9: Rotated Blocks

Directions: This test measures your ability to visualize and manipulate objects in space. For each question in this test, you will be shown a picture of a block. You must find a second block that is identical to the first. You will have thirteen (13) minutes to work the following problems.

Questions: 15
Time: 13 minutes

For sample Rotated Block questions, see page 53.

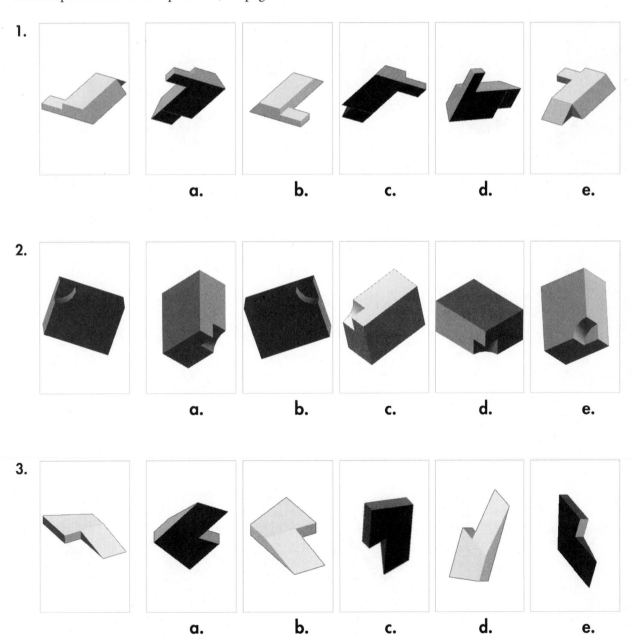

1.
    a.   b.   c.   d.   e.

2.
    a.   b.   c.   d.   e.

3.
    a.   b.   c.   d.   e.

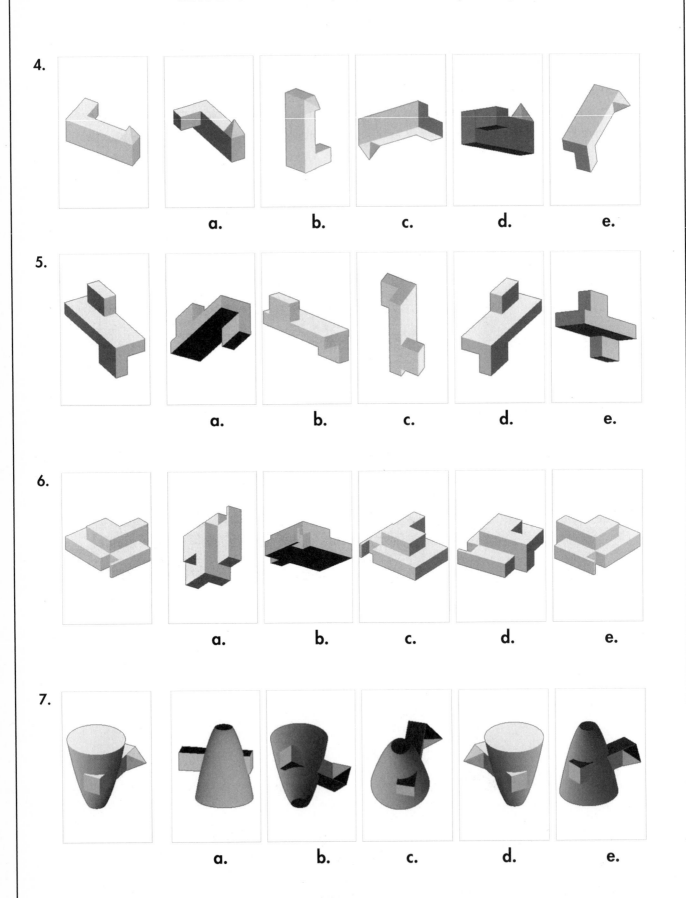

4.

a.   b.   c.   d.   e.

5.

a.   b.   c.   d.   e.

6.

a.   b.   c.   d.   e.

7.

a.   b.   c.   d.   e.

8.

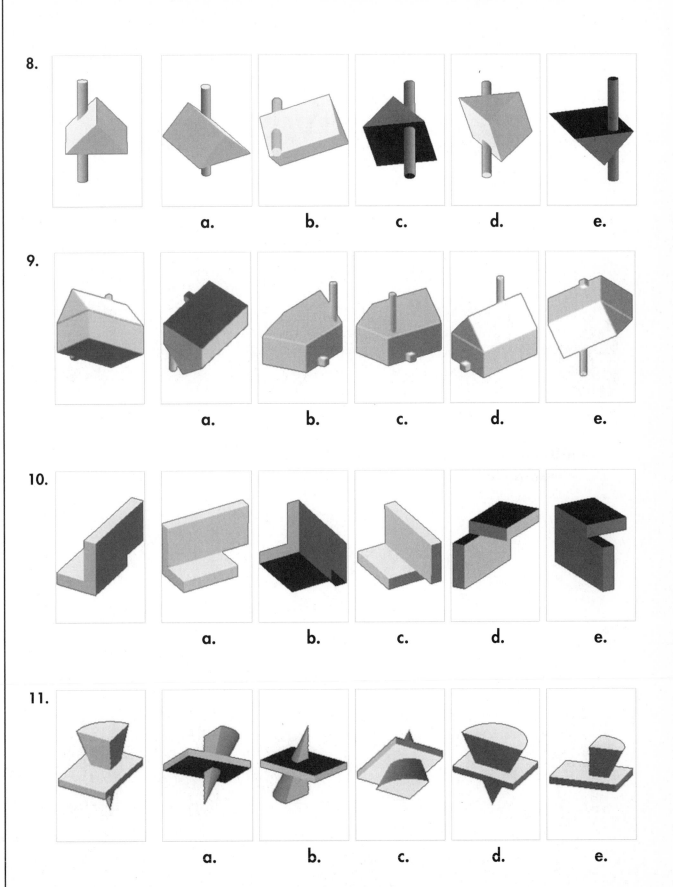

a.   b.   c.   d.   e.

9.

a.   b.   c.   d.   e.

10.

a.   b.   c.   d.   e.

11.

a.   b.   c.   d.   e.

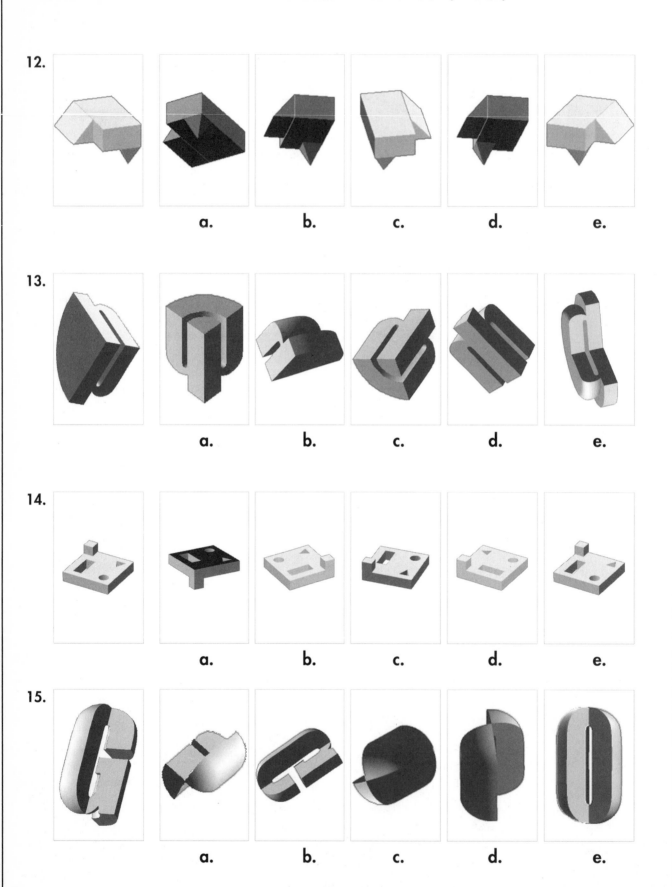

12.   a.   b.   c.   d.   e.

13.   a.   b.   c.   d.   e.

14.   a.   b.   c.   d.   e.

15.   a.   b.   c.   d.   e.

Section 10: General Science

Directions: This part of the test measures your knowledge in the area of science. Each of the questions or incomplete statements is followed by five choices. You must decide which one of the choices best answers the question or completes the statement. Again, if you are unsure of an answer, use the process of elimination. Remember, there are no penalties for guessing. You have ten (10) minutes to complete this section of the test.

Questions: 20
Time: 10 minutes

For sample General Science questions, see page 55.

1. The element _____ is the most abundant component of air.
   a. helium
   b. hydrogen
   c. nitrogen
   d. oxygen
   e. carbon

2. According to Boyle's law, if the pressure of a fixed mass of gas is kept constant but the temperature is allowed to increase, the volume of gas will
   a. not increase.
   b. decrease in proportion to the change in temperature.
   c. increase in proportion to the change in temperature.
   d. increase at twice the rate of change in temperature.
   e. There is not enough information to complete the statement.

3. Ohm's law describes how, if voltage is kept constant, an increase in current results in
   a. an increase in resistance.
   b. a decrease in resistance.
   c. an increase or decrease in resistance.
   d. no change in resistance.
   e. There is not enough information to complete the statement.

4. _____ wavelengths are longer than visible light and therefore have lower frequencies.
   a. Infrared
   b. Ultraviolet
   c. X-ray
   d. Gamma ray
   e. none of the above

5. If a substance has a pH of 1.0, it can be classified as a(n)
   a. acid.
   b. base.
   c. solvent.
   d. neutral compound.
   e. There is not enough information to complete the statement.

6. _____ in an atom's nucleus have a positive electrical charge.
   a. Electrons
   b. Neutrons
   c. Ions
   d. Photons
   e. Protons

7. A vector is defined by
   a. length.
   b. direction.
   c. neither length or direction.
   d. both length and direction.
   e. none of the above

8. The organ that is responsible for the production of insulin is the
  a. spleen.
  b. kidney.
  c. pancreas.
  d. liver.
  e. intestine.

9. The four planets in the solar system that are considered the gas giants are
  a. Mercury, Venus, Jupiter, Saturn.
  b. Jupiter, Saturn, Uranus, Neptune.
  c. Venus, Saturn, Uranus, Neptune.
  d. Jupiter, Saturn, Neptune, Pluto.
  e. Saturn, Uranus, Neptune, Pluto.

10. Carbon dioxide is made up of
  a. carbon.
  b. oxygen.
  c. both carbon and oxygen.
  d. both carbon and nitrogen.
  e. none of the above

11. What is a solution called when it can dissolve no more solutes?
  a. unsaturated
  b. supersaturated
  c. saturated
  d. volatile
  e. stable

12. What is the total number of atoms present in the molecule CH_3NH_2?
  a. 4
  b. 5
  c. 6
  d. 7
  e. 8

13. On the Celsius temperature scale, at what temperatures does water freeze and boil?
  a. It freezes at $-10°$ and boils at $100°$.
  b. It freezes at $32°$ and boils at $100°$.
  c. It freezes at $0°$ and boils at $212°$.
  d. It freezes at $32°$ and boils at $212°$.
  e. It freezes at $0°$ and boils at $100°$.

14. It is harder to stop a car moving at 60 miles per hour than a car moving at 15 miles per hour because the car moving at 60 miles per hour has more
  a. momentum.
  b. deceleration.
  c. mass.
  d. velocity.
  e. density.

15. What is the scientific notation for 617,000?
  a. 6.17×10^{-5}
  b. $.617 \times 10^2$
  c. $.617 \times 10^3$
  d. $.617 \times 10^4$
  e. 6.17×10^5

16. If you throw a baseball forward, it will accelerate downward because of
  a. orbital motion.
  b. terminal velocity.
  c. increase in resistance.
  d. Newton's third law of motion.
  e. gravity.

17. What type of rock is formed by the cooling of lava? (An example is granite.)
  a. metamorphic
  b. sedimentary
  c. igneous
  d. salt
  e. sandstone

18. One hundred centimeters equals how many kilometers?
   a. 0.001
   b. 0.01
   c. 0.1
   d. 1.0
   e. 10

19. Which of the following contains fiber?
   a. chicken breast
   b. raspberries
   c. steak
   d. butter
   e. yogurt

20. Which of the following ecosystems could be described as having a temperate climate and many leaf-shedding trees?
   a. a deciduous forest
   b. a tropical rain forest
   c. a tundra
   d. a taiga
   e. a prairie

Section 11: Hidden Figures

Directions: This part of the test measures your ability to see a simple figure in a complex drawing. Above each group of questions are five figures, lettered A, B, C, D, and E. Below this set of figures are several numbered drawings. You are to determine which lettered figure is contained in each of the numbered drawings. Each numbered drawing contains only ONE of the lettered figures. The correct figure in each drawing will always be of the same size and in the same position as it appears in the top set of figures. Look at each numbered drawing and decide which one of the five lettered figures is contained in it.

Questions: 15
Time: 8 minutes

For sample Hidden Figures questions, see page 56.

Use Figure J-1 for questions 1–5.

Figure J-1

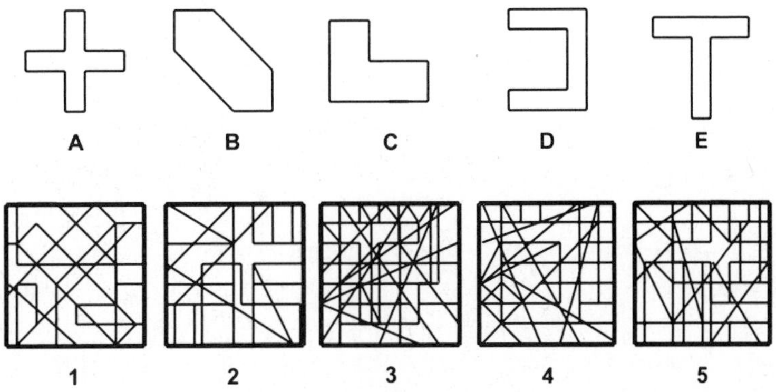

1. The hidden figure in block 1 is _____.
   a. A
   b. B
   c. C
   d. D
   e. E

2. The hidden figure in block 2 is _____.
   a. A
   b. B
   c. C
   d. D
   e. E

3. The hidden figure in block 3 is _____.
   a. A
   b. B
   c. C
   d. D
   e. E

4. The hidden figure in block 4 is _____.
   a. A
   b. B
   c. C
   d. D
   e. E

5. The hidden figure in block 5 is _____.
   a. A
   b. B
   c. C
   d. D
   e. E

Use Figure J-2 for questions 6–10.

Figure J-2

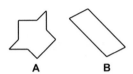

A   B   C   D   E

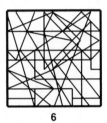 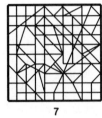 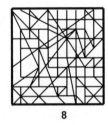

6   7   8

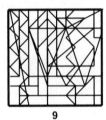 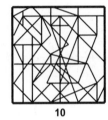

9   10

6. The hidden figure in block 6 is _____.
   a. A
   b. B
   c. C
   d. D
   e. E

7. The hidden figure in block 7 is _____.
   a. A
   b. B
   c. C
   d. D
   e. E

8. The hidden figure in block 8 is _____.
   a. A
   b. B
   c. C
   d. D
   e. E

9. The hidden figure in block 9 is _____.
   a. A
   b. B
   c. C
   d. D
   e. E

10. The hidden figure in block 10 is _____.
   a. A
   b. B
   c. C
   d. D
   e. E

Use Figure J-3 for questions 11–15.

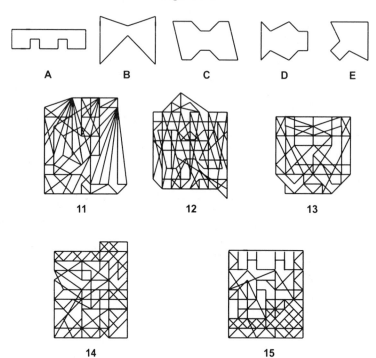

Figure J-3

11. The hidden figure in block 11 is _____.
    a. A
    b. B
    c. C
    d. D
    e. E

12. The hidden figure in block 12 is _____.
    a. A
    b. B
    c. C
    d. D
    e. E

13. The hidden figure in block 13 is _____.
    a. A
    b. B
    c. C
    d. D
    e. E

14. The hidden figure in block 14 is _____.
    a. A
    b. B
    c. C
    d. D
    e. E

15. The hidden figure in block 15 is _____.
    a. A
    b. B
    c. C
    d. D
    e. E

AFOQT ANSWERS

Section 1: Verbal Analogies

1. b. Coffee goes into a cup and soup goes into a bowl. Choices **a**, **c**, and **e** are incorrect because they are other utensils. The answer is not choice **d** because the word *food* is too general.

2. c. A bicycle is put in motion by means of a pedal. A canoe is put into motion by means of an oar. The answer is not choice **a** or **e** because the substance water does not necessarily put the canoe into motion. Kayak (choice **b**) is incorrect because it is a type of boat similar to a canoe. Choice **d** is incorrect because a fleet is a group of boats.

3. d. A window is made up of panes, and a book is made up of pages. The answer is not choice **a**, because a novel is a type of book. The answer is not choice **b**, because glass has no relationship to a book. Choices **c** and **e** are incorrect because a book is not made up of covers or indexes.

4. b. An actor performs in a play. A musician performs at a concert. Choices **a**, **c**, **d**, and **e** are incorrect because none include people who perform.

5. e. A group of lions is called a pride. A group of fish swim in a school. Teacher (choice **a**) and student (choice **b**) refer to another meaning of the word *school*. The answer is not choice **c** or **d** because self-respect and learning have no obvious relationship to this particular meaning of school.

6. b. *Elated* is the opposite of *despondent*; *enlightened* is the opposite of *ignorant*.

7. a. If someone has been humiliated, they have been greatly embarrassed. If someone is terrified, they are extremely frightened. Choice **e** may be related to a feeling of fright, but it is not an extreme emotion and therefore is not as good a match as choice **a**. The answer is not choice **b** because an agitated person is not necessarily frightened. Choices **c** and **d** are incorrect because neither word expresses a state of being frightened.

8. d. An odometer is an instrument used to measure mileage. A compass is an instrument used to determine direction. Choices **a**, **b**, **c**, and **e** are incorrect because none is an instrument.

9. c. *Fray* and *ravel* are synonyms, as are *jolt* and *shake*.

10. c. An elephant is a pachyderm; a kangaroo is a marsupial.

11. a. A psychologist treats a neurosis; an ophthalmologist treats a cataract.

12. c. Upon harvesting, cotton is gathered into bales; grain is gathered into shocks.

13. a. *Division* and *section* are synonyms; *layer* and *tier* are synonyms.

14. d. A mechanic works in a garage; a surgeon works in a hospital.

15. c. A chickadee is a type of bird; a Siamese is a type of cat.

16. e. To saunter is to walk slowly; to drizzle is to rain slowly.

17. b. To tailor a suit is to alter it; to edit a manuscript is to alter it.

18. a. Jaundice is an indication of a liver problem; rash is an indication of a skin problem.

19. c. Obsession is a greater degree of interest; fantasy is a greater degree of dream.

20. e. Slapstick results in laughter; horror results in fear.

21. b. *Verve* and *enthusiasm* are synonyms; *devotion* and *reverence* are synonyms.

22. a. A conviction results in incarceration; a reduction results in diminution.

23. b. Being erudite is a trait of a professor; being imaginative is a trait of an inventor.

24. d. *Dependable* and *capricious* are antonyms; *capable* and *inept* are antonyms.

25. c. *Hegemony* means *dominance*; *autonomy* means *independence*.

Section 2: Arithmetic Reasoning

1. c. Round 157 to 200 and round 817 to 800: $200 \times 800 = 160,000$.

2. d. It is important to remember to include all three telephone sets ($375 total), both computers ($2,600 total), and both monitors ($1,900 total) in the total value.

3. e. To solve this problem, you must convert $3\frac{1}{2}$ to $\frac{7}{2}$ and then divide $\frac{7}{2}$ by $\frac{1}{4}$. The answer, $\frac{28}{4}$, is then reduced to the number 14.

4. d. Mixed numbers must be converted to fractions, and you must use the least common denominator in this case 8: $\frac{18}{8} + \frac{37}{8} + \frac{4}{8} = \frac{59}{8}$ which is $7\frac{3}{8}$ after it is reduced.

5. b. You can't just take 25% off the original price, because the 10% discount after three years of service is taken off the price that has already been reduced by 15%. Figure the problem in two steps: After the 15% discount, the price is $71.83. 90% of that—subtracting 10%—is $64.65.

6. c. The problem is solved by dividing 204 by 1,700. The answer, 0.12, is then converted to a percentage—12%.

7. c. Use the equation $.05(1) = .02(x)$, where x is the total amount of water in the resulting 2% solution. Solving for x, you get 2.5. Subtracting the 1 liter of water already present in the 5% solution, you will find that 1.5 liters need to be added.

8. e. Each 9-foot wall has an area of 9(8), or 72 square feet. There are two such walls, so those two walls combined have an area of 144 square feet. Each 11-foot wall has an area of 11(8), or 88 square feet, and again there are two such walls: 88(2) = 176. Finally, add 144 and 176 to get 320 square feet.

9. e. Substituting 40 for C in the equation yields $F = (\frac{9}{5})(40) + 32 = 72 + 32 = 104$.

10. a. The woman will have traveled 3.5 hours at 45 miles per hour for a distance of 157.5 miles. To reach her in 3 hours, the man must travel at 157.5 miles per 3 hours, or 52.5 mph.

11. a. J = 6K. J + 2 = 2(K + 2), so 6K + 2 = 2K + 4, which means K equals $\frac{1}{2}$. J equals 6K, or 3.

12. e. The 827,036 bytes free on the flash drive plus 542,159 bytes freed when the file was deleted equals 1,369,195 bytes: 1,369,195 bytes minus 489,986 bytes put into the new file leaves 879,209 bytes free.

13. d. First, add the number of patients to find the total: 63. Then, divide the number of patients by the number of nursing assistants: 63 divided by 7 is 9.

14. c. Let E = emergency room cost; H = hospice cost, which is $\frac{1}{4}$E; N = home nursing cost, which is 2H, or $2(\frac{1}{4})$E. The total bill is E + H + N, which is E + $\frac{1}{4}$E + $\frac{2}{4}$E = 140,000. Add the left side of the equation to get $\frac{7}{4}$E = 140,000. To solve for E, multiply both sides of the equation by $\frac{4}{7}$. E = 140,000($\frac{4}{7}$), or 80,000. H = $\frac{1}{4}$E, or 20,000, and N = 2H, or 40,000.

15. b. If half the students are female, then you would expect half of the out-of-state students to be female. One-half of $\frac{1}{12}$ is $\frac{1}{24}$.

16. c. A foot in height makes a difference of 60 pounds, or 5 pounds per inch of height over 5' A person who is 5'5" is (5)(5 pounds), or 25 pounds, heavier than the person who is 5', so add 25 pounds to 110 pounds to get 135 pounds.

17. d. The difference between 220 and this person's age is 190. The maximum heart rate is 90% of this: (0.9)(190) = 171.

18. e. An amount equaling 30 ppm of the pollutant would have to be removed to bring the 50 ppm down to 20 ppm (30 ppm is 60% of 50 ppm).

19. e. Let E = the estimate. One-fifth more than the estimate would be $\frac{6}{5}$, or 120%, of E, so 600,000 = (1.20)(E). Dividing both sides by 1.2 leaves E = 500,000.

20. b. In terms of grams, 250 milligrams is $\frac{250}{1000}$ gram, or 0.250 g.

21. c. Three tons = 6,000 pounds. At 16 ounces per pound, 6,000 pounds = 96,000 ounces that can be carried by the truck. The total weight of each daily ration is 12 ounces + 18 ounces = 18 ounces = 48 ounces per soldier per day, and $\frac{96,000}{48}$ = 2,000. So $\frac{2,000}{10 \text{ days}}$ = 200 soldiers supplied.

22. e. Multiply the weight of each recyclable by the best price it will bring and add the amount together: 2,200(0.07) = $154; $154 + 1,400(0.04) = $210; $210 + 3,100(0.08) = $458; $458 + $900(0.03) = $485.

23. d. The total number of miles, 3,450, divided by 6 days is 575 miles.

24. b. The present number of men, 30, multiplied by 42 square feet of space is 1,260 square feet of space; 1,260 square feet divided by 35 men is 36 square feet, so each man will have 6 square feet of space less.

25. c. Let T = Ted's age; S = Sam's age = 3T; R = Ron's age = $\frac{S}{2}$, or $\frac{3T}{2}$. The sum of the ages is 55, which means T + 3T + $\frac{3T}{2}$ = 55. To find the common denominator (2), you can add to the left side of the equation: T = 10. If Ted is 10, then Sam is 30, and Ron is $\frac{3T}{2}$, which is 15 years old.

Section 3: Instrument Comprehension

Question	Answer	Heading	Pitch	Roll
1	D	68° East-Northeast	None	Right
2	C	090° East	None	Left
3	B	170° South	Down	Right
4	A	235° Southwest	Up	Right
5	B	45° Northeast	Up	Left
6	C	270° West	None	None
7	C	225° Southwest	Down	Left
8	B	270° West	Up	Left
9	B	180° South	Down	None
10	B	270° West	Up	Left
11	A	135° Southeast	Down	Left
12	A	270° West	Down	Right
13	C	180° South	Down	None
14	C	255° West-Southwest	Up	Left
15	A	270° West	Up	Right
16	A	45° Northeast	Up	Right
17	B	090° East	Up	None
18	A	180° South	Down	Right
19	C	270° West	Up	Right
20	D	180° South	Up	Left

Section 4: Block Counting

1. **b.** Block 1 touches one block to the left, one below, and one to the right.
2. **a.** Block 2 touches one block to the right and one below.
3. **c.** Block 3 touches one block above, two below, and one to the right.
4. **c.** Block 4 touches two above, one to the left, and one below.
5. **b.** Block 5 touches two to the left, and one below.
6. **b.** Block 6 touches one block to the left, one block to the right, and one block below.
7. **e.** Block 7 touches two blocks below, one block to the right, and three blocks above.
8. **d.** Block 8 touches two blocks below, two blocks to the left, and one block above.
9. **d.** Block 9 touches two blocks below, one block to the left, one block to the right, and one block above.
10. **c.** Block 10 touches three blocks above and one block to the right.
11. **b.** Block 11 touches two blocks below and one block to the right.
12. **e.** Block 12 touches three blocks above, one block to the left, and two blocks below.

13. e. Block 13 touches three blocks above, one block to the right, and two blocks below.

14. d. Block 14 touches two blocks above, one block below, one block to the right, and one block to the left.

15. b. Block 15 touches one block above and two blocks to the left.

16. c. Block 16 touches two blocks above, one block to the left, and one block below.

17. c. Block 17 touches one block above, one block to the left, and two blocks below.

18. a. Block 18 touches one block to the right and one block below.

19. b. Block 19 touches two blocks to the left and one block below.

20. a. Block 20 touches one block above and one block to the right.

Section 5: Word Knowledge

1. a. To be gauche is to lack social experience, grace, or aplomb; not tactful.

2. b. To enumerate is to ascertain the number of; to count.

3. c. To be triumphant is to rejoice for a celebrating victory.

4. c. To be magnanimous is to be noble of mind or generous.

5. d. To have an aversion to something is to have a feeling of repugnance for it or to dislike it.

6. d. To be poignant is to be pungently pervasive.

7. e. An antagonist is an opponent.

8. c. Perseverance means to be steadfast in your course or to have persistence.

9. a. Homogeneous means of the same or a similar kind; alike.

10. c. To be conspicuous is to be obvious to the eye or mind.

11. d. A recluse is a person who lives withdrawn from the world; a hermit.

12. e. To tote something is to haul or carry it.

13. e. To be preminent is to have outstanding or supreme rank.

14. c. Something that is grotesque is distorted, misshapen, or bizarre.

15. c. To be outmoded is to be out-of-date or obsolete.

16. b. A statement that is garbled is scrambled and confusing, or unintelligible.

17. b. If something is frail, it is easily broken or delicate.

18. e. To be vindictive is to be revengeful or spiteful.

19. c. An oration is a formal speech or an address.

20. b. A glib remark is quick and insincere, or superficial.

21. e. To be eccentric is to be unconventional or peculiar.

23. a. To be detrimental is to be obviously damaging and harmful.

24. b. To be ostentatious is to be showy or pretentious.

25. a. To be negligible is to be unimportant or insignificant.

Section 6: Table Reading

1. **c.** In Table B-1, the X values are listed horizontally across the top. The Y values are listed vertically along the left margin. Finding the intersection of the −3 column with the 2 row yields an answer of 23.

2. **c.** Finding the intersection of the 2 column with the −2 row yields an answer of 48.

3. **a.** Finding the intersection of the −2 column with the 3 row yields an answer of 44.

4. **e.** Finding the intersection of the 0 column with the −1 row yields an answer of 14.

5. **c.** Finding the intersection of the 3 column with the 1 row yields an answer of 32.

6. **e.** Finding the intersection of the 2 column with the −1 row yields an answer of 14.

7. **d.** Finding the intersection of the 0 column with the 0 row yields an answer of 61.

8. **e.** Finding the intersection of the −2 column with the −1 row yields an answer of 49.

9. **e.** Finding the intersection of the -1 column with the 2 row yields an answer of 99.

10. **b.** Finding the intersection of the 3 column with the 3 row yields an answer of 53.

11. **b.** Finding the intersection of the −1 column with the −1 row yields an answer of 43.

12. **a.** Finding the intersection of the −2 column with the 1 row yields an answer of 49.

13. **a.** Finding the intersection of the −3 column with the 0 row yields an answer of 18.

14. **e.** Finding the intersection of the 1 column with the 3 row yields an answer of 57.

15. **b.** Finding the intersection of the −3 column with the −2 row yields an answer of 86.

16. **a.** Finding the intersection of the −3 column with the −3 row yields an answer of 24.

17. **a.** Finding the intersection of the 2 column with the 2 row yields an answer of 14.

18. **d.** Finding the intersection of the −2 column with the 3 row yields an answer of 74.

19. **e.** Finding the intersection of the −1 column with the 0 row yields an answer of 43.

20. **c.** Finding the intersection of the 0 column with the 2 row yields an answer of 64.

21. **b.** Finding the intersection of the 2 column with the −3 row yields an answer of 43.

22. **b.** Finding the intersection of the −1 column with the 3 row yields an answer of 88.

23. **b.** Finding the intersection of the 2 column with the 2 row yields an answer of 22.

24. **c.** Finding the intersection of the −3 column with the 1 row yields an answer of 81.

25. **d.** Finding the intersection of the 2 column with the 3 row yields an answer of 11.

26. **c.** Finding the intersection of the 9 column with the -4 row yields an answer of 52.

27. **a.** Finding the intersection of the −5 column with the 9 row yields an answer of 54.

28. **b.** Finding the intersection of the −1 column with the −4 row yields an answer of 93.

29. **a.** Finding the intersection of the -3 column with the 8 row yields an answer of 29.

30. **e.** Finding the intersection of the 5 column with the −3 row yields an answer of 43.

31. **e.** Finding the intersection of the 0 column with the 7 row yields an answer of 21.

32. **e.** Finding the intersection of the 4 column with the -4 row yields an answer of 34.

33. **e.** Finding the intersection of the 7 column with the −3 row yields an answer of 51.

34. **b.** Finding the intersection of the −9 column with the 3 row yields an answer of 74

35. **d.** Finding the intersection of the 1 column with the −8 row yields an answer of 12.

36. **c.** Finding the intersection of the 0 column with the 0 row yields an answer of 18.

37. b. Finding the intersection of the –5 column with the 0 row yields an answer of 74.

38. c. Finding the intersection of the –2 column with the 7 row yields an answer of 11.

39. a. Finding the intersection of the –8 column with the 5 row yields an answer of 55.

40. b. Finding the intersection of the –6 column with the 4 row yields an answer of 68.

Section 7: Math Knowledge

1. c. When a number is marked off in groups of two digits each, starting at the decimal point, the square root of the largest square in the left hand group, whether one or two digits, is the first digit of the square root of the number. In this case (11-20-92), 9 is the largest square in 11, and 3 is the square root of 9.

2. b. A proportion can find an unknown side of a figure using known sides of a similar figure; a proportion can also find an unknown side using known perimeters. $\frac{93}{24} = \frac{31}{s}$. Cross-multiply: $93s = (31)(24)$.

3. d. Perimeter uses a single measurement such as an inch to describe the outline of a figure. Area and surface area use square measurements, an inch times an inch, to describe two-dimensional space. Volume uses the largest measurement; it uses the cubic measurement, an inch times an inch times an inch. Volume is three-dimensional; its measurement must account for each dimension.

4. b. The circumference of a circle is two times the radius times pi. So, in this case, the distance is 2 times 49, times 22, divided by 7, or 308 miles.

5. a. First, change (B) and (C) to decimals: 5% = 0.05; $\frac{1}{5}$ = 0.2. Then, find out which choice is true.

6. d. (B) and (C) are equal to $n \times n$.

7. b. You are given the diameter, so use $C = \pi d$. Plug in the diameter and pi and multiply: $(3.14)(10) = 31.4$. So your answer is choice **b**, 31.4 cm.

8. e. Obtuse angles are greater than 90°. Only one answer choice, **e**, is greater than 90°.

9. c. When dividing variables with exponents, if the variables are the same, you subtract the exponents to arrive at your answer: $\frac{n^5}{n^2} = \frac{n \cdot n \cdot n \cdot n}{n \cdot n} = n^{5-2} = n^3$.

10. a. First, factor the radicand:
$\sqrt{3n^2} = \sqrt{3 \cdot n \cdot n}$
Now take out the square root of the perfect square: $\sqrt{3 \cdot n \cdot n} = n\sqrt{3}$
You arrive at $n\sqrt{3}$, choice **a**.

11. c. This is a simple addition series. Each number increases by $\frac{1}{6}$.

12. b. *Volume* = 4.6 cubic feet. This is a square based pyramid; its volume is a third of a cube's volume with the same base measurements, or $\frac{1}{3}bh$. Plug its measurements into the formula: $\frac{1}{3}(2.4$ ft.$)2.4$ ft. *Volume of square pyramid* = $\frac{1}{3}(5.76$ sq. ft.$)2.4$ ft. = $\frac{1}{3}(13.824$ cubic ft.$) = 4.608$ cubic ft.

13. c. In this question, $\frac{1}{5}$ of 820 = 164; 164 – 42 = 122.

14. e. Simplify the second term of the expression by factoring the radicand:
$2\sqrt{7} - 3\sqrt{28} = 2\sqrt{7} - 3\sqrt{4 \cdot 7}$
Now simplify the radicand:
$\sqrt{7} - 3\sqrt{4 \cdot 7} = 2\sqrt{7} - 3 \cdot 2\sqrt{7}$
Finally, combine "like terms":
$2\sqrt{7} - 6\sqrt{7} = -4\sqrt{7}$, choice **e**.

15. d. Divide numerical terms: $\frac{8xy^2}{2xy} = \frac{4xy^2}{xy}$. When similar factors, or bases, are being divided, subtract the exponent in the denominator from the exponent in the numerator. $\frac{4xy^2}{xy} = 4x^{1-1}y^{2-1}$. Simplify: $4x^0y^1 = 4(1)y = 4y$. The answer is $4y$, choice **d.**

16. c. In this question, $\frac{2}{5}$ of $25 = 10$; $10 - 6 = 4$.

17. a. In this question, 4% of $20 = 0.8$; $3 \times 0.8 = 2.4$.

18. c. First, solve for (A), (B), and (C): (A) = 49, (B) = 64, (C) = 15. Then, find out which choice is true.

19. d. The factorial of a positive integer is that integer times each of the integers between it and 1. In this case, 5 times 4 times 3 times 2 equals 120.

20. d. In this question, 15% of $30 = 4.5$; $20 - 4.5 = 15.5$, choice **d.**

21. a. The reciprocal of a number is that number divided into one. In this case, that is $\frac{1}{10}$, or 0.1.

22. b. First, set up the equation: $n + 2n = 99$. Then, solve: $3n = 99$; $n = 33$.

23. b. First, solve for (A), (B), and (C): (A) = 40, (B) = 40, (C) = 20. Then, find out which choice is true.

24. d. Using a proportion, find x: $\frac{12}{36} = \frac{4.5}{x}$. Cross-multiply: $12x = 36(4.5)$; $x = 13.5$. Polygon *CRXZ* is a rectangle whose sides measure 13.5, 54, 13.5, and 54. To find the perimeter of rectangle *CRXZ*, add the measures of its sides together.

25. a. You are given the radius, so use $C = 2\pi r$. Plug in the radius and pi and multiply: (2)(3.14)(22) = 157. So your answer is 157 cm, or 1.57 m, choice **a.**

Section 8: Aviation Information

1. d. The rudder is the control surface on the vertical stabilizer or tail. Any deflection of the rudder makes the aircraft move about the yaw, or vertical axis.

2. b. The elevator is the control surface on the horizontal stabilizer. Any deflection of the elevator makes the aircraft move about the pitch axis. The pitch axis runs from one wingtip to the other, passing through the aircraft's center of gravity.

3. c. The aileron is the control surface on the trailing edge of the wings. Any deflection of the aileron makes the aircraft move about the roll axis. The roll axis runs the length of the aircraft from nose to tail, passing through the center of gravity.

4. b. Pushing the right rudder pedal causes the rudder control surface to move into the windstream to the right, which *pushes the tail of the airplane left, and the nose of the airplane right.*

5. a. Angle of attack is defined as the angle between the airfoil chord and the direction of relative motion.

6. c. *Drag* refers to the rearward force on an aircraft caused by air friction and lift. More specifically, *parasite drag* refers to the component of drag associated with friction, and *induced drag* refers to the component associated with lift.

7. a. *Camber* refers to the side (cross-section) view of a wing's shape. This shape causes the air to travel faster over the top portion of the wing and therefore causes lift.

8. **e.** Pulling back on the aircraft controls causes the elevators to deflect. By pulling back, the *elevators* are deflected up into the airstream, which pushes the tail of the aircraft down and the nose of the aircraft up.

9. **b.** Increasing the *angle of attack* of an aircraft will eventually cause a stall as the airflow over the wing detaches from the wing's surface.

10. **b.** One knot (nautical mile per hour) is equal to approximately $\frac{8}{7}$ of a mph (mile per hour). A nautical mile is approximately 6,080 feet, but a statute mile is approximately 5,280 feet. The ratio of these distances can be approximated with the ratio of 8:7. Therefore 100 knots is a *faster* speed than 100 mph.

11. **c.** Transponder codes are as follows:

Hijacking 7500

Loss of comms 7600

Emergency 7700

12. **d.** *Zulu time* refers to the time in Greenwich England, commonly known as *Greenwich Mean Time*. Zulu time is commonly used for aviation, especially when several time zones will be crossed.

13. **a.** The Pitot system measures *airspeed* by measuring the impact pressure of the relative wind and comparing it to the static pressure. The static system measures static pressure, which indicates *altitude*.

14. **b.** Pitch angle of an aircraft refers to the angle between the extended fuselage of the aircraft and the *horizon*. For example, an aircraft flying straight up would have a pitch angle of 90°.

15. **a.** A wing with flaps fully extended will generally produce *more lift and more drag*. The flaps increase the wing's camber, which causes more lift and more induced drag.

16. **d.** The wind flowing over a wing, which is creating lift, moves *faster* than the wind flowing beneath the wing. This increased velocity causes a lower air pressure on the top of the wing compared with the air pressure below the wing. This difference in air pressure is lift.

17. **c.** Airport runways are numbered according to the first two digits of compass heading, with the zero omitted for headings between 010 and 090.

18. **c.** Wake turbulence is caused by the higher-pressure air under a wing "escaping" in an outward direction from the wingtip to the lower-pressure air flowing above the wing. This "escaping" air will swirl upward causing *vortices*, known as wake turbulence.

19. **b.** The port running lights are red; the starboard lights are green. Positional lights are white.

20. **b.** Mach 1 is the *speed of sound* for a given air density.

Section 9: Rotated Blocks

1. a.
2. a.
3. e.
4. c.
5. c.
6. d.
7. b.
8. c.
9. a.
10. b.
11. b.
12. a.
13. b.
14. a.
15. c.

Section 10: General Science

1. c. Air consists of 78% nitrogen, 21% oxygen, and the remainder is made up of noble gases and rare earth elements.

2. c. Boyle's law states that for a given pressure, temperature and volume are directly proportional.

3. b. Ohm's law states that current and resistance are inversely proportional. Therefore, any increase in one would result in a corresponding decrease in the other.

4. a. Ultraviolet, X-ray, and gamma ray wavelengths are all shorter than visible light. Infrared wavelengths are slightly longer than visible light on the electromagnetic spectrum.

5. a. The pH scale ranges from 0 to 14. If a substance has a pH of 7.0, it is considered neutral; pH values of less than 7 indicate acids, and values greater than 7 are bases.

6. e. Protons are subatomic particles located in the nucleus of an atom and have positive electrical charges.

7. d. Vectors are defined by both length and direction.

8. c. The pancreas is the organ responsible for insulin production.

9. b. The four planets in our solar system that are considered gas giants are Jupiter, Saturn, Uranus, and Neptune.

10. c. Carbon dioxide, or CO_2, is made up of both carbon and oxygen.

11. c. The dissolved solution is in equilibrium with the undissolved in saturated solutions.

12. d. The molecule CH_3NH_2 contains one atom of carbon, one atom of nitrogen, and five atoms of hydrogen, for a total of seven atoms.

13. e. The Celsius scale is part of the metric system. On the Celsius scale, the freezing point of water is 0°; the boiling point is 100°.

14. a. Momentum equals mass (amount of matter in an object) times velocity (speed in a given direction).

15. e. To express a number in scientific notation, you move the decimal as many places as necessary until there is only one digit to the left of the decimal. For 617,000, you move the decimal to the left by five decimal places. The fact that you had to move it to the left means that the 10 should be raised to a positive power, so the result is 6.17×10^5.

16. e. Gravity pulls the ball downward as it moves forward.

17. c. Igneous rocks make up a group of rocks formed from the crystallization of magma (lava).

18. a. One hundred centimeters equals 1 meter, and 1,000 meters equals 1 kilometer.

19. b. Fiber is found only in plants. Raw vegetables, fruit with seeds, whole cereals, and bread are possible sources of fiber.

20. a. Deciduous forests are characterized by having mild temperatures and many trees that periodically shed leaves.

Section 11: Hidden Figures

1. b.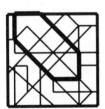

2. c.

3. e.

4. d.

5. a.

6. d.

7. e.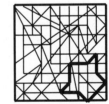

8. a.

9. c.

10. b.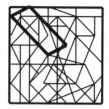

11. d.

12. c.

13. b.

14. e.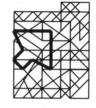

15. a.

8 ▶ Alternate Flight Aptitude Selection Test (AFAST)

This sample Alternate Flight Aptitude Selection Test tests you on instrument comprehension, complex movements, helicopter knowledge, cyclic orientation, and mechanical functions—all skills needed by an Army aviator.

SECTION 1: INSTRUMENT COMPREHENSION

1.	ⓐ ⓑ ⓒ ⓓ		6.	ⓐ ⓑ ⓒ ⓓ		11.	ⓐ ⓑ ⓒ ⓓ
2.	ⓐ ⓑ ⓒ ⓓ		7.	ⓐ ⓑ ⓒ ⓓ		12.	ⓐ ⓑ ⓒ ⓓ
3.	ⓐ ⓑ ⓒ ⓓ		8.	ⓐ ⓑ ⓒ ⓓ		13.	ⓐ ⓑ ⓒ ⓓ
4.	ⓐ ⓑ ⓒ ⓓ		9.	ⓐ ⓑ ⓒ ⓓ		14.	ⓐ ⓑ ⓒ ⓓ
5.	ⓐ ⓑ ⓒ ⓓ		10.	ⓐ ⓑ ⓒ ⓓ		15.	ⓐ ⓑ ⓒ ⓓ

SECTION 2: COMPLEX MOVEMENTS

1.	ⓐ ⓑ ⓒ ⓓ ⓔ		11.	ⓐ ⓑ ⓒ ⓓ ⓔ		21.	ⓐ ⓑ ⓒ ⓓ ⓔ
2.	ⓐ ⓑ ⓒ ⓓ ⓔ		12.	ⓐ ⓑ ⓒ ⓓ ⓔ		22.	ⓐ ⓑ ⓒ ⓓ ⓔ
3.	ⓐ ⓑ ⓒ ⓓ ⓔ		13.	ⓐ ⓑ ⓒ ⓓ ⓔ		23.	ⓐ ⓑ ⓒ ⓓ ⓔ
4.	ⓐ ⓑ ⓒ ⓓ ⓔ		14.	ⓐ ⓑ ⓒ ⓓ ⓔ		24.	ⓐ ⓑ ⓒ ⓓ ⓔ
5.	ⓐ ⓑ ⓒ ⓓ ⓔ		15.	ⓐ ⓑ ⓒ ⓓ ⓔ		25.	ⓐ ⓑ ⓒ ⓓ ⓔ
6.	ⓐ ⓑ ⓒ ⓓ ⓔ		16.	ⓐ ⓑ ⓒ ⓓ ⓔ		26.	ⓐ ⓑ ⓒ ⓓ ⓔ
7.	ⓐ ⓑ ⓒ ⓓ ⓔ		17.	ⓐ ⓑ ⓒ ⓓ ⓔ		27.	ⓐ ⓑ ⓒ ⓓ ⓔ
8.	ⓐ ⓑ ⓒ ⓓ ⓔ		18.	ⓐ ⓑ ⓒ ⓓ ⓔ		28.	ⓐ ⓑ ⓒ ⓓ ⓔ
9.	ⓐ ⓑ ⓒ ⓓ ⓔ		19.	ⓐ ⓑ ⓒ ⓓ ⓔ		29.	ⓐ ⓑ ⓒ ⓓ ⓔ
10.	ⓐ ⓑ ⓒ ⓓ ⓔ		20.	ⓐ ⓑ ⓒ ⓓ ⓔ		30.	ⓐ ⓑ ⓒ ⓓ ⓔ

SECTION 3: HELICOPTER KNOWLEDGE

1.	ⓐ ⓑ ⓒ ⓓ ⓔ		11.	ⓐ ⓑ ⓒ ⓓ ⓔ
2.	ⓐ ⓑ ⓒ ⓓ ⓔ		12.	ⓐ ⓑ ⓒ ⓓ ⓔ
3.	ⓐ ⓑ ⓒ ⓓ ⓔ		13.	ⓐ ⓑ ⓒ ⓓ ⓔ
4.	ⓐ ⓑ ⓒ ⓓ ⓔ		14.	ⓐ ⓑ ⓒ ⓓ ⓔ
5.	ⓐ ⓑ ⓒ ⓓ ⓔ		15.	ⓐ ⓑ ⓒ ⓓ ⓔ
6.	ⓐ ⓑ ⓒ ⓓ ⓔ		16.	ⓐ ⓑ ⓒ ⓓ ⓔ
7.	ⓐ ⓑ ⓒ ⓓ ⓔ		17.	ⓐ ⓑ ⓒ ⓓ ⓔ
8.	ⓐ ⓑ ⓒ ⓓ ⓔ		18.	ⓐ ⓑ ⓒ ⓓ ⓔ
9.	ⓐ ⓑ ⓒ ⓓ ⓔ		19.	ⓐ ⓑ ⓒ ⓓ ⓔ
10.	ⓐ ⓑ ⓒ ⓓ ⓔ		20.	ⓐ ⓑ ⓒ ⓓ ⓔ

SECTION 4: CYCLIC ORIENTION

See pages 178–192 to fill in cyclic orientation grid.

SECTION 5: MECHANICAL FUNCTIONS

1.	ⓐ	ⓑ	ⓒ	ⓓ	ⓔ	11.	ⓐ	ⓑ	ⓒ	ⓓ	ⓔ
2.	ⓐ	ⓑ	ⓒ	ⓓ	ⓔ	12.	ⓐ	ⓑ	ⓒ	ⓓ	ⓔ
3.	ⓐ	ⓑ	ⓒ	ⓓ	ⓔ	13.	ⓐ	ⓑ	ⓒ	ⓓ	ⓔ
4.	ⓐ	ⓑ	ⓒ	ⓓ	ⓔ	14.	ⓐ	ⓑ	ⓒ	ⓓ	ⓔ
5.	ⓐ	ⓑ	ⓒ	ⓓ	ⓔ	15.	ⓐ	ⓑ	ⓒ	ⓓ	ⓔ
6.	ⓐ	ⓑ	ⓒ	ⓓ	ⓔ	16.	ⓐ	ⓑ	ⓒ	ⓓ	ⓔ
7.	ⓐ	ⓑ	ⓒ	ⓓ	ⓔ	17.	ⓐ	ⓑ	ⓒ	ⓓ	ⓔ
8.	ⓐ	ⓑ	ⓒ	ⓓ	ⓔ	18.	ⓐ	ⓑ	ⓒ	ⓓ	ⓔ
9.	ⓐ	ⓑ	ⓒ	ⓓ	ⓔ	19.	ⓐ	ⓑ	ⓒ	ⓓ	ⓔ
10.	ⓐ	ⓑ	ⓒ	ⓓ	ⓔ	20.	ⓐ	ⓑ	ⓒ	ⓓ	ⓔ

Section 1: Instrument Comprehension

DIRECTIONS: This test measures your ability to determine the position of an aircraft in flight by reading instruments showing its compass heading, its amount of climb or dive, and its degree of bank to right or left. In each test item, the left-hand dial is labeled ARTIFICIAL HORIZON. The small aircraft silhouette remains stationary on the face of this dial, while the positions of the heavy black line and black pointer vary with the changes in the position of the aircraft in which the instrument is located.

The heavy black line represents the HORIZON LINE, and the black pointer shows the degree of BANK to right or left. If the aircraft is neither climbing nor diving, the horizon line is directly on the silhouette's fuselage. If the aircraft has no bank, the black pointer will point to zero (Dial 1).

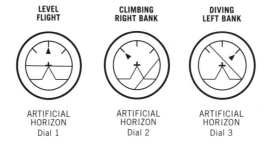

If the aircraft is climbing, the fuselage silhouette is seen between the horizon line and the pointer. The greater the amount of climb, the greater the distance between the horizon line and the fuselage silhouette. If the aircraft is banked to the pilot's right, the pointer will point to the left of zero (Dial 2).

If the aircraft is diving, the horizon line is between the fuselage silhouette and the pointer. The greater the amount of dive, the greater the distance between the horizon line and the fuselage silhouette. If the aircraft is banked to the pilot's left, the pointer will point to the right of zero (Dial 3).

The HORIZON LINE tilts as the aircraft is banked. It is always at a right angle to the pointer.

On each test item, the right-hand dial is the COMPASS. This dial shows the direction in which the aircraft is headed. Dial 4 shows north, Dial 5 is west, and Dial 6 is northwest.

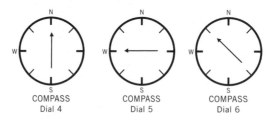

Each example in this test consists of two dials and four silhouettes of aircraft in flight. Your task is to determine which of the four aircraft is closest to the position indicated by the two dials. Remember, you are always looking NORTH at the same altitude as each plane. East is always to the RIGHT as you look at the page.

You will have nine (9) minutes to complete this portion of the test.

Questions: 15
Time: 9 minutes

For sample Instrument Comprehension questions, see page 47.

1.

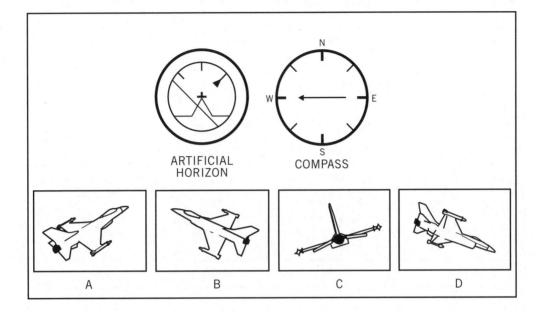

2.

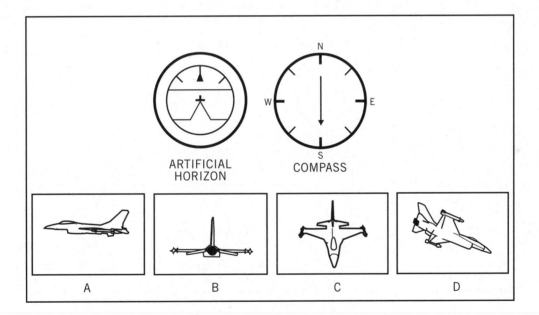

3.

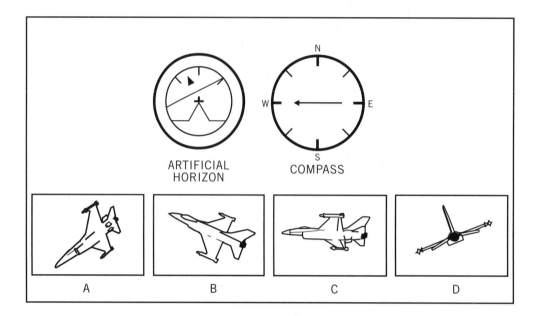

ARTIFICIAL HORIZON

COMPASS

A   B   C   D

4.

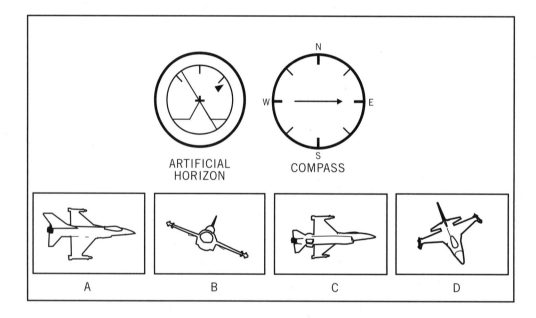

ARTIFICIAL HORIZON

COMPASS

A   B   C   D

5.

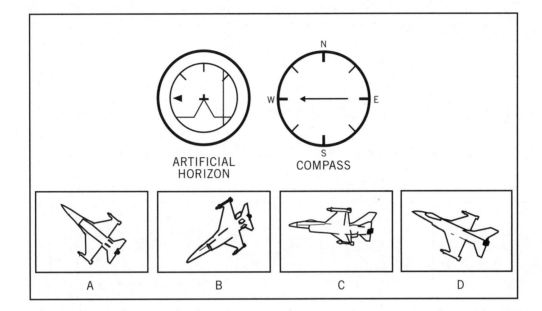

ARTIFICIAL HORIZON   COMPASS

A   B   C   D

6.

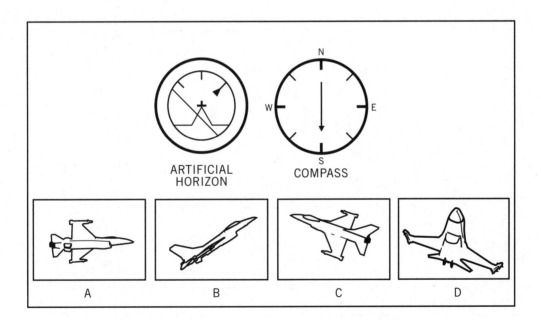

ARTIFICIAL HORIZON   COMPASS

A   B   C   D

7.

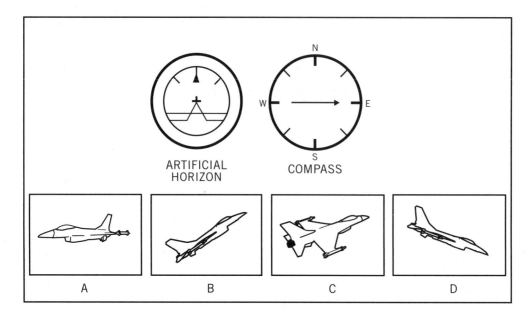

8.

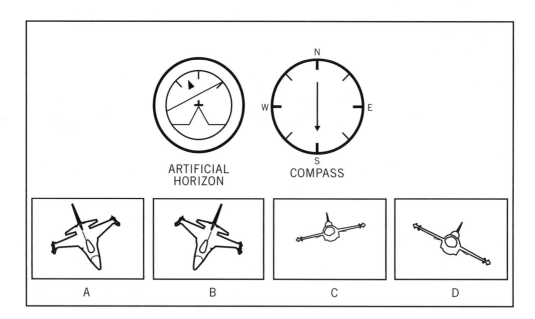

9.

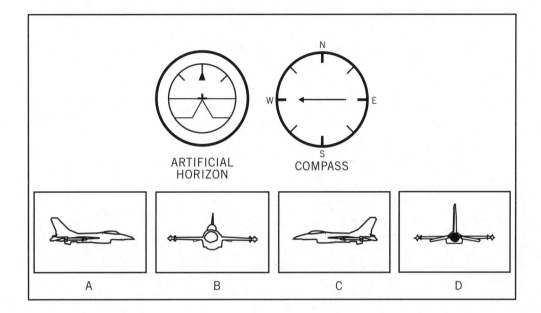

10.

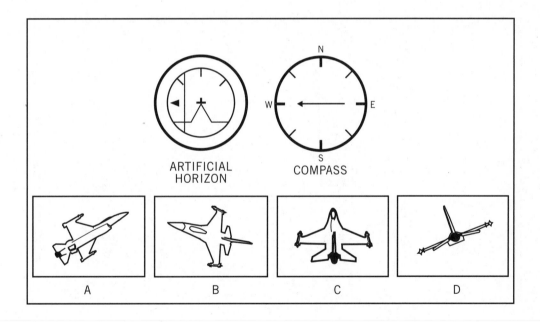

11.

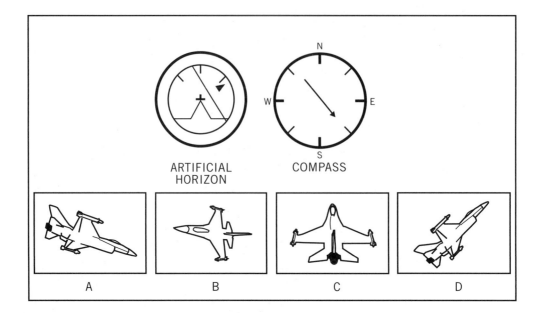

12.

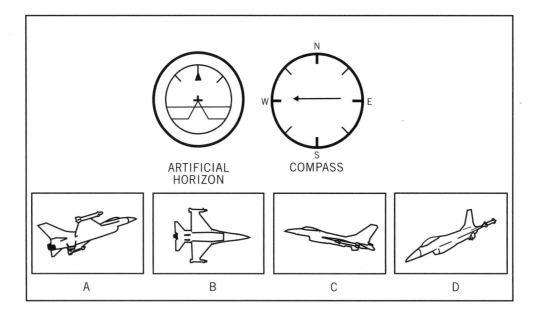

13.

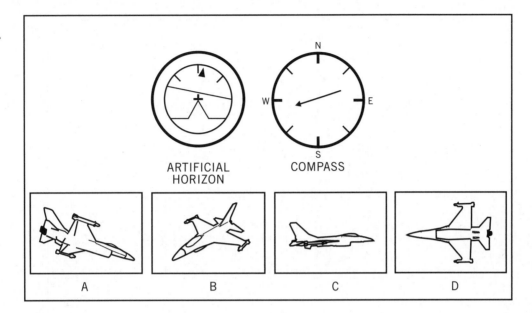

14.

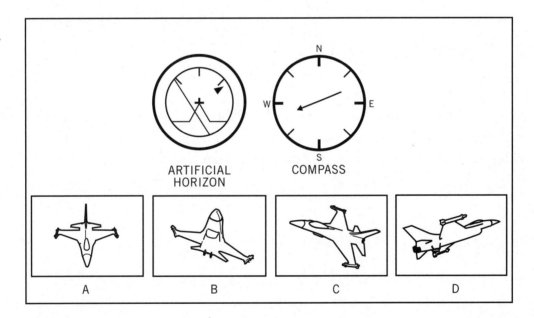

15.

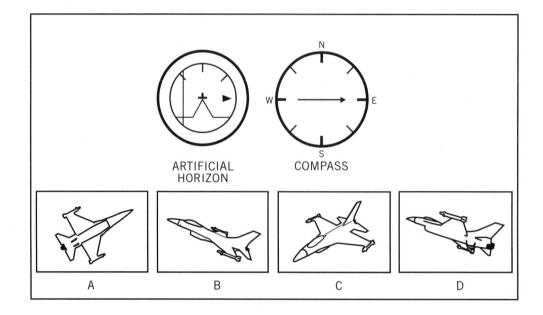

ARTIFICIAL HORIZON   COMPASS

A   B   C   D

Section 2: Complex Movements

DIRECTIONS: The questions in this subtest measure your ability to judge distance and visualize motion. Nine symbols are given, representing direction and distance. You are to choose the one set that represents the amount and direction of movement necessary to move a dot from outside a circle into the center of the circle. You will have five (5) minutes to complete this portion of the test.

Questions: 30
Time: 5 minutes

For sample Complex Movements questions, see page 58.

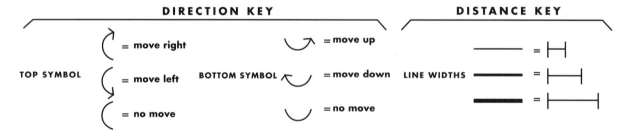

1.

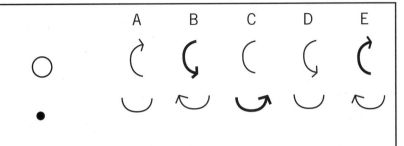

2.

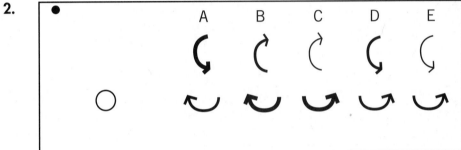

3.

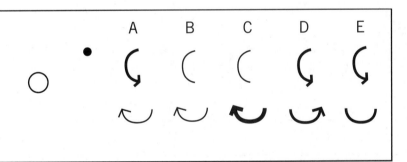

4.

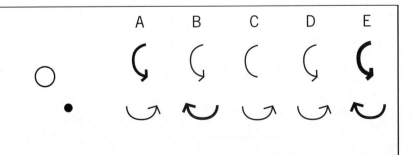

5.

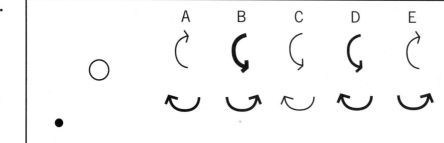

6.

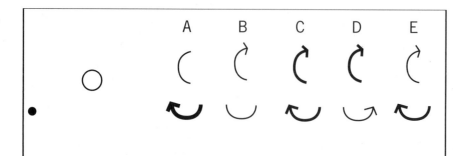

7.

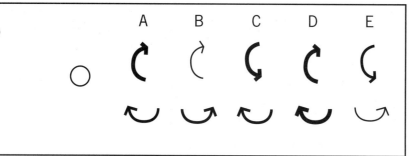

8.

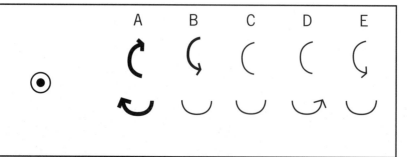

9.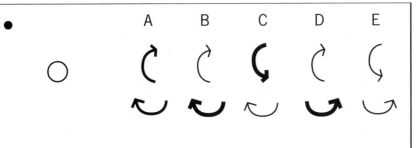

10.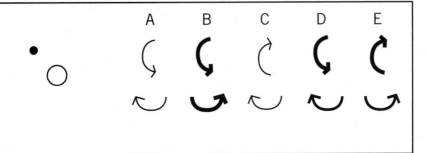

11.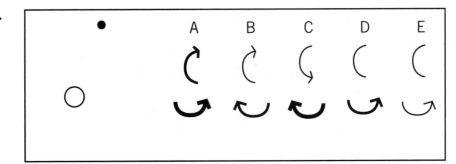

12.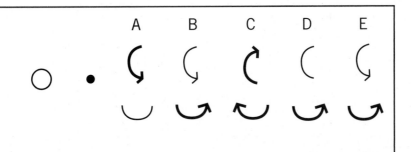

13.

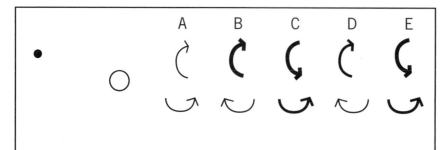

14.

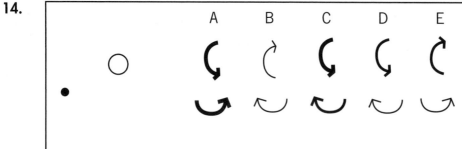

15.

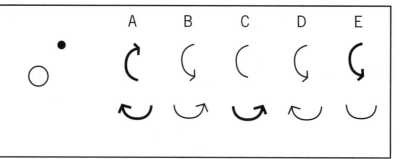

16.

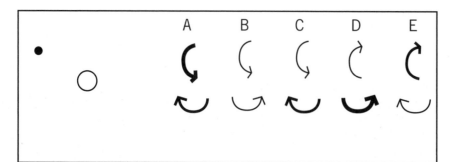

17.

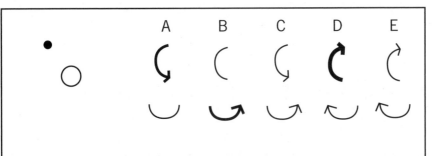

18.

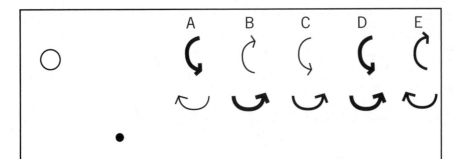

19.

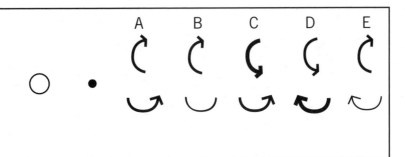

20.

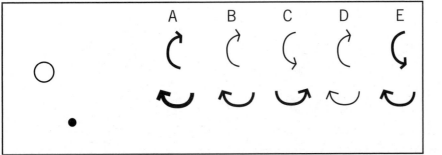

21.

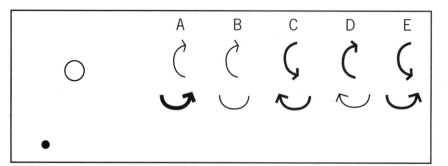

22.

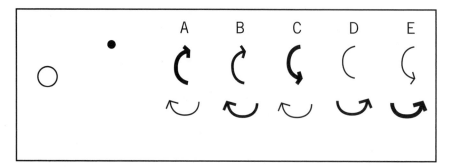

23.

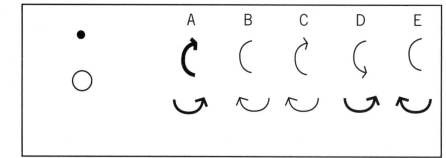

24.

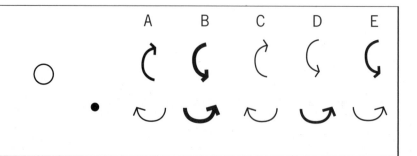

25.

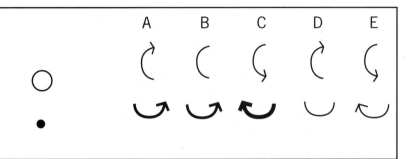

26.

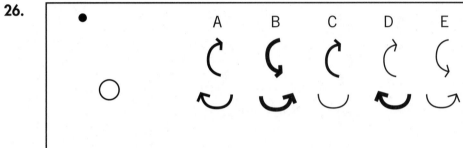

27.

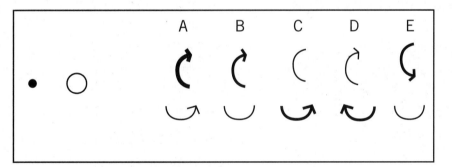

28.

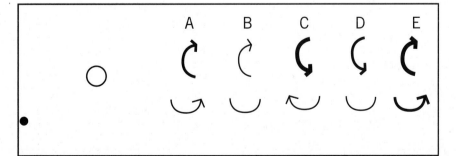

29.

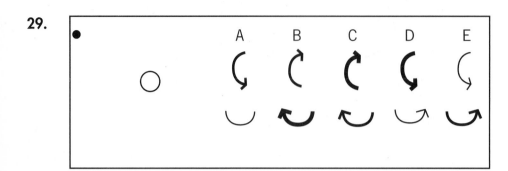

30.

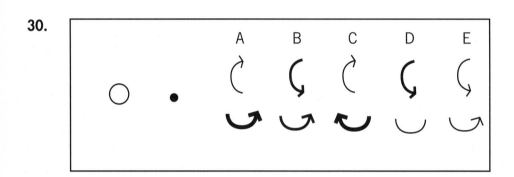

Section 3: Helicopter Knowledge

DIRECTIONS: This segment deals with your understanding of the principles of helicopter flight. You must decide which one of the five choices best completes each statement. You will have ten (10) minutes to complete this portion of the test.

Questions: 20
Time: 10 minutes

For sample Helicopter Knowledge questions, see page 59.

1. Altitude in a helicopter is controlled by
   a. the collective lever.
   b. the foot pedals.
   c. the cyclic stick.
   d. the altimeter.
   e. none of the above

2. The foot pedals in the cockpit control
   a. altitude.
   b. the tail rotor.
   c. speed.
   d. all of the above
   e. none of the above

3. Which of these conditions can adversely affect a helicopter's performance?
   a. moderate winds
   b. low temperatures
   c. light weight
   d. low-density altitude
   e. high-density altitude

4. During flight, lift and centrifugal force cause the rotor blades to bend upward. This effect is known as
   a. blade flapping.
   b. lift vector.
   c. coning.
   d. transverse flow effect.
   e. angle of attack.

5. The downward airflow created by the rotor is called
   a. downwash.
   b. drag.
   c. centrifugal force.
   d. sheer.
   e. none of the above

6. In a tandem rotor configuration, which way do the helicopter blades rotate?
   a. both clockwise
   b. both counter clockwise
   c. opposite directions
   d. There are no tandem rotor helicopters.
   e. none of the above

7. Given a constant power setting and a straight and level flight, what will happen when the nose of a helicopter is tilted downward? The altitude will
   a. initially increase.
   b. initially decrease.
   c. remain the same.
   d. initially decrease and then remain the same
   e. none of the above

8. Ground effect
   a. is only effective on rotors prior to lifting off.
   b. is the condition of increased performance when operating within half-rotor diameter of the ground.
   c. increases drag on airframe while operating within half-rotor diameter of the ground
   d. has no effect on helicopters, only on fixed-wing aircraft.
   e. can be experienced at high altitudes.

9. What does the cyclic stick control?
   a. altitude
   b. direction
   c. speed
   d. disc attitude
   e. all of the above

10. The tail rotor on a helicopter serves to
   a. control height.
   b. control speed.
   c. counteract drag.
   d. control torque.
   e. all of the above

11. Controlled descent with the engine disengaged is called
   a. crashing.
   b. autorotation.
   c. stalled descent.
   d. RPM decay.
   e. none of the above

12. Retreating blade stall
   a. can limit forward speed.
   b. is the tendency of the retreating blade to stall in forward flight.
   c. can be indicated by abnormal vibration, nose pitchup, and roll in the direction of stall.
   d. none of the above
   e. all of the above

13. For a helicopter to hover, what two forces must be in balance?
   a. lift and weight
   b. lift and drag
   c. drag and weight
   d. torque and antitorque
   e. none of the above

14. The amount of lift and drag produced by an airfoil is largely affected by
   a. coning.
   b. centrifugal force.
   c. gravity.
   d. blade flapping.
   e. angle of attack.

15. Which of these factors can affect the angle of attack?
   a. blade flexing
   b. collective pitch controls
   c. blade flapping
   d. turbulent air conditions
   e. all of the above

16. The dominant force that affects the rotor system is
   a. centrifugal force.
   b. friction.
   c. vertical force.
   d. centripetal force.
   e. none of the above.

17. Angle of attack is the angle between
   a. airfoil chord and relative direction of motion.
   b. blade center and angle of incidence.
   c. airfoil chord and angle of incidence.
   d. induced air flow and relative direction of motion.
   e. none of the above

18. Total drag is a combination of
   a. parasite drag, vertical drag, profile drag.
   b. induced drag, parasite drag, vertical drag.
   c. profile drag, induced drag, parasite drag.
   d. vertical drag, profile drag, parasite drag.
   e. none of the above

19. Drag that results from the production of lift is called
   a. profile drag.
   b. induced drag.
   c. vertical drag.
   d. parasite drag.
   e. none of the above

20. The collective pitch controls
   a. heading.
   b. starting and stopping.
   c. speed.
   d. starting, stopping, and speed.
   e. heading, starting, and stopping.

Section 4: Cyclic Orientation

DIRECTIONS: This is a test of your ability to recognize simple changes in helicopter position and to indicate the corresponding cyclic (stick) movement. You will look at a series of three sequential pictures that represent the pilot's view through the helicopter windshield. The three pictures change from top to bottom, showing the view from an aircraft in a climb, a dive, a bank to the left or right, or a combination of these maneuvers. For each question, you will determine how the cyclic (stick) would be positioned in order to perform the maneuver indicated by the pictures.

You will have five (5) minutes to complete this section of the test.

Questions: 15
Time: 5 minutes

For sample Cyclic Orientation questions, see page 60.

1.

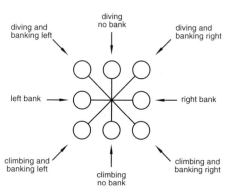

2.

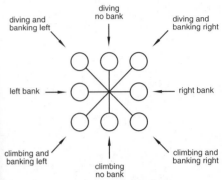

3.

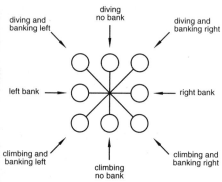

4.

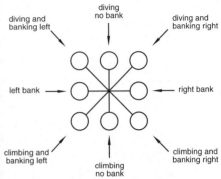

5.

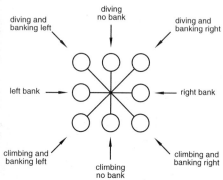

6.

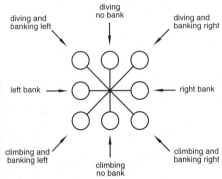

7.

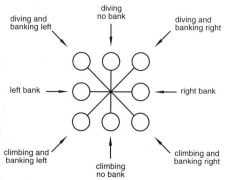

8.

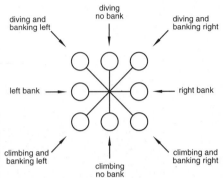

9.

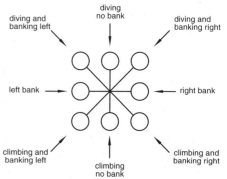

10.

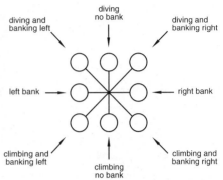

11.

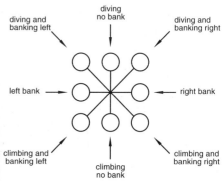

12.

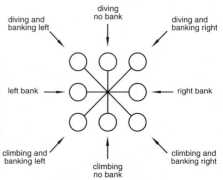

13.

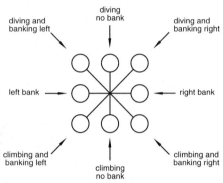

14.

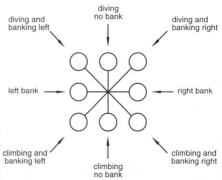

15.

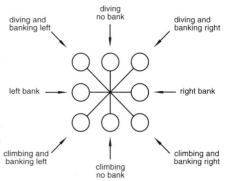

Section 5:
Mechanical Functions

DIRECTIONS: This part of the test measures your ability to understand and reason with mechanical terms. Included in this part of the test are diagrams showing various mechanical devices. Following each diagram are several questions or incomplete statements. Study each diagram carefully, as details do make a difference in how each device operates, and then select the choice that best answers the question or completes the statement. You will have ten (10) minutes to complete this section of the test.

Questions: 20

Time: 10 minutes

For sample Mechanical Functions questions, see page 45.

Figure G-1

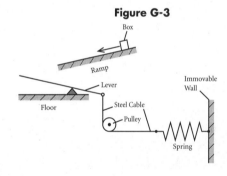

1. In Figure G-1 shown here, all valves are initially closed. Gravity will cause water to drain down into the barrels when valves are opened. Which barrels will be filled if valves B, D, and F are opened and valves A, C, E, and G are left closed?
   a. barrels #3 and #4
   b. barrels #1 and #2
   c. barrel #1
   d. barrel #3
   e. barrels #1, #2, #3, and #4

Figure G-2

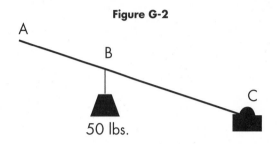

50 lbs.

2. In Figure G-2, the distance from A to B is three feet, and the distance from B to C is 7 feet. How much force must be applied at A to lift the 50 lbs. at point B?
   a. 25 lbs.
   b. 35 lbs.
   c. 45 lbs.
   d. 55 lbs.
   e. 65 lbs.

Figure G-3

3. In Figure G-3 shown here, if the box slides down the ramp and drops onto the left side of the lever, what will happen to the spring?
   a. It will touch the box.
   b. It will remain as it is.
   c. It will be compressed, or shortened.
   d. It will be stretched, or lengthened.
   e. none of these things

Figure G-4

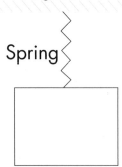

Spring

4. The spring in Figure G-4 has a stiffness of 20 lbs./in. How much is the spring stretched if the weight of the block is 400 lbs.?

a.   2 inches

b.   4 inches

c.   10 inches

d.   20 inches

e.   .5 inch

Figure G-5

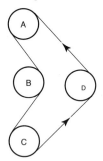

5. In figure G-5 shown here, which gears are turning counterclockwise?

a.   B

b.   B and D

c.   D

d.   A, B, C, and D

e.   A, C, and D

Figure G-6

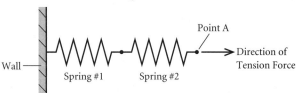

3 feet

6. If the tire in Figure G-6 is three feet in diameter and is turning at 500 revolutions per minute, what speed (in feet/minutes) is the tire traveling down the road?

a.   500 ft./min.

b.   1,500 ft./min.

c.   1,860 ft./min.

d.   2,355 ft./min.

e.   4,710 ft./min.

Figure G-7

Wall — Spring #1   Spring #2   Point A → Direction of Tension Force

7. Two springs are arranged in a series as shown in Figure G-7. Spring #1 is very stiff and will become one inch longer when a tension force of 10 pounds is applied to it. Spring #2 is very soft and will become two inches longer when a tension force of five pounds is applied to it. What will be the change in length of the two springs when a force of 20 pounds is applied— that is, how far will point A move to the right?

a.   10 inches

b.   8 inches

c.   6 inches

d.   4 inches

e.   3 inches

Figure G-8

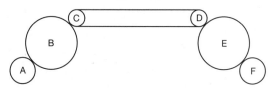

8. Figure G-8 shows a series of gears A, B, and C, which are connected by a conveyor belt to gears D, E, and F. If gear A turns clockwise, what direction do gears E and F turn?

   a. clockwise, clockwise

   b. counterclockwise, counterclockwise

   c. clockwise, counterclockwise

   d. counterclockwise, clockwise

   e. not enough information

Figure G-9

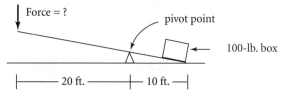

9. In Figure G-9, Joe must lift a 100-lb. box using a lever. How many pounds of force must he apply to the left side of the lever to lift the box? (The product of the weight of the box times the distance of the box from the pivot point must be equal to the product of the required force times the distance from the force to the pivot point: $w \times d_1 = f \times d_2$.)

   a. 100 lbs.

   b. 200 lbs.

   c. 50 lbs.

   d. 33 lbs.

   e. 15 lbs.

Figure G-10

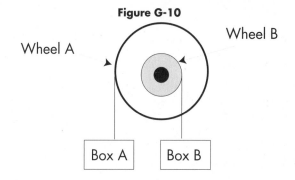

10. In Figure G-10, Box A weighs 75 lbs. The radius of Wheel A is six feet, and the radius of Wheel B is two feet. If both wheels are balanced, what must Box B weigh?

   a. 75 lbs.

   b. 150 lbs.

   c. 225 lbs.

   d. 300 lbs.

   e. 375 lbs.

Figure G-11

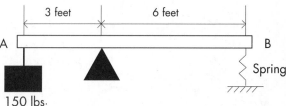

11. The 150-lb. weight at point A is supported by a spring at point B, as depicted in Figure G-11. The spring has a stiffness of 25 lbs./in. How many inches is the spring stretched?

   a. 1 inch

   b. 1.5 inches

   c. 2.0 inches

   d. 2.5 inches

   e. 3.0 inches

Figure G-12

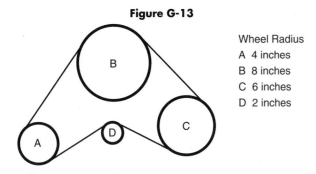

Dam Shapes

12. You have been instructed to build a dam on the river as depicted in Figure G-12. What shape should you make the dam for the given dam site?

a. shape A
b. shape B
c. shape C
d. shape D
e. shape E

Figure G-13

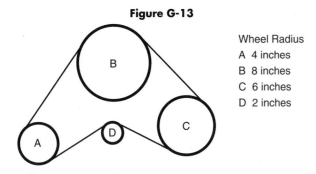

Wheel Radius
A 4 inches
B 8 inches
C 6 inches
D 2 inches

13. All four gears are connected by the same fan belt in Figure G-13. What gear is turning at the highest revolution per minute (rpm)?

a. gear A
b. gear B
c. gear C
d. gear D
e. They all turn at the same rpm.

Figure G-14

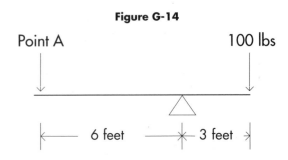

14. If you intend to keep the bar level, as depicted in Figure G-14, what force must you use at point A to counterbalance the 100 lbs. at the other end?

a. 10 lbs.
b. 50 lbs.
c. 100 lbs.
d. 150 lbs.
e. 200 lbs.

Figure G-15

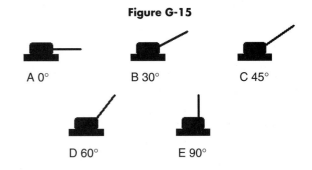

15. Neglecting air resistance, which gun angle in Figure G-15 will shoot the farthest projectile?

a. A
b. B
c. C
d. D
e. E

Figure G-16

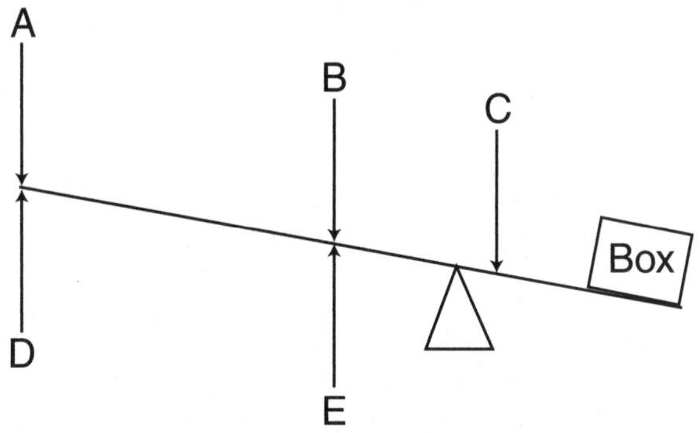

A

B

C

Box

D

E

16. You want to lift the box in Figure G-16. At what point and in what direction would you get the maximum leverage to lift the box?

  a. point A
  b. point B
  c. point C
  d. point D
  e. point E

Figure G-17

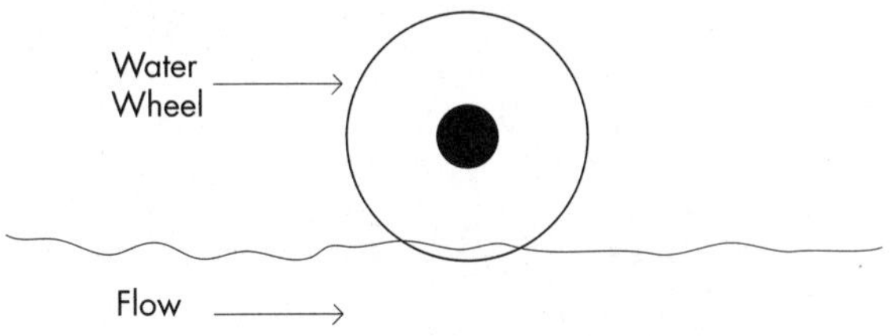

Water Wheel →

Flow →

17. The water wheel in Figure G-17 has a diameter of nine feet. The flow of the river is 300 feet/minute. Approximately how many revolutions per minute is the water wheel turning and in what direction?

  a. 10 rpm, counterclockwise
  b. 10 rpm, clockwise
  c. 33 rpm, counterclockwise
  d. 33 rpm, clockwise
  e. 100 rpm, counterclockwise

Figure G-18

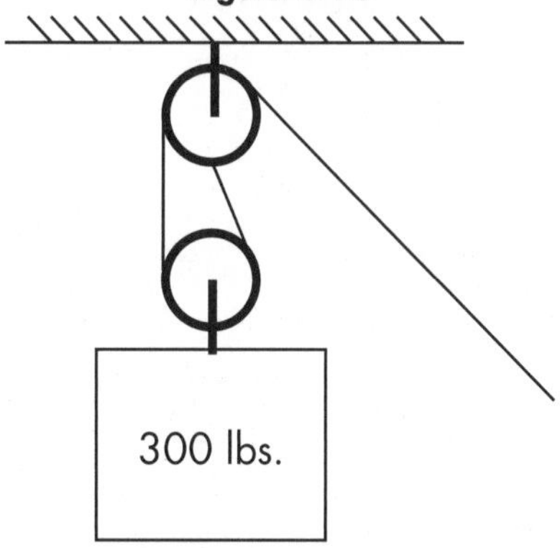

300 lbs.

18. How much effort must be used to raise the 360-lb. weight in Figure G-18?

  a. 50 lbs.
  b. 90 lbs.
  c. 100 lbs.
  d. 120 lbs.
  e. 150 lbs.

Figure G-19

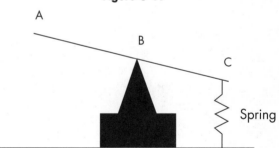

A

B

C

Spring

19. Given the lever in Figure G-19, determine how much force you must push down on point A to stretch the spring 10 inches. (The distance from A to B is six feet, and the distance from B to C is four feet. The spring has a stiffness of 20 lbs./in.)

  a. 110.0 lbs.
  b. 120.5 lbs.
  c. 133.3 lbs.
  d. 142.5 lbs.
  e. 155.5 lbs.

Figure G-20

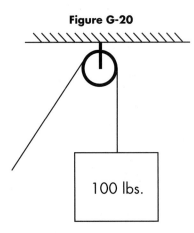

100 lbs.

20. How much effort must be used to raise the 100-lb. weight in Figure G-20?
   a. 50 lbs.
   b. 100 lbs.
   c. 150 lbs.
   d. 200 lbs.
   e. 250 lbs.

AFAST ANSWERS

Section 1: Instrument Comprehension

Question	Answer	Heading	Pitch	Roll
1	B	270° West	Up	Left
2	C	180° South	Down	None
3	A	270° West	Down	Right
4	C	90° East	None	Left
5	A	270° Northeast	Up	Right
6	D	180° South	Up	Left
7	B	90° East	Up	None
8	A	180° West	Down	Right
9	C	270° West	None	None
10	B	270° West	Up	Left
11	A	135° Southeast	Down	Left
12	C	270° West	Up	None
13	B	260° West-Southwest	Down	Left
14	C	255° West-Southwest	Up	Left
15	A	90° East	Up	Left

Section 2: Complex Movements

1. **c.** To center the dot in the circle, you had to move a medium distance up and none to the right or left.

2. **b.** To center the dot in the circle, you had to move a medium distance to the right and a long distance down.

3. **a.** To center the dot in the circle, you had to move a medium distance to the left and a small distance down.

4. **d.** To center the dot in the circle, you had to move a small distance to the left and a small distance up.

5. **d.** To center the dot in the circle, you had to move a medium distance to the right and a small distance up.

6. **e.** To center the dot in the circle, you had to move a short distance to the right and a medium distance up.

7. **a.** To center the dot in the circle, you had to move a long distance to the right and a medium distance down.

8. **c.** The dot is already centered in the circle, none to the left or right, none up or down.

9. **a.** To center the dot in the circle, you had to move a medium distance to the right and a medium distance down.

10. **c.** To center the dot in the circle, you had to move a short distance to the right and a short distance down.

11. **c.** To center the dot in the circle, you had to move a short distance to the left and a long distance down.

12. **a.** To center the dot in the circle, you had to move a medium distance to the left and none up or down.

13. **b.** To center the dot in the circle, you had to move a long distance to the right and a short distance down.

14. **e.** To center the dot in the circle, you had to move a medium distance to the right and a short distance up.

15. **d.** To center the dot in the circle, you had to move a short distance to the left and a short distance down.

16. **e.** To center the dot in the circle, you had to move a medium distance to the right and a short distance down.

17. **e.** To center the dot in the circle, you had to move a short distance to the right and a short distance down.

18. **d.** To center the dot in the circle, you had to move a long distance to the left and a long distance up.

19. **b.** To center the dot in the circle, you had to move a medium distance to the left and none up and down.

20. **c.** To center the dot in the circle, you had to move a short distance to the left and a medium distance up.

21. **a.** To center the dot in the circle, you had to move a short distance to the right and a long distance up.

22. **c.** To center the dot in the circle, you had to move a long distance to the left and a short distance down.

23. **e.** To center the dot in the circle, you had to move a medium distance down and none to the right or left.

24. **e.** To center the dot in the circle, you had to move a medium distance to the left and a short distance up.

25. **b.** To center the dot in the circle, you had to move a medium distance up and none to the right or left.

26. **d.** To center the dot in the circle, you had to move a short distance to the right and a long distance down.

27. **b.** To center the dot in the circle, you had to move a medium distance to the right and none up or down.

28. **e.** To center the dot in the circle, you had to move a long distance to the right and a medium distance up.

29. **c.** To center the dot in the circle, you had to move a long distance to the right and a medium distance down.

30. **d.** To center the dot in the circle, you had to move a medium distance to the left and none up and down.

Section 3: Helicopter Knowledge

1. **a.** The collective lever controls the pitch of the main rotor blades. An increase in pitch increases altitude, while a decrease in pitch decreases altitude.

2. **b.** The foot pedals control the tail rotor, which counteracts the torque created by the main rotor. Purposely overcompensating for the torque effect causes the helicopter to turn. In this way the pedals can help to control the helicopter's heading.

3. **e.** Helicopter performance is reduced by a high-density altitude. The other choices available all fall into favorable conditions for flight.

4. **c.** The correct term for this effect is *coning*.

5. **a.** The downwash is the induced downward flow of air created by the main rotors. When hovering, the pilot must increase the collective pitch to compensate for this factor.

6. **c.** The rear rotor spins in the opposite direction of the main forward rotor, to control the torque effect.

7. **b.** When the nose of a helicopter is tilted downward, the altitude will initially decrease.

8. **b.** Ground effect in helicopters is an improved performance condition that is encountered within half-rotor diameter of the ground.

9. **e.** The cyclic stick controls the attitude, or direction, which then affects the helicopter's direction and speed. Pulling back on the stick increases altitude while decreasing speed. Pushing the stick forward decreases altitude while increasing speed. Left or right movement causes the helicopter to move in the corresponding direction.

10. **d.** The tail rotor counteracts the torque effect of the main rotor and can help to control heading during flight by over-compensating for the torque effect. It has no effect on height, speed, or drag.

11. **b.** *Autorotation* is a term used for a controlled descent with the engine disengaged. The airflow created by the descent sustains the rpms required to provide control of the craft by the pilot.

12. **e.** All of the above. Retreating blade stall is the tendency for the retreating blade to stall in forward flight, and is a limiting factor in determining forward speed. Major indications can include abnormal vibration, nose pitchup, and a roll toward the stalled side.

13. a. The forces of lift and weight must be in balance for a helicopter to hover. If lift exceeds weight, the helicopter will rise, while if weight exceeds lift, it will descend.

14. e. The angle of attack helps determine the amount of lift and drag produced by an airfoil. For example, an increase in the angle of attack will increase the amount of lift.

15. e. All of these factors, some within pilot control, some not, can affect the angle of attack.

16. a. Centrifugal force is the main force acting on the rotor system. Centripetal force acts to modify this driving force.

17. a. Angle of attack is defined as the angle between the airfoil chord and the direction of relative motion.

18. c. Total drag is a combination of profile, induced, and parasite drag. Profile drag is created by the drag of the helicopter blades. The production of lift creates induced drag. The body of the helicopter creates parasite drag as the helicopter flies.

19. b. Induced drag results from the production of lift. Induced drag flows in the opposite direction of airfoil movement.

20. d. Starting, stopping, and speed are all controlled by the collective pitch. Heading is controlled by the foot pedals.

Section 4: Cyclic Orientation

1. Diving no bank.

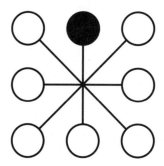

2. Diving no bank.

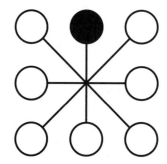

3. Diving bank right.

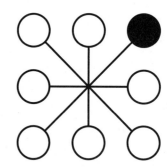

4. Climbing no bank.

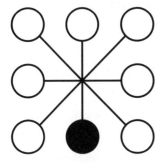

5. Climbing no bank.

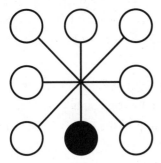

6. Diving bank right.

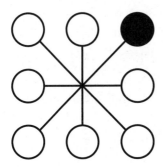

7. Diving no bank.

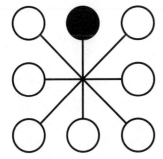

8. Climbing bank right.

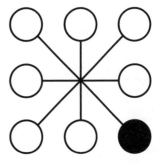

9. Diving no bank.

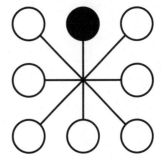

10. Diving bank left.

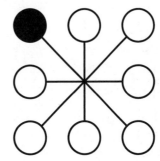

11. Diving bank right.

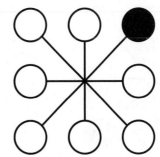

12. Climbing bank left.

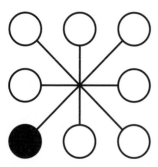

13. Diving bank left.

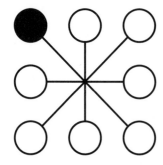

14. Climbing bank left.

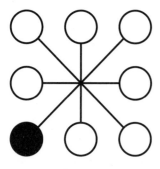

15. Climbing bank right.

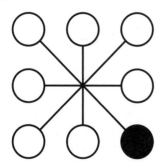

Section 5:
Mechanical Functions

1. d. Because valves D and F are opened, water will flow to barrel #3. With only valve B open, a closed valve C will prevent water from flowing to barrel #2.

2. b. The 50-lb. weight at B creates a moment about the fulcrum of 350 feet-lbs. (50 lbs. × 7 feet = 350 feet-lbs.). If the distance from the fulcrum to the lifting point is 10 feet, then only 35 lbs. of force must be used to lift the block (350 feet-lbs./10 feet = 35 lbs.).

3. d. The box will force the left side of the lever down and the right side of the lever up, which will pull the cable up. The cable will pass across the pulley and apply a pulling force on the spring, so the spring will stretch.

4. d. If the block weighs 400 lbs. and the stiffness of the spring is 20 lbs./in., then the spring will stretch [(400 lbs.)/(20 lbs./in.)] = 20 inches.

5. e. Gears A, C, and D are turning counterclockwise. B is turning clockwise. It helps to follow the direction of the chain, which is connected to all the gears.

6. e. If the tire is 3 feet in diameter, then the circumference is 3 feet × (3.14) = 9.42 feet. The circumference is also the same distance as one revolution of the tire. So if the tire is turning at 500 revolutions per minute and the circumference is 9.42 feet, then the tire is traveling at 4,710 ft./min. down the road (500 rev/min. × 9.42 ft./rev = 4,710 ft./min.).

7. a. Because the springs are in series, their amount of stretch is additive. Spring #1 will stretch 1 inch under 10 pounds, so its total stretch under 20 pounds will be 2 inches. Spring #2 is being subjected to a load of 20 pounds, which is four times the load that will stretch it 2 inches. Therefore, its total stretch will be 8 inches. Adding the amount of stretch for the two springs together gives you 10 inches.

8. d. Gears E and F turn counterclockwise and clockwise, respectively.

9. c. The distance from the pivot point to the point of application of the force (20 feet) is twice the distance from the pivot point to the box (10 feet). Therefore, in order to lift the box, the required force will be one-half of the weight of the box (100 lbs.), or 50 lbs.

10. c. Box A creates a moment about the axel of 450 feet-lbs. (75 lbs. × 6 feet). Since box B is supported by the smaller two-foot wheel, box B must weigh 225 lbs. in order to create an equal moment about the axel (225 lbs. × 2 feet).

11. e. The first step is determining the moment about the fulcrum created by the weight (150 lbs. × 3 feet = 450 feet-lbs.). Next, apply this same moment to the opposite end of the lever to calculate the force applied to the spring (450 feet-lbs.)/(6 feet) = 75 lbs. If you apply this 75-lb. force to the spring with a stiffness of 25 lbs./inch, the spring will move only 3 inches (75 lbs.)/(25 lbs./inch) = 3 inches.

12. d. Shape D is the best shape to make the dam, because as the flow of the water pushes against it, the arch distributes the force equally and directs it into the banks of the river instead of the center of the dam, which would cause it to collapse.

13. d. Since all the gears in Figure G-13 are connected by the same fan belt, their circumferences are all moving at the same speed. However, since all the gears have different radii and, therefore, different circumferences, the gear with the smallest size (gear D) must turn at the highest rpm to match the speed of the fan belt.

14. b. The 100 lbs. at the right end of the lever creates a moment about the fulcrum of 300 feet-lbs. (100 lbs. × 3 feet). To counterbalance this moment, a 50-lb. force must be applied at the opposite end to create the equal 300 feet-lb. moment (50 lbs. × 6 feet).

15. c. Neglecting air resistance, a 45° angle will give a projectile the most distance. Angles greater than this will shoot higher, but not travel downrange as far. Likewise, angles less than this will shoot lower, but impact the ground before reaching the distance shot by the 45° gun.

16. a. Point A delivers the maximum leverage in the correct direction, because it is as far from the fulcrum as possible.

17. a. Looking at Figure G-17, the flow of the water pushing against the bottom of the water wheel would cause the water wheel to turn counterclockwise. The flow of the water is 300 feet/minute. This is also the speed that the circumference of the wheel is turning. So if the circumference of the wheel is 28.26 feet (9 feet × 3.14), then the revolutions per minute are (300 feet/minute)/ (28.26 feet/revolution) = 10.6 revolutions/ minute, or approximately 10 rpm.

18. **e.** In Figure G-18, the top pulley is fixed, but the bottom pulley is raised. This arrangement creates a mechanical advantage of 2. Therefore, the required force to lift the weight is equal to half the weight itself. In this problem, that equals 150 lbs.

19. **c.** The first step is determining how much force at point C it takes to stretch the spring itself the required 10 inches. If the stiffness of the spring is 20 lbs./inch, then 200 lbs. (20 lbs./inch $\times$ 10 inches = 200 lbs.) of force must be applied at point C. To calculate the required force at point A, you must determine the moment about the fulcrum created by the 200-lb. force at C. This is done by multiplying 200 lbs. at point C by the distance from C to the fulcrum (4 feet). The result is 200 lbs. $\times$ 4 feet = 800 feet-lbs. Now, taking this moment about the fulcrum and applying it to the part of the lever from A to B, you calculate the required force at A as 133.3 lbs. (800 feet-lbs./6 feet = 133.3 lbs.).

20. **b.** Since the pulley in Figure G-20 is fixed, there is no additional mechanical advantage, and it still requires 100 lbs. of force to lift the 100-lb. weight.

9 ▶ Aviation Selection Test Battery (ASTB)

In the Aviation Selection Test Battery, you will be tested on mathematical and verbal reasoning, mechanical comprehension, spatial apperception, and aviation and nautical knowledge.

SECTION 1: MATH SKILLS

1.	ⓐ	ⓑ	ⓒ	ⓓ	14.	ⓐ	ⓑ	ⓒ	ⓓ	27.	ⓐ	ⓑ	ⓒ	ⓓ
2.	ⓐ	ⓑ	ⓒ	ⓓ	15.	ⓐ	ⓑ	ⓒ	ⓓ	28.	ⓐ	ⓑ	ⓒ	ⓓ
3.	ⓐ	ⓑ	ⓒ	ⓓ	16.	ⓐ	ⓑ	ⓒ	ⓓ	29.	ⓐ	ⓑ	ⓒ	ⓓ
4.	ⓐ	ⓑ	ⓒ	ⓓ	17.	ⓐ	ⓑ	ⓒ	ⓓ	30.	ⓐ	ⓑ	ⓒ	ⓓ
5.	ⓐ	ⓑ	ⓒ	ⓓ	18.	ⓐ	ⓑ	ⓒ	ⓓ					
6.	ⓐ	ⓑ	ⓒ	ⓓ	19.	ⓐ	ⓑ	ⓒ	ⓓ					
7.	ⓐ	ⓑ	ⓒ	ⓓ	20.	ⓐ	ⓑ	ⓒ	ⓓ					
8.	ⓐ	ⓑ	ⓒ	ⓓ	21.	ⓐ	ⓑ	ⓒ	ⓓ					
9.	ⓐ	ⓑ	ⓒ	ⓓ	22.	ⓐ	ⓑ	ⓒ	ⓓ					
10.	ⓐ	ⓑ	ⓒ	ⓓ	23.	ⓐ	ⓑ	ⓒ	ⓓ					
11.	ⓐ	ⓑ	ⓒ	ⓓ	24.	ⓐ	ⓑ	ⓒ	ⓓ					
12.	ⓐ	ⓑ	ⓒ	ⓓ	25.	ⓐ	ⓑ	ⓒ	ⓓ					
13.	ⓐ	ⓑ	ⓒ	ⓓ	26.	ⓐ	ⓑ	ⓒ	ⓓ					

SECTION 2: READING SKILLS

1.	ⓐ	ⓑ	ⓒ	ⓓ	11.	ⓐ	ⓑ	ⓒ	ⓓ	21.	ⓐ	ⓑ	ⓒ	ⓓ
2.	ⓐ	ⓑ	ⓒ	ⓓ	12.	ⓐ	ⓑ	ⓒ	ⓓ	22.	ⓐ	ⓑ	ⓒ	ⓓ
3.	ⓐ	ⓑ	ⓒ	ⓓ	13.	ⓐ	ⓑ	ⓒ	ⓓ	23.	ⓐ	ⓑ	ⓒ	ⓓ
4.	ⓐ	ⓑ	ⓒ	ⓓ	14.	ⓐ	ⓑ	ⓒ	ⓓ	24.	ⓐ	ⓑ	ⓒ	ⓓ
5.	ⓐ	ⓑ	ⓒ	ⓓ	15.	ⓐ	ⓑ	ⓒ	ⓓ	25.	ⓐ	ⓑ	ⓒ	ⓓ
6.	ⓐ	ⓑ	ⓒ	ⓓ	16.	ⓐ	ⓑ	ⓒ	ⓓ	26.	ⓐ	ⓑ	ⓒ	ⓓ
7.	ⓐ	ⓑ	ⓒ	ⓓ	17.	ⓐ	ⓑ	ⓒ	ⓓ	27.	ⓐ	ⓑ	ⓒ	ⓓ
8.	ⓐ	ⓑ	ⓒ	ⓓ	18.	ⓐ	ⓑ	ⓒ	ⓓ					
9.	ⓐ	ⓑ	ⓒ	ⓓ	19.	ⓐ	ⓑ	ⓒ	ⓓ					
10.	ⓐ	ⓑ	ⓒ	ⓓ	20.	ⓐ	ⓑ	ⓒ	ⓓ					

SECTION 3: MECHANICAL COMPREHENSION

1.	ⓐ	ⓑ	ⓒ	ⓓ	ⓔ	11.	ⓐ	ⓑ	ⓒ	ⓓ	ⓔ	21.	ⓐ	ⓑ	ⓒ	ⓓ	ⓔ
2.	ⓐ	ⓑ	ⓒ	ⓓ	ⓔ	12.	ⓐ	ⓑ	ⓒ	ⓓ	ⓔ	22.	ⓐ	ⓑ	ⓒ	ⓓ	ⓔ
3.	ⓐ	ⓑ	ⓒ	ⓓ	ⓔ	13.	ⓐ	ⓑ	ⓒ	ⓓ	ⓔ	23.	ⓐ	ⓑ	ⓒ	ⓓ	ⓔ
4.	ⓐ	ⓑ	ⓒ	ⓓ	ⓔ	14.	ⓐ	ⓑ	ⓒ	ⓓ	ⓔ	24.	ⓐ	ⓑ	ⓒ	ⓓ	ⓔ
5.	ⓐ	ⓑ	ⓒ	ⓓ	ⓔ	15.	ⓐ	ⓑ	ⓒ	ⓓ	ⓔ	25.	ⓐ	ⓑ	ⓒ	ⓓ	ⓔ
6.	ⓐ	ⓑ	ⓒ	ⓓ	ⓔ	16.	ⓐ	ⓑ	ⓒ	ⓓ	ⓔ	26.	ⓐ	ⓑ	ⓒ	ⓓ	ⓔ
7.	ⓐ	ⓑ	ⓒ	ⓓ	ⓔ	17.	ⓐ	ⓑ	ⓒ	ⓓ	ⓔ	27.	ⓐ	ⓑ	ⓒ	ⓓ	ⓔ
8.	ⓐ	ⓑ	ⓒ	ⓓ	ⓔ	18.	ⓐ	ⓑ	ⓒ	ⓓ	ⓔ	28.	ⓐ	ⓑ	ⓒ	ⓓ	ⓔ
9.	ⓐ	ⓑ	ⓒ	ⓓ	ⓔ	19.	ⓐ	ⓑ	ⓒ	ⓓ	ⓔ	29.	ⓐ	ⓑ	ⓒ	ⓓ	ⓔ
10.	ⓐ	ⓑ	ⓒ	ⓓ	ⓔ	20.	ⓐ	ⓑ	ⓒ	ⓓ	ⓔ	30.	ⓐ	ⓑ	ⓒ	ⓓ	ⓔ

SECTION 4: SPATIAL APPERCEPTION

1. (a) (b) (c) (d) (e)	11. (a) (b) (c) (d) (e)	21. (a) (b) (c) (d) (e)
2. (a) (b) (c) (d) (e)	12. (a) (b) (c) (d) (e)	22. (a) (b) (c) (d) (e)
3. (a) (b) (c) (d) (e)	13. (a) (b) (c) (d) (e)	23. (a) (b) (c) (d) (e)
4. (a) (b) (c) (d) (e)	14. (a) (b) (c) (d) (e)	24. (a) (b) (c) (d) (e)
5. (a) (b) (c) (d) (e)	15. (a) (b) (c) (d) (e)	25. (a) (b) (c) (d) (e)
6. (a) (b) (c) (d) (e)	16. (a) (b) (c) (d) (e)	
7. (a) (b) (c) (d) (e)	17. (a) (b) (c) (d) (e)	
8. (a) (b) (c) (d) (e)	18. (a) (b) (c) (d) (e)	
9. (a) (b) (c) (d) (e)	19. (a) (b) (c) (d) (e)	
10. (a) (b) (c) (d) (e)	20. (a) (b) (c) (d) (e)	

SECTION 5: AVIATION AND NAUTICAL INFORMATION

1. (a) (b) (c) (d) (e)	11. (a) (b) (c) (d) (e)	21. (a) (b) (c) (d) (e)
2. (a) (b) (c) (d) (e)	12. (a) (b) (c) (d) (e)	22. (a) (b) (c) (d) (e)
3. (a) (b) (c) (d) (e)	13. (a) (b) (c) (d) (e)	23. (a) (b) (c) (d) (e)
4. (a) (b) (c) (d) (e)	14. (a) (b) (c) (d) (e)	24. (a) (b) (c) (d) (e)
5. (a) (b) (c) (d) (e)	15. (a) (b) (c) (d) (e)	25. (a) (b) (c) (d) (e)
6. (a) (b) (c) (d) (e)	16. (a) (b) (c) (d) (e)	26. (a) (b) (c) (d) (e)
7. (a) (b) (c) (d) (e)	17. (a) (b) (c) (d) (e)	27. (a) (b) (c) (d) (e)
8. (a) (b) (c) (d) (e)	18. (a) (b) (c) (d) (e)	28. (a) (b) (c) (d) (e)
9. (a) (b) (c) (d) (e)	19. (a) (b) (c) (d) (e)	29. (a) (b) (c) (d) (e)
10. (a) (b) (c) (d) (e)	20. (a) (b) (c) (d) (e)	30. (a) (b) (c) (d) (e)

Section 1: Math Skills

DIRECTIONS: The Math Skills section of the test measures mathematical reasoning. It is concerned with your ability to arrive at solutions to problems. Each problem is followed by four possible answers. Decide which one of the answers is most nearly correct. A method for attacking each of these questions is given in the answer block at the end of this chapter.

You will have twenty-five (25) minutes to complete this portion of the test.

Questions: 30
Time: 25 minutes

For sample Math Skills questions, see pages 42 and 45.

1. What is the estimated product when 174 and 362 are rounded to the nearest hundred and multiplied?
   a. 160,000
   b. 180,000
   c. 16,000
   d. 80,000

2. Mr. Richard Tupper is purchasing gifts for his family. He stops to consider what else he has to buy. A quick mental inventory of his shopping bag so far reveals the following:

   1 cashmere sweater, valued at $260
   3 diamond bracelets, each valued at $365
   1 computer game, valued at $78
   1 cameo brooch, valued at $130

Later, having coffee in the food court, he suddenly remembers that he has purchased only two diamond bracelets, not three, and that the cashmere sweater was on sale for $245. What is the total value of the gifts Mr. Tupper has purchased so far?
   a. $833
   b. $1,183
   c. $1,198
   d. $1,563

3. One lap on a particular outdoor track measures a quarter of a mile around. To run a total of five-and-three-quarter miles, how many laps must a person complete?
   a. 7
   b. 10
   c. 23
   d. 35

4. Body mass index (BMI) is equal to weight in kilograms/(height in meters)^2. A man who weighs 64.8 kilograms has a BMI of 20. How tall is he?
   a. 1.8 meters
   b. .9 meters
   c. 2.16 meters
   d. 3.24 meters

5. A floor plan is drawn to scale so that $\frac{1}{4}$ inch represents two feet. If a hall on the plan is four inches long, how long will the actual hall be when it is built?
   a. 2 feet
   b. 8 feet
   c. 16 feet
   d. 32 feet

6. Newly hired referees have to buy uniforms at the full price of $116.75, but those who have worked at least a year get a 10% discount. Those who have worked at least three years get an additional 15% off the discounted price. How much does a referee who has worked at least three years have to pay for uniforms?

   a. $87.56
   b. $89.32
   c. $93.40
   d. $105.08

7. The condition Down syndrome occurs in about one in 1,500 children when the mothers are in their twenties. About what percentage of all children born to mothers in their twenties are likely to have Down syndrome?

   a. .0067%
   b. .67%
   c. 6.7%
   d. .067%

8. If a population of yeast cells grows from 10 to 320 in a period of five hours, what is the rate of growth?

   a. It doubles its numbers every hour.
   b. It triples its numbers every hour.
   c. It doubles its numbers every two hours.
   d. It triples its numbers every two hours.

9. How much water must be added to one liter of a 9% saline solution to get a 3% saline solution?

   a. 1 liter
   b. 1.5 liter
   c. 2 liters
   d. 2.5 liters

10. In the first week of his exercise program, John went on a 15-mile hike. The next week, he increased the length of his hike by 20%. How long was his hike in the second week?

    a. 17 miles
    b. 18 miles
    c. 30 miles
    d. 35 miles

11. All of the rooms in a building are rectangular, with nine-foot ceilings. One room is 10 feet wide by 14 feet long. What is the combined area of the four walls, including doors and windows?

    a. 99 square feet
    b. 160 square feet
    c. 320 square feet
    d. 72 square feet

12. A child has a temperature of 39.6° C. What is the child's temperature in degrees Fahrenheit? $(F = \frac{9}{5}C + 32)$

    a. 101.2° F
    b. 102° F
    c. 103.3° F
    d. 104.1° F

13. A dosage of a certain medication is 12 cc per 100 pounds. What is the dosage for a patient who weighs 175 pounds?

    a. 15 cc
    b. 18 cc
    c. 21 cc
    d. 24 cc

14. A hiker walks 40 miles on the first day of a five-day trip. On each day after that, he can walk only half as far as he did the day before. On average, how far does he walk each day?
    a. 10 miles
    b. 15.5 miles
    c. 20 miles
    d. 24 miles

15. A fugitive drives west at 50 miles per hour. After an hour, the police start to follow her. How fast must the police drive to catch up to her 4 hours after they start?
    a. 52.5 mph
    b. 55 mph
    c. 60 mph
    d. 62.5 mph

16. Jason is six times as old as Kate. In two years, Jason will be twice as old as Kate is then. How old is Jason now?
    a. 3 years old
    b. 6 years old
    c. 9 years old
    d. 12 years old

17. During her first three months at college, a student's long distance phone bills are $103.30, $71.60, and $84.00. Her local phone bill is $18.00 each month. What is her average total monthly phone bill?
    a. $86.30
    b. $92.30
    c. $98.30
    d. $104.30

18. A car uses 16 gallons of gas to travel 448 miles. How many miles per gallon does the car get?
    a. 22 miles per gallon
    b. 24 miles per gallon
    c. 26 miles per gallon
    d. 28 miles per gallon

19. A hard drive has 962,342 bytes free. If you delete a file of 454,783 bytes and create a new file of 315,926 bytes, how many free bytes will the hard drive have?
    a. 677,179 free bytes
    b. 881,525 free bytes
    c. 1,101,199 free bytes
    d. 1,417,125 free bytes

20. Jackie is paid $822.40 twice a month. If she saves $150.00 per paycheck and pays $84.71 on her student loan each month, how much does she have left to spend each month?
    a. $1,175.38
    b. $1,260.09
    c. $1,410.09
    d. $1,310.29

21. $(.4)2 =$
    a. .016
    b. .8
    c. .08
    d. .16

22. A fuel additive requires that four parts be added per 12 gallons of fuel. How many parts need to be added for 51 gallons of fuel?
    a. 4 parts
    b. 5 parts
    c. 17 parts
    d. 48 parts

23. An aerial refueling tanker departs two hours prior to a fighter jet. If the tanker maintains a constant speed of 300 mph, how fast does the fighter jet have to fly to rendezvous with the tanker in two hours after the jet's takeoff?
    a. 300 mph
    b. 450 mph
    c. 600 mph
    d. 900 mph

24. A fighter jet burns 4,800 lbs. of fuel per hour. The fuel has a specific density of six lbs. per gallon. How much fuel will need to be requested for the aircraft to complete a three-hour flight and still have 3,000 lbs. of fuel remaining upon landing?
    a. 2,900 lbs.
    b. 2,400 gallons
    c. 2,000 lbs.
    d. 2,900 gallons

25. An aerial tanker's refueling orbit is six miles in circumference. To fly 54 miles, how many orbits must the tanker complete?
    a. 9 orbits
    b. 10 orbits
    c. 12 orbits
    d. 14 orbits

26. A model plane is built scale so that .5 inch equals five feet. If the model plane is 10 inches long, how long is the actual airplane?
    a. 10 feet
    b. 20 feet
    c. 50 feet
    d. 100 feet

27. Bonnie has twice as many cousins as Robert. George has five cousins, which is 11 less than Bonnie has. How many cousins does Robert have?
    a. 17
    b. 21
    c. 4
    d. 8

28. Oscar sold two glasses of milk for every five sodas he sold. If he sold 10 glasses of milk, how many sodas did he sell?
    a. 45
    b. 20
    c. 25
    d. 10

29. Justin earned scores of 85, 92, and 95 on his science tests. What does he need to earn on his next science test to have an average (arithmetic mean) of 93%?
    a. 93
    b. 100
    c. 85
    d. 96

30. Which expression has an answer of 18?
    a. $2 \times 5 + 4$
    b. $2 \times (4 + 5)$
    c. $5 \times (2 + 4)$
    d. $4 \times 2 + 5$

Section 2: Reading Skills

DIRECTIONS: The Reading Skills section measures your ability to read and understand paragraphs. For each question, choose the answer that best completes the meaning of the paragraph. Pay close attention as you read, and try to find the point that the author was trying to make. Once you have read the paragraph all the way through, you will find that one or two of the possible answers can be quickly eliminated based on the context.

You will have twenty-five (25) minutes to complete this portion of the test.

Questions: 27
Time: 25 minutes

For sample Reading Skills questions, see pages 43.

Anyone who lives in a large, modern city has heard the familiar sound of electronic security alarms. Although these mechanical alarms are fairly recent, the idea of a security system is not new. The oldest alarm system was probably a few strategically placed dogs that would discourage intruders with a loud warning cry.

1. The paragraph best supports the statement that
   a. dogs are more reliable than electronic alarms.
   b. city dwellers would be wise to use dogs for security.
   c. mechanical alarm systems break down, but dogs do not.
   d. a dog is an older alarm device than is a mechanical alarm.

In cities throughout the country, there is a new direction in local campaign coverage. Frequently, in local elections, journalists are not giving voters enough information to understand the issues and evaluate the candidates. The local news media devotes too much time to scandal and not enough time to policy.

2. This paragraph best supports the statement that the local news media
   a. is not doing an adequate job when it comes to covering local campaigns.
   b. does not understand either campaign issues or politics.
   c. should learn how to cover politics by watching the national news media.
   d. has no interest in covering stories about local political events.

Many office professionals today have an interest in replacing the currently used keyboard, known as the QWERTY keyboard, with a keyboard that can keep up with technological changes and make offices more efficient. The best choice is the Dvorak keyboard. Studies have shown that people using the Dvorak keyboard can type 20 to 30% faster and cut their error rate in half. Dvorak puts vowels and other frequently used letters right under the fingers (on the home row), where typists make 70% of their keystrokes.

3. The paragraph best supports the statement that the Dvorak keyboard
   a. is more efficient than the QWERTY.
   b. has more keys right under the typists' fingers than the QWERTY.
   c. is favored by more typists than the QWERTY.
   d. is, on average, 70% faster than the QWERTY.

Every year Americans use over one billion sharp objects to administer health care in their homes. These sharp objects include lancets, needles, and syringes. If not disposed of in puncture-resistant containers, they can injure sanitation workers. Sharp objects should be disposed of in hard plastic or metal containers with secure lids. The containers should be clearly marked and be puncture resistant.

4. The paragraph best supports the idea that sanitation workers can be injured if they
   a. do not place sharp objects in puncture-resistant containers.
   b. come in contact with sharp objects that have not been placed in secure containers.
   c. are careless with sharp objects such as lancets, needles, and syringes in their homes.
   d. do not mark the containers they pick up with a warning that those containers contain sharp objects.

Close-up images of Mars by the *Mariner 9* probe indicated networks of valleys that looked like the stream beds on Earth. These images also implied that Mars once had an atmosphere that was thick enough to trap the sun's heat. If this is true, something must have happened to Mars billions of years ago that stripped away the planet's atmosphere.

5. The paragraph best supports the statement that
   a. Mars once had a thicker atmosphere than earth does.
   b. the *Mariner 9* probe took the first pictures of Mars.
   c. Mars now has little or no atmosphere.
   d. Mars is closer to the sun than Earth is.

After a snow or ice fall, the city streets are treated with ordinary rock salt. In some areas, the salt is combined with calcium chloride, which is more effective in below-zero temperatures and which melts ice better. This combination of salt and calcium chloride is also less damaging to foliage along the roadways.

6. In deciding whether to use ordinary rock salt or the salt and calcium chloride mixture on a particular street, which of the following is NOT a consideration?
   a. the temperature at the time of treatment
   b. the plants and trees along the street
   c. whether there is ice on the street
   d. whether the street is a main or a secondary road

The city has distributed standardized recycling containers to all households with directions that read: "We would prefer that you use this new container as your primary recycling container, as this will expedite pickup of recyclables. Additional recycling containers may be purchased from the city."

7. According to the directions, each household
   a. may use only one recycling container.
   b. must use the new recycling container.
   c. should use the new recycling container.
   d. must buy a new recycling container.

It is well known that the world urgently needs adequate distribution of food so that everyone gets enough. Adequate distribution of medicine is just as urgent. Medical expertise and medical supplies need to be redistributed throughout the world so that people in emerging nations will have proper medical care.

8. This paragraph best supports the statement that
   a. the majority of the people in the world have no medical care.
   b. medical resources in emerging nations have diminished in the past few years.
   c. not enough doctors give time and money to those in need of medical care.
   d. many people who live in emerging nations are not receiving proper medical care.

In the past, suggesting a gas tax has usually been thought of as political poison. But that doesn't seem to be the case today. Several states are pushing bills in their state legislatures that would cut income or property taxes and make up the revenue with taxes on fossil fuel.

9. The paragraph best supports the statement that
   a. gas taxes produce more revenue than income taxes.
   b. states with low income tax rates are increasing their gas taxes.
   c. state legislators no longer fear increasing gas taxes.
   d. taxes on fossil fuels are more popular than property taxes.

Lawyer bashing is on the increase in the United States. Lawyers are accused of lacking principles, clogging the justice system, and increasing the cost of liability insurance. Lawyers have received undeserved criticism. A lawyer is more likely than not to try to dissuade a client from litigation by offering to arbitrate and settle conflict.

10. The main idea of the paragraph is best expressed in which of the following statements from the passage?
   a. Lawyer bashing is on the increase in the United States.
   b. Lawyers have received undeserved criticism.
   c. Lawyers are accused of lacking principles.
   d. A lawyer is more likely than not to try to dissuade a client from litigation by offering to arbitrate and settle conflict.

Generation Xers are those people born roughly between 1965 and 1981. As employees, Generation Xers tend to be more challenged when they can carry out tasks independently. This makes Generation Xers the most entrepreneurial generation in history.

11. This paragraph best supports the statement that Generation Xers
   a. work harder than people from other generations.
   b. have a tendency to be self-directed workers.
   c. tend to work in jobs that require risk-taking behavior.
   d. like to challenge their bosses' work attitudes.

Electronic mail (e-mail) has been in widespread use for more than a decade. E-mail simplifies the flow of ideas, connects people from distant offices, eliminates the need for meetings, and often boosts productivity. But e-mail should be carefully managed to avoid unclear and inappropriate communication. E-mail messages should be concise and limited to one topic. When complex issues need to be addressed, phone calls are still best.

12. The main idea of the paragraph is that e-mail
 a. is not always the easiest way to connect people from distant offices.
 b. has changed considerably since it first began a decade ago.
 c. causes people to be unproductive when it is used incorrectly.
 d. is effective for certain kinds of messages, but only if managed wisely.

Children start out in a world where fantasy and imagination are not substantially different from experience. But as they get older, they are shocked to discover that the world in which people reliably exist is the physical world. Computer games and virtual reality are two ways in which children can come to terms with this dilemma.

13. The main idea of the paragraph is that computer games and virtual reality
 a. can be important tools in children's lives.
 b. keep children from experiencing reality.
 c. help children to uncover shocking truths about the world.
 d. should take the place of children's fantasy worlds.

Native American art often incorporates a language of abstract visual symbols. The artist gives a poetic message to the viewer, communicating the beauty of an idea by using either religious symbols or a design from nature such as rain on leaves or sunshine on water. The idea communicated may even be purely whimsical, in which case the artist might start out with symbols developed from a bird's tracks or a child's toy.

14. The main idea of the passage is that Native American art
 a. is purely poetic and dreamlike.
 b. is usually abstract, although it can also be poetic and beautiful.
 c. communicates the beauty of ideas through the use of symbols.
 d. is sometimes purely whimsical.

The supervisors have received numerous complaints over the last several weeks about buses on several routes running hot. Drivers are reminded that each route has several checkpoints at which drivers should check the time. If the bus is ahead of schedule, drivers should delay at the checkpoint until it is the proper time to leave.

15. In the passage, saying a bus is "running hot" means
 a. the engine is overheating.
 b. the bus is running ahead of schedule.
 c. the air conditioning is not working.
 d. there is no more room for passengers.

Hazardous waste is defined as any waste designated by the U.S. Environmental Protection Agency as hazardous. If a worker is unclear whether a particular item, is hazardous, he or she should not handle the item, but should instead notify the supervisor and ask for directions.

16. Hazardous waste is
  a. anything too dangerous for workers to handle.
  b. picked up by special trucks.
  c. defined by the United States Environmental Protection Agency.
  d. not allowed with regular residential garbage.

In the summer, the northern hemisphere is slanted toward the sun, making the days longer and warmer than in winter. The summer solstice is the first day of summer and the longest day of the year. However, June 21 marks the beginning of winter in the southern hemisphere, when that hemisphere is tilted away from the sun.

17. According to the passage, when it is summer in the northern hemisphere, in the southern hemisphere it is
  a. spring.
  b. summer.
  c. autumn.
  d. winter.

An ecosystem is a group of animals and plants living in a specific region and interacting with one another and with their physical environment. Ecosystems include physical and chemical components, such as soils, water, and nutrients, that support the organisms living there. These organisms may range from large animals to microscopic bacteria. Ecosystems can also be thought of as the interactions among all organisms in a given habitat; for instance, one species may serve as food for another.

18. An ecosystem can most accurately be defined as a
  a. geographical area.
  b. community.
  c. habitat.
  d. protected environment.
  e. specific location.

The English-language premiere of Samuel Beckett's play *Waiting for Godot* took place in London in August 1955. *Godot* is an avant-garde play with only five characters (not counting Mr. Godot, who never arrives) and a minimal setting (one rock and one bare tree). The play has two acts. The second act repeats what little action occurs in the first with few changes; the tree, for instance, acquires one leaf. The play initially met with bafflement and derision. However, Harold Hobson, in his review in *The Sunday Times,* managed to recognize the play for what history has proven it to be: a revolutionary moment in theater.

19. Which of the following best describes the attitude of the author of the passage toward the play *Waiting for Godot?*
  a. It was a curiosity in theater history.
  b. It is the most important play of the twentieth century.
  c. It had no effect on theater.
  d. It represented a turning point in theater history.
  e. It was a mediocre play.

Everyone is sensitive to extreme weather conditions. But with age, the body may become less able to respond to long exposure to very hot or very cold temperatures. Some older people might develop hypothermia when exposed to cold weather. Hypothermia is a drop in internal body temperature, which can be fatal if not detected and treated.

20. This paragraph best supports the statement that
   a. cold weather is more dangerous for older people than warm weather.
   b. hypothermia is a condition that only affects older people.
   c. older people who live in warm climates are healthier than older people who live in cold climates.
   d. an older person is more susceptible to hypothermia than a younger person.
   e. young people prefer cold weather.

In the United States, the most frequently used nutritional standard for maintaining optimal health is known as the Recommended Dietary Allowance, otherwise known as the "RDA." The RDA specifies the recommended amount of nutrients for people in many different age and gender groups. While the basic premise of an RDA is a good one, the current model has a number of shortcomings. First, it is based on the assumption that it is possible to define nutritional requirements accurately for a given group. However, individual nutritional requirements can vary widely within each group. The efficiency with which a person converts food intake into nutrients can also vary widely. Certain foods when eaten in combination actually prevent the absorption of nutrients. For example, spinach combined with milk reduces the amount of calcium available to the body from the milk. Also, the RDA approach specifies a different dietary requirement for each age and gender, and it is clearly unrealistic to prepare a different menu for each family member. Still, although we cannot rely solely upon the RDA to ensure our overall long-term health, it can be a useful guide so long as its limitations are recognized.

21. With which of the following would the author most likely agree?
   a. The RDA approach should be replaced by a more realistic nutritional guide.
   b. The RDA approach should be supplemented with more specific nutritional guides.
   c. In spite of its flaws, the RDA approach is definitely the best guide to good nutrition.
   d. The RDA approach is most suitable for a large family.
   e. The RDA approach is outdated.

The coast of Maine is one of the most irregular in the world. This irregularity is the result of what is called a *drowned coastline*. The term comes from the glacial activity of the Ice Age. During the Ice Age, the whole area that is now Maine was part of a mountain range that towered above the sea. As the glacier descended, however, it expended enormous force on those mountains, and they sank into the sea. As the mountains sank, ocean water charged over the lowest parts of the remaining land, forming a series of twisting inlets and lagoons. Once the glacier receded, the highest parts of the former mountain range that were nearest the shore remained as islands. Although the mountain ranges were never to return, the land rose somewhat over the centuries. On one of these islands, marine fossils have been found at 225 feet above today's sea level.

22. According to the passage, when the glacier moved over what is now the state of Maine, it helped to create all of the following EXCEPT
   a. an irregular coastline.
   b. coastal islands.
   c. a mountain range.
   d. inlets.
   e. lagoons.

Light pollution is a growing problem worldwide. Like other forms of pollution, light pollution degrades the quality of the environment. Where once it was possible to look up at the night sky and see thousands of twinkling stars in the inky blackness, one now sees little more than the yellow glare of urban sky-glow. When we lose the ability to connect visually with the vastness of the universe by looking up at the night sky, we lose our connection with something profoundly important to the human spirit, our sense of wonder.

23. The passage implies that the most serious damage done by light pollution is to our
    a. artistic appreciation.
    b. sense of physical well-being.
    c. cultural advancement.
    d. aesthetic sensibilities.
    e. spiritual selves.

Law enforcement officers often do not like taking time from their regular duties to testify in court, but testimony is an important part of an officer's job. To be good witnesses, officers should keep complete notes detailing any potentially criminal or actionable incidents. When on the witness stand, officers may refer to those notes to refresh their memories about particular events. It is also very important for officers to listen carefully to the questions asked by the lawyers and to provide only the information requested. Officers should never volunteer opinions or any extra information that is beyond the scope of a question.

24. The paragraph best supports the statement that a poor police witness might
    a. rely on memory alone when testifying in court.
    b. hold an opinion about the guilt or innocence of a suspect before the trial is over.
    c. rely too much on notes and not enough on experience at the crime scene.

    d. be unduly influenced by prosecution lawyers when giving testimony.
    e. not offer extra information on the stand which would help the prosecution's case.

The Competitive Civil Service system is designed to give applicants fair and equal treatment and to ensure that federal applicants are hired based on objective criteria. Hiring has to be based solely on candidates' knowledge, skills, and abilities (which you will sometimes see abbreviated as *ksa*) and not on any external factors such as race, religion, sex, and so on. Whereas employers in the private sector can hire employees for subjective reasons, federal employers must be able to justify their decisions with objective evidence that the candidate is qualified.

25. The federal government's practice of hiring on the basis of *ksa* frequently results in the hiring of employees
    a. based on race, religion, sex, and so forth.
    b. who are unqualified for the job.
    c. who are qualified for the job.
    d. on the basis of subjective judgment.
    e. based on the unequal treatment of applicants.

On occasion, corrections officers may be involved in receiving a confession from an inmate under their care. Sometimes, one inmate may confess to another inmate, who may be motivated to pass the information on to correction officers. Often, however, these confessions are obtained by placing an undercover agent, posing as an inmate, in a cell with the prisoner. On the surface, this may appear to violate the principles of the constitutional Fifth Amendment privilege against self-incrimination. However, the courts have found that the Fifth Amendment is intended to protect suspects from coercive interrogation, which is present when a person is in custody and is subject to official questioning. In the case of an undercover officer posing as an inmate, the questioning does not appear to be official; therefore, confessions obtained in this manner are not considered coercive.

26. The privilege against self-incrimination can be found in
  a. a Supreme Court opinion.
  b. prison rules and regulations.
  c. state law governing prisons.
  d. the U.S. Constitution.
  e. Congressional legislature.

One of the most hazardous conditions a firefighter will ever encounter is a backdraft (also known as a smoke explosion). Firefighters should be aware of the conditions that indicate the possibility for a backdraft to occur. When there is a lack of oxygen during a fire, the smoke becomes filled with carbon dioxide or carbon monoxide and turns dense gray or black. Other warning signs of a potential backdraft are little or no visible flame, excessive heat, smoke leaving the building in puffs, muffled sounds, and smoke-stained windows.

27. Which of the following is NOT mentioned as a potential backdraft warning sign?
  a. windows stained with smoke
  b. flames shooting up from the building
  c. puffs of smoke leaving the building
  d. more intense heat than usual
  e. muffled sounds coming from the building

Section 3: Mechanical Comprehension

DIRECTIONS: This part of the test measures your ability to learn and reason with mechanical terms. Included in this part of the test are diagrams showing various mechanical devices. Following each diagram are several questions or incomplete statements. Study each diagram carefully, as details do make a difference in how each device operates, and then select the choice that best answers the question or completes the statement. You will have fifteen (15) minutes to complete this section of the test.

Questions: 30
Time: 15 minutes

For sample Mechanical Comprehension questions, see page 45.

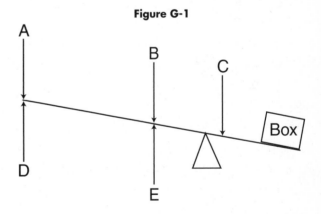

Figure G-1

1. In Figure G-1, you want to lift the box. At what point and in what direction would you get the maximum leverage to lift the box?
  a. point A
  b. point B
  c. point C
  d. point D
  e. point E

Figure G-2

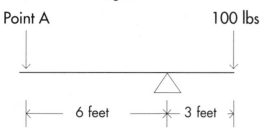

Point A   100 lbs

|← 6 feet →|← 3 feet →|

2. If you intend to keep the bar level, as depicted in Figure G-2, what force must you use at point A to counter balance the 100 lbs. at the other end?

   a. 10 lbs.

   b. 50 lbs.

   c. 100 lbs.

   d. 150 lbs.

   e. 200 lbs.

Figure G-3

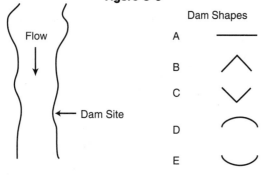

3. You have been instructed to build a dam on the river, as depicted in Figure G-3. What shape should you make the dam for the given dam site?

   a. shape A

   b. shape B

   c. shape C

   d. shape D

   e. shape E

Figure G-4

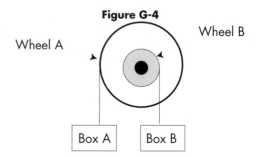

4. In Figure G-4, box A weighs 75 lbs. The radius of wheel A is six feet and the radius of wheel B is two feet. If both wheels are balanced, what must box B weigh?

   a. 75 lbs.

   b. 150 lbs.

   c. 225 lbs.

   d. 300 lbs.

   e. 375 lbs.

Figure G-5

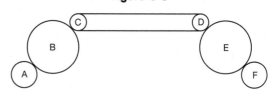

5. Figure G-5 shows a series of gears, A, B, and C, that are connected by a conveyor belt to gears D, E, and F. If gear A turns clockwise, what direction do gears E and F turn?

   a. clockwise, clockwise

   b. counterclockwise, counterclockwise

   c. clockwise, counterclockwise

   d. counterclockwise, clockwise

   e. not enough information

Figure G-6

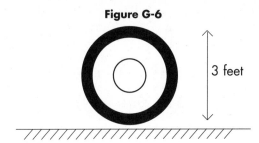

3 feet

6. If the tire in Figure G-6 is 3 feet in diameter and is turning at 500 revolutions per minute, what speed (in feet/minutes) is the tire traveling down the road?

   a. 500 ft./min.

   b. 1,500 ft./min.

   c. 1,860 ft./min.

   d. 2,355 ft./min.

   e. 4,710 ft./min.

Figure G-7

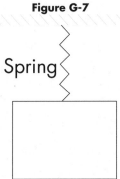

Spring

7. The spring in Figure G-7 has a stiffness of 16 lbs./in. How much is the spring stretched if the weight of the block is 98 lbs.?

   a. $4\frac{7}{8}$ inches

   b. $5\frac{3}{4}$ inches

   c. $6\frac{1}{8}$ inches

   d. $7\frac{1}{4}$ inches

   e. $7\frac{5}{8}$ inches

Figure G-8

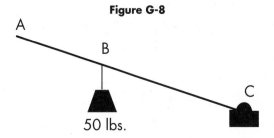

A

B

C

50 lbs.

8. In Figure G-8, the distance from A to B is three feet, and the distance from B to C is seven feet. How much force must be applied at A to lift the 50 lbs. at point B?

   a. 25 lbs.

   b. 35 lbs.

   c. 45 lbs.

   d. 55 lbs.

   e. 65 lbs.

Figure G-9

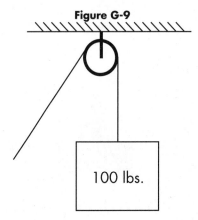

100 lbs.

9. How much effort must be used to raise the 100-lb. weight in Figure G-9?

   a. 50 lbs.

   b. 100 lbs.

   c. 150 lbs.

   d. 200 lbs.

   e. 250 lbs.

Figure G-10

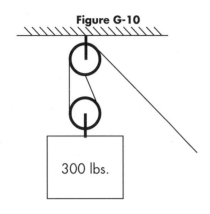

300 lbs.

10. How much effort must be used to raise the 360-lb. weight in Figure G-10?

   a. 50 lbs.

   b. 90 lbs.

   c. 100 lbs.

   d. 120 lbs.

   e. 150 lbs.

Figure G-11

A

     B

        C

          Spring

11. Given the lever in Figure G-11, determine how much force you must push down on point A to stretch the spring 10 inches. (The distance from A to B is 6 feet and the distance from B to C is 4 feet. The spring has a stiffness of 20 lbs./in.)

   a. 110.0 lbs.

   b. 120.5 lbs.

   c. 133.3 lbs.

   d. 142.5 lbs.

   e. 155.5 lbs.

Figure G-12

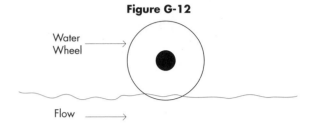

Water Wheel →

Flow →

12. In Figure G-12, the water wheel has a diameter of nine feet. The flow of the river is 300 feet/minute. Approximately how many revolutions per minute is the water wheel turning and in what direction?

   a. 10 rpm, counterclockwise

   b. 10 rpm, clockwise

   c. 33 rpm, counterclockwise

   d. 33 rpm, clockwise

   e. 100 rpm, counterclockwise

Figure G-13

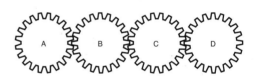

13. If gear C rotates five revolutions counterclockwise in Figure G-13, what will gear D do?

   a. rotate one revolution clockwise

   b. rotate five revolutions clockwise

   c. rotate five revolutions counter clockwise

   d. none of the above

Figure G-14

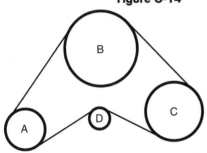

Wheel Radius
A 4 inches
B 8 inches
C 6 inches
D 2 inches

14. All four gears are connected by the same fan belt in Figure G-14. What gear is turning at the highest revolution per minute (rpm)?

a. gear A
b. gear B
c. gear C
d. gear D
e. They all turn at the same rpm.

Figure G-15

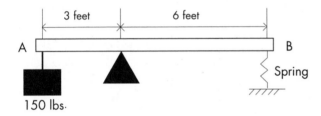

15. The 150 lb. weight at point A is supported by a spring at point B, as depicted in Figure G-15. The spring has a stiffness of 25 lbs./inch. How many inches is the spring stretched?

a. 1 inch
b. 1.5 inches
c. 2.0 inches
d. 2.5 inches
e. 3.0 inches

Figure G-16

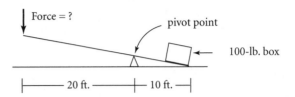

16. In Figure G-16 shown here, Joe must lift a 100-lb. box using a lever. How many pounds of force must he apply to the left side of the lever to lift the box? (The product of the weight of the box times the distance of the box from the pivot point must be equal to the product of the required force times the distance from the force to the pivot point: $w \times d_1 = f \times d_2$.)

a. 100 lbs.
b. 200 lbs.
c. 50 lbs.
d. 33 lbs.
e. 15 lbs.

Figure G-17

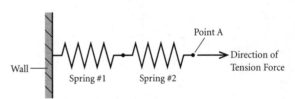

17. Two springs are arranged in series as shown in Figure G-17. Spring #1 is very stiff and will become 1 inch longer when a tension force of 10 pounds is applied to it. Spring #2 is very soft and will become two inches longer when a tension force of five pounds is applied to it. What will be the change in length of the two springs when a force of 20 pounds is applied—that is, how far will point A move to the right?

a. 10 inches
b. 8 inches
c. 6 inches
d. 4 inches
e. 3 inches

Figure G-18

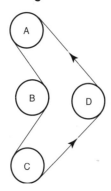

18. Which gears are turning clockwise?

   a. B

   b. B and D

   c. D

   d. A, B, C, and D

   e. A, C, and D

Figure G-19

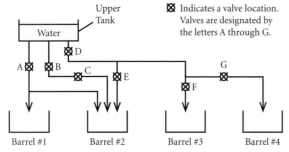

19. In Figure G-19, all valves are initially closed. Gravity will cause the water to drain down into the barrels when the valves are opened. Which barrels will be filled if valves A, B, E, F, and G are opened and valves C and D are left closed?

   a. barrels #1 and #2

   b. barrels #3 and #4

   c. barrels #1, #2, #3, and #4

   d. barrels #1, #2, and #3

   e. barrels #1 and #4

Figure G-20

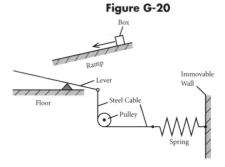

20. In Figure G-20, if the box slides down the ramp and drops onto the left side of the lever, what will happen to the spring?

   a. It will touch the box.

   b. It will remain as it is.

   c. It will be compressed or shortened.

   d. It will be stretched or lengthened.

   e. none of the above

Figure G-21

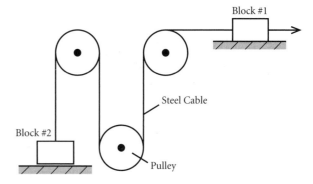

21. In Figure G-21, if block #1 is moved 10 feet to the right, how far upward is block #2 lifted?

   a. 3 feet

   b. 5 feet

   c. 10 feet

   d. 15 feet

   e. 20 feet

Figure G-22

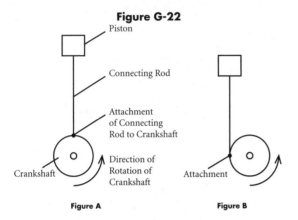

Figure A

Figure B

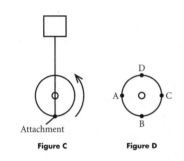

Figure C

Figure D

22. In Figure G-22, Figure A shows the initial position of a piston that is connected to a crankshaft by a connecting rod; Figure B shows the relative positions after the crankshaft is rotated 90° (one quarter of a revolution) in the direction shown; and Figure C shows the relative positions after another 90° of rotation. In Figure D, what will be the position of the connecting rod attachment to the crankshaft after yet another 90° rotation?

  a. position A

  b. position B

  c. position C

  d. position D

  e. none of the above

Figure G-23

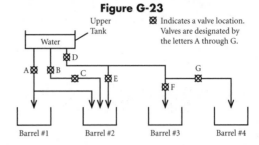

23. In Figure G-23, all valves are initially closed. Gravity will cause the water to drain down into the barrels when the valves are opened. Which barrels will be filled if valves A, B, E, F, and G are opened and valves C and D are left closed?

  a. barrels #1 and #2

  b. barrels #3 and #4

  c. barrels #1, #2, #3, and #4

  d. barrels #1, #2, and #3

Figure G-24

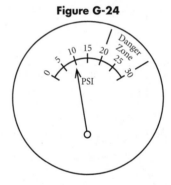

24. On the gauge in Figure G-24, what is the maximum recommended operating pressure in psi (pounds per square inch) for the needle to remain in a safe zone?

  a. 10 psi

  b. 15 psi

  c. 20 psi

  d. 25 psi

  e. 30 psi

Figure G-25

Lift = 95,000 lbs

Force on Elevator

Weight = 92,000 lbs

25. In Figure G-25, an aircraft is flying in a straight and level profile. The weight of the aircraft is 73,000 lbs., and the wings are generating 75,000 lbs. of lift. The distance between the lift force and the weight force is 2.5 feet. Since the lift force and the weight force are not equal, the elevator must apply some force to maintain the straight and level profile. Determine what force is necessary from the elevator and if that force is in the up or down direction. The distance from the elevator to the weight force is 23 feet.

a. 217.4 lbs./up
b. 217.4 lbs./down
c. 2,174.3 lbs./up
d. 2,174.3 lbs./down
e. 4,348.6 lbs./down

Figure G-26

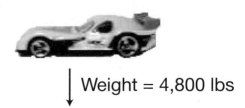

Weight = 4,800 lbs

26. The car in Figure G-26 weighs 4,800 lbs. How much weight does each tire support?

a. 1,200 lbs.
b. 2,400 lbs.
c. 3,600 lbs.
d. 4,800 lbs.
e. 6,000 lbs.

Figure G-27

	Weight	Spring Resistance
A	25 lbs.	10 lbs./inch
B	15 lbs.	5 lbs./inch
C	35 lbs.	20 lbs./inch
D	10 lbs.	15 lbs./inch
E	50 lbs.	25 lbs./inch

A B C D E

27. Figure G-27 depicts a series of weights suspended from a bar, using springs. Using the given weights and spring resistances, determine which weight will stretch its respective spring the most.

a. weight A
b. weight B
c. weight C
d. weight D
e. weight E

Figure G-28

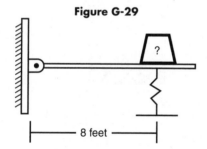

Figure G-30

300 lbs.

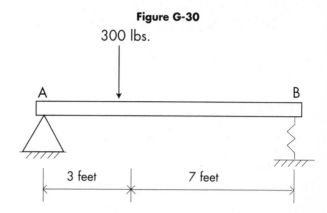

3 feet   7 feet

28. Wheel A in Figure G-28 turns clockwise. All the wheels are connected by the same fan belt. Determine the direction of rotation for all the other wheels.

  a. clockwise: B, C, counterclockwise: D, E
  b. clockwise: D, E, counterclockwise: B, C
  c. clockwise: C, D, E counterclockwise: B
  d. clockwise: B, counterclockwise: C, D, E
  e. clockwise: B, C, D, counterclockwise: E

30. In Figure G-30, a 300-lb. force is applied to a bar supported at points A and B. The force is applied three feet from point A and seven feet from point B. The support at point B is a spring with a resistance of 15 lbs./inch. Determine how much the spring will be compressed in this configuration.

  a. 2 inches
  b. 3 inches
  c. 4 inches
  d. 5 inches
  e. 6 inches

Figure G-29

?

8 feet

29. Using Figure G-29, determine how much weight must be applied to compress the spring 10 inches. Neglect the weight of the bar and use 20 lbs./inch for the resistance of the spring. Assume the weight is placed directly over the spring, eight feet from the hinge.

  a. 25 lbs.
  b. 50 lbs.
  c. 100 lbs.
  d. 200 lbs.
  e. 400 lbs.

Section 4: Spatial Apperception

DIRECTIONS: This test measures your ability to determine the position of an aircraft in flight in relation to a ship on the water. You are to determine whether it is climbing, diving, banking to right or left, or in level flight. For each question, select the choice that most nearly represents the aircraft's position in relation to the position of the ship. You will have ten (10) minutes to complete this section of the test.

Questions: 25
Time: 10 minutes

For sample Spatial Apperception questions, see page 61.

1.

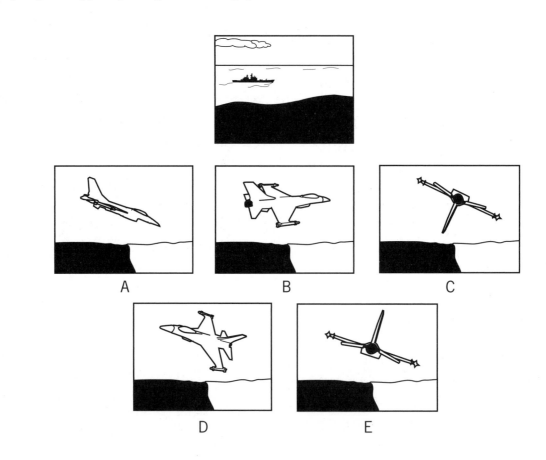

2.

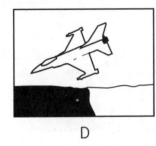 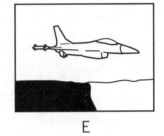 

A   B   C

 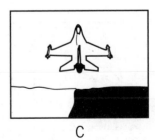

D   E

3.

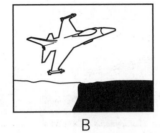

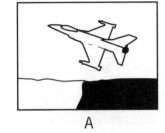 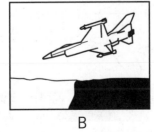 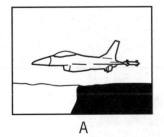

A   B   C

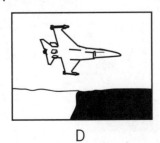 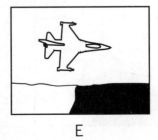

D   E

4.

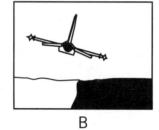
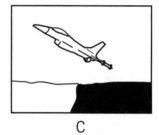

A   B   C

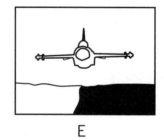

D   E

5.

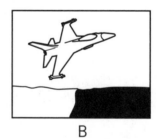

A   B   C

6.

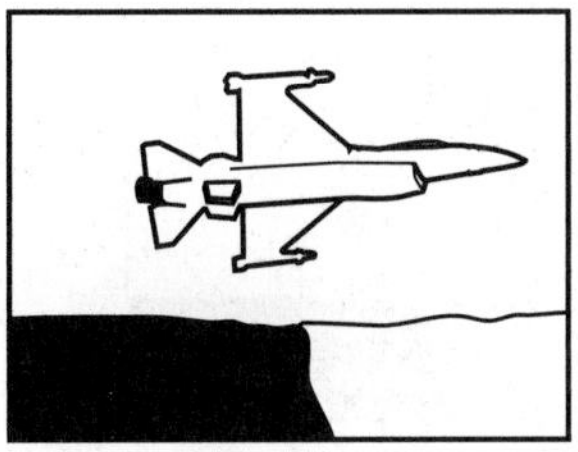

A    B    C

D    E

7.

A    B    C

D    E

8.

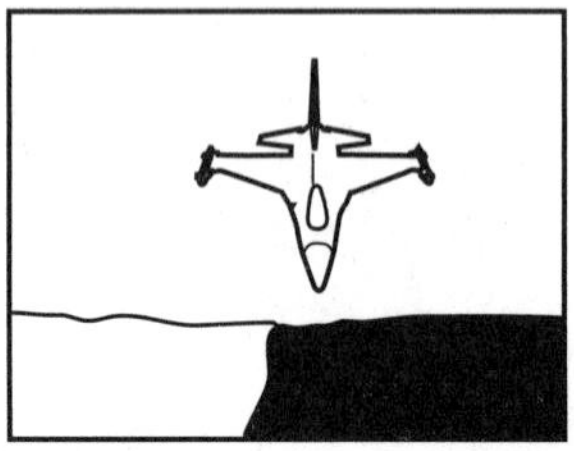

A    B    C

D    E

9.

A    B    C

D    E

10.

A    B    C

D    E

11.

A    B    C

D    E

12.

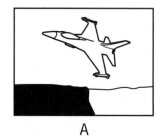 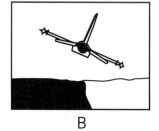 

A   B   C

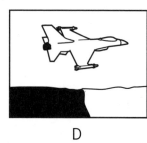 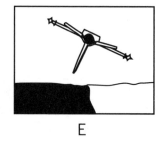

D   E

13.

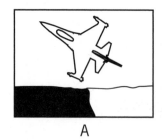 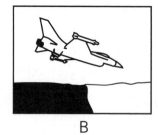 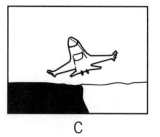

A   B   C

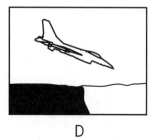 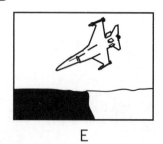

D   E

14.

A  B 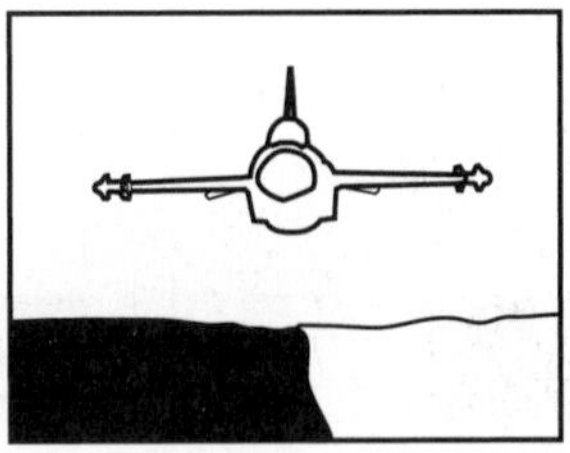 C

D  E

15.

A  B  C

D  E

16.

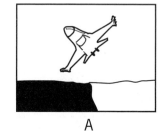

A

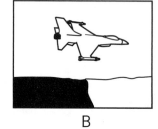

B

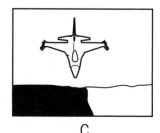

C

D

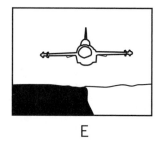

E

17.

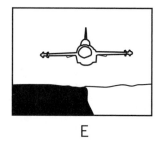

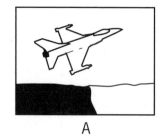

A

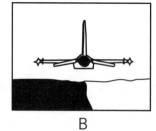

B

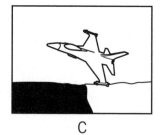

C

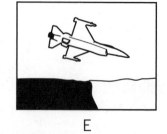

D

E

18.

A

B

C

D

E

19.

A

B

C

D

E

20.

A    B    C

D    E

21.

A    B    C

D    E

22.

A	B	C

D	E

23.

A	B	C

D	E

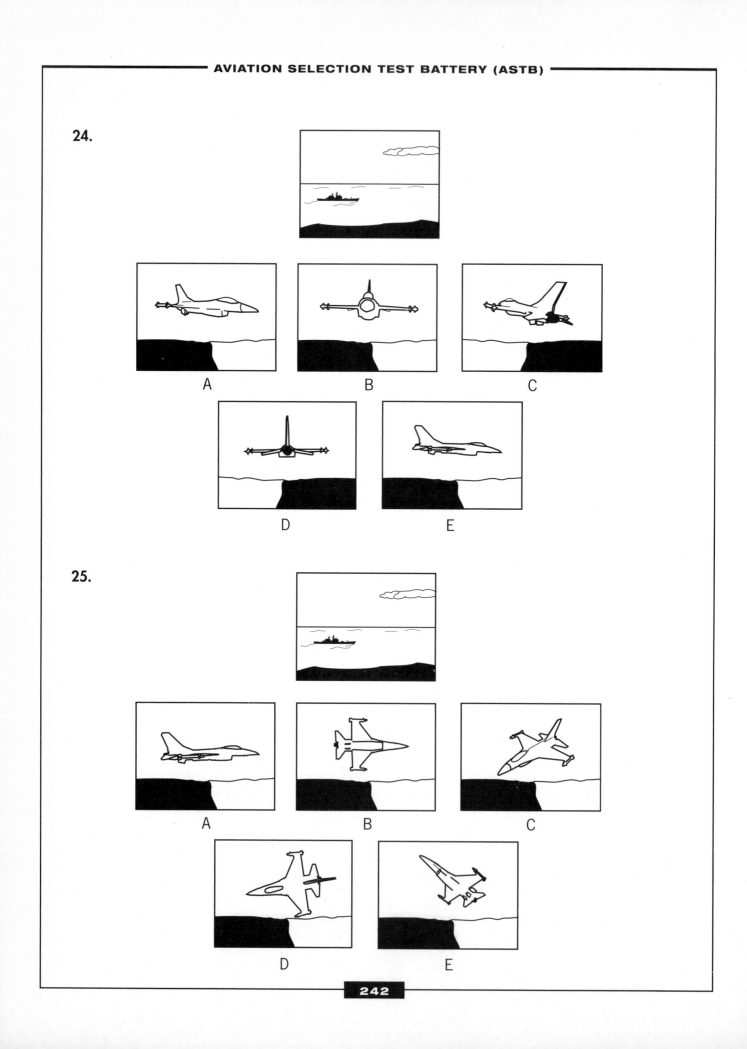

24.

A   B   C

D   E

25.

A   B   C

D   E

Section 5: Aviation and Nautical Information

DIRECTIONS: This part of the test measures your aviation and nautical knowledge. Each of the questions or incomplete statements is followed by several choices. You must decide which one of the choices best completes the statement or answers the question. Eliminating any obviously incorrect choices first will increase your chances of selecting the right answer. You will have fifteen (15) minutes to complete these questions.

Questions: 30

Time: 15 minutes

For sample Aviation and Nautical Information questions, see page 52.

1. The front section of a ship is known as the
   a. port side.
   b. starboard side.
   c. bow.
   d. stern.
   e. keel.

2. The rear section of a ship is known as the
   a. port side.
   b. starboard side.
   c. bow.
   d. stern.
   e. keel.

3. The right-hand side of a ship is known as the
   a. port side.
   b. starboard side.
   c. bow.
   d. stern.
   e. keel.

4. The left-hand side of a ship is known as the
   a. port side.
   b. starboard side.
   c. bow.
   d. stern.
   e. keel.

For questions 5–8, refer to Figure 1.

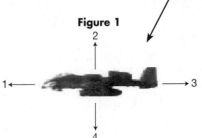

Figure 1

5. The force represented by arrow #1 is
   a. lift.
   b. weight.
   c. drag.
   d. thrust.
   e. none of the above

6. The force represented by arrow #2 is
   a. lift.
   b. weight.
   c. drag.
   d. thrust.
   e. none of the above

7. The force represented by arrow #3 is
   a. lift.
   b. weight.
   c. drag.
   d. thrust.
   e. none of the above

8. The force represented by arrow #4 is
   a. lift.
   b. weight.
   c. drag.
   d. thrust.
   e. none of the above

For questions 9–12, refer to Figure 2.

Figure 2

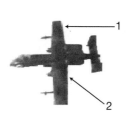 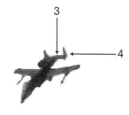

9. Arrow #1 is pointing to the
   a. aileron.
   b. flap.
   c. rudder.
   d. elevator.
   e. fuselage.

10. Arrow #2 is pointing to the
   a. aileron.
   b. flap.
   c. rudder.
   d. elevator.
   e. fuselage.

11. Arrow #3 is pointing to the
   a. aileron.
   b. flap.
   c. rudder.
   d. elevator.
   e. fuselage.

12. Arrow #4 is pointing to the
   a. aileron.
   b. flap.
   c. rudder.
   d. elevator.
   e. fuselage.

13. The _____ is the kitchen compartment of a ship.
   a. hull
   b. keel
   c. bulkhead
   d. galley
   e. forecastle

14. The _____ is the section of the upper deck of a ship located at the bow.
   a. hull
   b. keel
   c. bulkhead
   d. galley
   e. forecastle

15. The _____ is the body of a ship excluding masts, sails, yards, and riggings.
   a. hull
   b. keel
   c. bulkhead
   d. galley
   e. forecastle

16. A _____ is one of the straight upright partitions dividing a ship into compartments.
   a. hull
   b. keel
   c. bulkhead
   d. galley
   e. forecastle

17. The _____ is the principal structural member that forms the centerline of the hull running from bow to stern.
    a. hull
    b. keel
    c. bulkhead
    d. galley
    e. forecastle

18. _____ is the actual velocity of an aircraft traveling through the air.
    a. Indicated airspeed
    b. Calibrated airspeed
    c. Equivalent airspeed
    d. True airspeed
    e. Ground speed

19. _____ is the instrumental indication of the dynamic pressure of the airplane during flight.
    a. Indicated airspeed
    b. Calibrated airspeed
    c. Equivalent airspeed
    d. True airspeed
    e. Ground speed

20. _____ is a measure of the aircraft's actual speed over the ground.
    a. Indicated airspeed
    b. Calibrated airspeed
    c. Equivalent airspeed
    d. True airspeed
    e. Ground speed

21. _____ is the corrected airspeed taking into account instrumental error.
    a. Indicated airspeed
    b. Calibrated airspeed
    c. Equivalent airspeed
    d. True airspeed
    e. Ground speed

22. _____ is found by correcting calibrated airspeed for compressibility error.
    a. Indicated airspeed
    b. Calibrated airspeed
    c. Equivalent airspeed
    d. True airspeed
    e. Ground speed

23. A jet is flying straight and level at 10,000 feet and 400 knots. If the pilot pulls back on the throttle but gives no input to the stick, how will the aircraft react?
    a. The jet will accelerate and climb.
    b. The jet will initially slow down and begin a gradual descent.
    c. The jet will remain level and slow down.
    d. The jet will remain level and accelerate.
    e. The jet will not experience any changes.

24. A jet is flying straight and level at 10,000 feet and 400 knots. If the pilot adds power and pushes the stick forward, how will the aircraft react?
    a. The jet will climb and accelerate.
    b. The jet will descend and slow down.
    c. The jet will descend and accelerate.
    d. The jet will climb and decelerate.
    e. The jet will remain level and decelerate.

25. The average lapse rate of temperature in the atmosphere is the decrease in the air temperature as you climb at a rate of 2° C per 1,000 feet. If the temperature at the airfield is 15° C and you plan to fly a mission with a cruise altitude of 20,000 feet, what temperature can you expect to find during the cruise portion of your flight? (The elevation of your airfield is 2,000 feet MSL.)

    a. −12° C
    b. −16° C
    c. −21° C
    d. −25° C
    e. −40° C

26. An aircraft's current heading is 180° and your navigator instructs you to turn left 45°, what would be your new heading?

    a. 225
    b. 135
    c. 145
    d. 45
    e. 315

27. An aircraft's current heading is 270°, and your navigator instructs you to turn right 100°, what would be your new heading?

    a. 010
    b. 370
    c. 100
    d. 260
    e. 170

28. Temperature is best described as
    a. the amount of water vapor in the air.
    b. the rate at which sound waves travel through an air mass.
    c. a measure of the average kinetic energy of the air particles.
    d. a measure of the air's resistance to flow and shearing.
    e. the total mass of air particles per unit volume.

29. Humidity is best described as
    a. the amount of water vapor in the air.
    b. the rate at which sound waves travel through an air mass.
    c. a measure of the average kinetic energy of the air particles.
    d. a measure of the air's resistance to flow and shearing.
    e. the total mass of air particles per unit volume.

30. Air density is best described as
    a. the amount of water vapor in the air.
    b. the rate at which sound waves travel through an air mass.
    c. a measure of the average kinetic energy of the air particles.
    d. a measure of the air's resistance to flow and shearing.
    e. the total mass of air particles per unit volume.

ASTB ANSWERS

Section 1: Math Skills

1. **d.** 174 is rounded to 200; 364 is rounded to 400. $(200)(400) = 80,000$.

2. **b.** Add the corrected value of the sweater ($245) to the value of the two, not three, bracelets ($730), plus the other two items ($78 and $130).

3. **d.** To solve this problem, convert $5\frac{3}{4}$ to $\frac{23}{4}$ and then divide $\frac{23}{4}$ by $\frac{1}{4}$. The answer is 23.

4. **a.** Substituting known quantities in the formula yields $20 = \frac{64.8}{x^2}$ Next, you must multiply through by x^2 to get $20x^2 = 64.8$. Now divide through by 20 to get $x^2 = \frac{64.8}{20} = 3.24$. Now take the square root of both sides to get x equals 1.8.

5. **d.** Four inches is equal to 16 quarter inches. Each quarter inch is 2 feet, so 16 quarter inches is 32 feet.

6. **b.** You can't just take 25% off the original price, because the 15% discount after three years of service is taken off the price that has already been reduced by 10%. Figure the problem in two steps: After the 10% discount, the price is $105.08. Subtracting 5% from that gives you $89.32.

7. **d.** The simplest way to solve this problem is to divide 1 by 1,500, which is .0006667, and then count off two decimal places to arrive at the percentage, which is .06667 percent. Since the question asks *about* what percentage, the nearest value is .067%.

8. **a.** You can use trial and error to arrive at a solution to this problem. After the first hour, the number would be 20, after the second hour 40, after the third hour 80, after the fourth hour 160, and after the fifth hour 320. The other answer choices do not have the same outcome.

9. **c.** Use the equation $.09(1) = .03(x)$, where x is the total amount of water in the resulting 3% solution. Solving for x, you get 3. Subtracting the 1 liter of water already present in the 9% solution, you will find that 2 liters need to be added.

10. **b.** On this question, 20% of 15 miles is 3 miles. Adding 3 to 15 gives 18 miles.

11. **d.** Each 10-foot wall has an area of $9(10)$, or 90 square feet. There are two such walls, so those two walls combined have an area of 180 square feet. Each 14-foot wall has an area of $14(10)$, or 140 square feet, and again there are two such walls: $140(2) = 280$. Finally, add 180 and 280 to get 460 square feet.

12. **c.** Substituting 39.6 for C in the equation yields $F = (\frac{9}{5})(39.6) + 32 = 71.28 + 32 = 103.3$.

13. **c.** The ratio is $\frac{12\,cc}{100}$ pounds $= \frac{x}{175}$ pounds, where x is the number of cc's per 175 pounds. Multiply both sides by 175 to get $(175)(\frac{12}{100})$ equals x, so x equals 21.

14. **b.** On the first day, the hiker walks 40 miles. On the second day, he walks 20 miles. On the third day, he walks 10 miles. On the fourth day, he walks 5 miles. On the fifth day, he walks 2.5 miles. The sum of the miles walked, then, is 77.5 miles. The average over five days is 77.5 divided by 5, or 15.5 miles per day.

15. d. The fugitive will have traveled 5 hours at 50 miles per hour for a distance of 250 miles. To reach her in 4 hours, the police must travel at 250 miles per 4 hours, or 62.5 mph.

16. a. $J = 6K$, and $J + 2 = 2(K + 2)$, so $6K + 2 = 2K + 4$, which means K equals $\frac{1}{2}$. J equals 6K, or 3.

17. d. Add each monthly bill plus $54 for total local service to get $312.90 for three months. Dividing by 3 gives an average of $104.30.

18. d. In this question, 448 miles divided by 16 gallons is 28 miles per gallon.

19. c. In this question, 962,342 bytes free plus 454,783 bytes freed when a file was deleted equals 1,417,125 bytes; 1,417,125 bytes minus 315,926 bytes put into the new file leaves 1,101,199 bytes free.

20. b. Jackie is paid and saves twice a month, while she pays her student loan only once a month. Her monthly salary is $1,644.80. Subtract $300 in savings and $84.71 for the student loan to get $1,260.09.

21. b. The answer to .4 squared is .8.

22. c. First, determine the lowest fraction of parts. Four parts to 12 gallons also equals one part to three gallons. Divide 51 gallons of fuel by a factor of 3 to determine 17 parts of fuel additive are required.

23. c. First, determine how long the tanker has been flying. Two hours prior to the fighter jet's takeoff, and an additional two hours until rendezvous, which equals four hours. Next, determine how far the tanker has flown in four hours. Four times 300 mph equals 1,200 miles. Finally, divide 1,200 miles by the fighter jet's duration of flight: $\frac{1,200}{2} = 600$ mph.

24. d. First, convert pounds to gallons for the fighter jet burn rate: 4,800 lbs. divided by 6 lbs./gallon equals 800 gallons. Multiply the burn rate of 800 gallons per hour times a three hour flight to get 2,400 gallons. Next, convert the landing fuel requirement: 3,000 lbs. divided by 6 lbs/gallon equals 500 gallons. Add 2,400 gallons plus 500 gallons to get the answer of 2,900 gallons.

25. a. Divide 54 miles by the six-mile orbit circumference to equal 9 orbits.

26. d. The model plane's 10 inches is equal to 20 one-half inches. Each of those is 5 feet. $20 \times 5 = 100$ ft.

27. d. Work backward to find the solution. George has five cousins, which is 11 fewer than Bonnie has; therefore, Bonnie has 16 cousins. Bonnie has twice as many as Robert has, so half of 16 is 8. Robert has eight cousins.

28. c. Set up a proportion with $\frac{milk}{soda}$; $\frac{2}{5} = \frac{10}{x}$. Cross-multiply and solve: $(5)(10) = 2x$. Divide both sides by 2: $\frac{50}{2} = \frac{2x}{2}$; $x = 25$ sodas.

29. b. To earn an average of 93% on four tests, the sum of those four tests must be (93)(4) or 372. The sum of the first three tests is $85 + 92 + 95 = 272$. The difference between the needed sum of four tests, and the sum of the first three tests is 100. He needs a 100 to earn a 93 average.

30. b. Use the order of operations and try each option. The first option results in 14 because $2 \times 5 = 10$, then $10 + 4 = 14$. This does not work. The second option does result in 18. The numbers in parentheses are added first and result in 9, which is then multiplied by 2 to get a final answer of 18. Choice **c** does not work because the operation in parentheses is done first, yielding 6, which is then multiplied by 5 to get a result of 30. Choice **d** does not work because the multiplication is done first, yielding 8, which is added to 5 for a final answer of 13.

Section 2: Reading Skills

1. d. The last sentence in the passage refers to dogs as probably the oldest alarm system. The other choices, even if true, are not in the passage.

2. a. This is the only choice reflected in the passage. Choice **d** may seem attractive at first, but the passage simply says that the local media does not cover local politics—it doesn't give the reason for their neglect.

3. a. The first sentence reflects the idea that the Dvorak keyboard is more efficient than the QWERTY. The other choices are not in the passage.

4. b. The other choices are incorrect because the passage is not concerned with how sanitation workers should deal with sharp objects, but with how everyone should dispose of sharp objects in order to avoid hurting sanitation workers.

5. c. The final sentence indicates that the atmosphere of Mars has been stripped away.

6. d. The directions mention nothing about main or secondary roads.

7. b. The directions indicate that the city prefers, but does not require, use of the new container provided by the city and that the customers may use more than one container if they purchase an additional one.

8. d. This answer is implied by the statement that redistribution is needed so that people in emerging nations can have proper medical care. Choices **a**, **b**, and **c** are not mentioned in the passage.

9. c. This choice is the best answer because the paragraph indicates that legislators once feared suggesting gas taxes, but now many of them are pushing bills in favor of these taxes. There is no indication that choice **a** is true. Choice **b** is incorrect because the paragraph doesn't say why more gas taxes are being proposed. There is no support for choice **d**.

10. b. Choices **a** and **c** are too narrow to be the main idea. Choice **d** simply supports the main idea that lawyers have received undeserved criticism.

11. b. The support for choice **b** is given in the second sentence of the paragraph. Generation Xers like to work independently, which means they are self-directed. No support is given for choice **a**. Choice **c** is not related to the paragraph. Although the paragraph mentions that Generation Xers liked to be challenged, it does not say they like to challenge their bosses' attitudes; therefore, choice **d** can be ruled out.

12. d. This choice encompasses the main information in the passage. Choices **a**, **b**, and **c** are not mentioned.

13. a. The final sentence states that computer games and virtual reality help children come to terms with the truths of the real world. The other choices are not reflected in the passage.

14. c. The first and second sentences reflect this idea. The passage does not say that Native American art is dreamlike (choice **a**). Choices **b** and **d** are too narrow to be main ideas.

15. b. The passage explains the procedure for bus drivers to follow when their bus gets ahead of schedule. Therefore, "running hot" means running ahead of schedule.

16. c. According to the passage, hazardous waste is defined by the U.S. Environmental Protection Agency.

17. d. The first day of summer in the north is the first day of winter in the south.

18. b. This is the only choice that reflects the idea of interaction among all members of the group spoken of in the first sentence. The other choices are only physical settings.

19. d. The final sentence indicates that the author agrees with the review in *The Sunday Times* that the play was revolutionary (a word which literally means a turning point). Choice **a** underplays and choice **b** overestimates the importance of the work to the author of the passage. Choices **c** and **e** are contradicted by the last sentence.

20. d. The paragraph specifically states that age makes a person less able to respond to long exposure to very hot or very cold temperatures. This would mean that older people are more susceptible to hypothermia. Choices **a**, **b**, and **c** are not supported by the information given in the paragraph.

21. b. Choice **b** is indicated by the final sentence, which indicates that the RDA approach is useful, but has limitations, implying that a supplemental guide would be a good thing. Choice **a** is contradicted by the final sentence of the passage. Choice **c** is incorrect because the passage says the RDA approach is a useful guide, but does NOT say it is the best guide to good nutrition. Choice **d** is contradicted by the next-to-last sentence of the passage.

22. c. Note that this question asked you to find the answer that is NOT included in the passage. Choice **c** is the best answer because the passage states that after the glacier, the mountain ranges were never to return.

23. e. This detail can be found in the final sentence of the passage.

24. a. The passage states that officers should keep complete notes and use them to refresh their memories about events. None of the other choices is reflected in the passage.

25. c. See the second sentence, which defines *ksa*. The other choices are refuted in the passage.

26. d. See the fourth sentence of the passage.

27. b. The last sentence indicates that there is little or no visible flame with a potential backdraft. The other choices are also listed at the end of the last sentence as warning signs of a potential backdraft.

Section 3:
Mechanical Comprehension

1. **a.** Point A delivers the maximum leverage in the correct direction, because it is as far from the fulcrum as possible.

2. **b.** The 100 lbs. at the right end of the lever creates a moment about the fulcrum of 300 feet-lbs. (100 lbs. × 3 feet). To counterbalance this moment, a 50-lb. force must be applied at the opposite end to create the equal 300 feet-lbs. moment (50 lbs. × 6 feet).

3. **d.** Shape D is the best shape to make the dam, because as the flow of the water pushes against it, the arch distributes the force equally and directs it into the banks of the river, instead of the center of the dam, which would cause it to collapse.

4. **c.** Box A creates a moment about the axle of 450 feet-lbs. (75 lbs. × 6 feet). Since box B is supported by the smaller 2-foot wheel, box B must weigh 225 lbs. in order to create an equal moment about the axle (225 lbs. × 2 feet).

5. **d.** Gears E and F turn counterclockwise and clockwise, respectively.

6. **e.** If the tire is 3 feet in diameter, then the circumference is 3 feet × pi (3.14) = 9.42 feet. The circumference is also the same distance as one revolution of the tire. So if the tire is turning at 500 revolutions per minute and the circumference is 9.42 feet, then the tire is traveling at 4,710 ft./min. down the road (500 rev/min. × 9.42 ft./rev = 4,710 ft./min.).

7. **c.** If the block weighs 98 lbs. and the stiffness of the spring is 16 lbs./inch, then the spring will stretch 6.125, or $6\frac{1}{8}$ inches [(98 lbs.)/(16 lbs./inch)] = 6.125 inches.

8. **b.** The 50-lb. weight at B creates a moment about the fulcrum of 350 feet-lbs. (50 lbs. × 7 feet = 350 feet-lbs.). If the distance from the fulcrum to the lifting point is 10 feet, then only 35 lbs. of force must be used to lift the block (350 feet-lbs./10 feet = 35 lbs.).

9. **b.** Since the pulley in Figure G-9 is fixed, there is no additional mechanical advantage, and it still requires 100 lbs. of force to lift the 100-lb. weight.

10. **e.** The top pulley is fixed, but the bottom pulley is raised in Figure G-10. This arrangement creates a mechanical advantage of 2. Therefore, the required force to lift the weight is equal to half the weight itself. In this problem, that equals 150 lbs.

11. **c.** The first step is determining how much force at point C it takes to stretch the spring itself the required 10 inches. If the stiffness of the spring is 20 lbs./inch, then 200 lbs. (20 lbs./inch × 10 inches = 200 lbs.) of force must be applied at point C. To calculate the required force at point A, you must determine the moment about the fulcrum created by the 200-lb. force at C. This is done by multiplying 200 lbs. at point C by the distance from C to the fulcrum (4 feet). The result is 200 lbs. × 4 feet = 800 feet-lbs. Now, taking this moment about the fulcrum and applying it to the part of the lever from A to B, you calculate the required force at A as 133.3 lbs. (800 feet-lbs./6 feet = 133.3 lbs.).

12. a. Looking at Figure G-12, the flow of the water pushing against the bottom of the water wheel would cause the water wheel to turn counterclockwise. The flow of the water is 300 feet/minute. This is also the speed that the circumference of the wheel is turning. So if the circumference of the wheel is 28.26 feet (9 feet × 3.14), then the revolutions per minute are (300 feet/minute)/(28.26 feet/revolution) = 10.6 revolutions/minute, or approximately 10 rpm.

13. b. Gear D will rotate clockwise five rotations.

14. d. Since all the gears in Figure G-14 are connected by the same fan belt, their circumferences are all moving at the same speed. However, since all the gears have different radii and, therefore, different circumferences, the gear with the smallest size (gear D) must turn at the highest rpm to match the speed of the fan belt.

15. e. The first step is determining the moment about the fulcrum created by the weight (150 lbs. × 3 feet = 450 feet-lbs.). Next, apply this same moment to the opposite end of the lever to calculate the force applied to the spring (450 feet-lbs.)/(6 feet) = 75 lbs. If you apply this 75-lb. force to the spring with a stiffness of 25 lbs./inch, the spring will move only 3 inches (75 lbs.)/(25 lbs./inch) = 3 inches.

16. c. The distance from the pivot point to the point of application of the force (20 feet) is twice the distance from the pivot point to the box (10 feet). Therefore, in order to lift the box, the required force will be one half of the weight of the box (100 lbs.), or 50 lbs.

17. a. Because the springs are in a series, their amount of stretch is additive. Spring #1 will stretch 1 inch under 10 pounds, so its total stretch under 20 pounds will be 2 inches. Spring #2 is being subjected to a load of 20 pounds, which is four times the load that will stretch it 2 inches. Therefore, its total stretch will be 8 inches. Adding the amount of stretch for the two springs together gives you 10 inches.

18. c. Gear B will rotate clockwise.

19. a. Since valve D is closed, water will not flow to barrels #3 and #4. Water will flow through valve B but be stopped at valve C. Water will flow through valve A into barrels #1 and #2.

20. d. The box will force the left side of the lever down and the right side of the lever up, which will pull the cable up. The cable will pass across the pulley and apply a pulling force on the spring, so the spring will stretch.

21. c. The two blocks are directly connected by a fixed length of steel cable. Therefore, regardless of the number of pulleys between the two blocks, the distance moved by one block will be the same as that moved by the other block.

22. c. Figure #3 shows the attachment of the connecting rod to the crankshaft at the bottom of the crankshaft. Another 90° counterclockwise rotation would place the attachment point on the right side of the crankshaft at position C.

23. a. Since valve D is closed, water will not flow to barrels #3 and #4. Water will flow through valve B but be stopped at valve C. Water will flow through valve A into barrels #1 and #2.

24. c. The gauge indicates that any pressure greater than 20 psi is in the danger zone.

25. b. The first step is determining the moment caused by the lift force. Since the lift and weight forces are in opposite directions, they must be subtracted (75,000 − 73,000 = 2,000 lbs.), resulting in a net 2,000-lb. force in the up direction. This force is 2.5 feet from the center of gravity of the aircraft, resulting in a moment of (2000 lbs. × 2.5 feet = 5,000 feet-lbs.). The force required at the elevator to balance the moment caused by the lift must be in the down direction. Since the distance from the center of gravity to the elevator is 23 feet, the force at the elevator must be (5,000 feet-lbs./23 feet = 217.4 lbs.).

26. a. Since the weight of the car is evenly distributed on the four wheels, each wheel supports 1,200 lbs. (4,800 lbs./4 wheels = 1,200 lbs./wheel).

27. b. In calculating the amount each spring will stretch, each weight must be divided by the corresponding spring resistance. In doing so, it is found that weight B has the greatest displacement with 3 inches [(15 lbs.)/(5 lbs./in) = 3 inches].

28. c. Wheel B is the only wheel in the diagram that turns counterclockwise. All the other wheels turn clockwise.

29. d. To calculate the required weight to compress the spring 10 inches, you must multiply the spring resistance by the amount of desired compression: (20 lbs./inch) × (10 inches) = 200 lbs. Since the weight is placed directly over the spring, the distance from the hinge does not matter.

30. e. The 300-lb. force creates a 900 feet-lbs. moment at point A. This results in a 90-lb. force being applied to the spring at point B [(900 feet-lbs.)/(10 feet) = 90 lbs.]. A 90-lb. force applied to the spring will compress it 6 inches [(90 lbs.)/(15 lbs./inch) = 6 inches].

Section 4: Spatial Apperception

Question	Answer	Pitch	Roll	Direction
1	A	diving	no bank angle	flying out to sea
2	C	diving	banking right	flying out to sea
3	B	diving	banking right	flying out to sea
4	E	level	no bank angle	coastline on left
5	E	level	banking right	coastline on left
6	B	level	banking left	coastline on right
7	B	climbing	banking left	flying out to sea
8	B	level	no bank angle	coastline on right
9	D	climbing	banking left	flying out to sea
10	B	level	banking right	coastline on right
11	A	level	banking right	coastline on right,
12	B	level	banking right	coastline on left
13	D	diving	no bank angle	flying out to sea
14	C	level	no bank angle	coastline on right
15	A	level	no bank angle	diagonal heading 45° coastline on right, ocean on left
16	C	diving	no bank angle	coastline on right
17	A	climbing	banking right	flying out to sea
18	E	climbing	banking right	flying out to sea
19	E	diving	banking left	flying out to sea
20	B	level	banking left	flying out to sea
21	A	diving	banking left	flying out to sea
22	D	level	no bank angle	coastline on left
23	B	level	banking right	coastline on right
24	E	level	no bank angle	flying out to sea
25	A	level	no bank angle	flying out to sea

Section 5: Aviation and Nautical Information

1. **c.** The front section of a ship is known as the bow.
2. **d.** The rear section of a ship is known as the stern.
3. **b.** The right-hand side of a ship is known as the starboard side.
4. **a.** The left-hand side of a ship is known as the port side.
5. **d.** Thrust acts in the direction of flight.
6. **a.** Lift acts perpendicular to the wings.
7. **c.** Drag acts in the opposite direction of flight.
8. **b.** Weight acts in the direction that always points to the center of the earth.
9. **a.** aileron
10. **b.** flap
11. **d.** elevator
12. **c.** rudder
13. **d.** The galley is the kitchen compartment of a ship.
14. **e.** The forecastle is the section of the upper deck of a ship located at the bow.
15. **a.** The hull is the body of a ship excluding masts, sails, yards, and riggings.
16. **c.** A bulkhead is one of the straight upright partitions dividing a ship into compartments.
17. **b.** The keel is the principal structural member that forms the centerline of the hull running from bow to stern.
18. **d.** True airspeed is the actual velocity of an aircraft traveling through the air.
19. **a.** Indicated airspeed is the instrumental indication of the dynamic pressure of the airplane during flight.
20. **e.** Ground speed is a measure of the aircraft's actual speed over the ground.
21. **b.** Calibrated airspeed is the corrected airspeed taking into account instrumental error.
22. **c.** Equivalent airspeed is found by correcting calibrated airspeed for compressibility error.
23. **b.** The jet will initially slow down due to the power reduction and will begin a gradual descent.
24. **c.** The jet will descend with the push forward on the stick and will accelerate with the addition of power.
25. **c.** If the airfield is located at an elevation of 2,000 feet MSL and your planned cruise altitude is 20,000 feet, this is a difference of 18,000 feet. Using the standard lapse rate of 2° C per 1,000 feet in altitude change, this results in a total change in temperature of 36° C. If the starting temperature at the airfield is 15° C, then the temperature at the cruise altitude is −21° C (15° C − 36° C = −21° C).
26. **b.** 180 minus a left turn of 45° equals a new heading of 135.
27. **a.** A heading of 270° added to a right turn of 100 degrees equals 370°. In a compass there are only 360° as you pass through north. 370 minus 360 equals 10°.
28. **c.** Temperature is best described as a measure of the average kinetic energy of the air particles.
29. **a.** Humidity is best described as the amount of water vapor in the air.
30. **e.** Air density is best described as the total mass of air particles per unit volume.

Additional
Online Practice

Whether you need help building basic skills or preparing for an exam, visit the LearningExpress Practice Center! On this site, you can access additional AFOQT practice materials by using the code below. This online practice will provide you with:

- **Immediate scoring**

- **Detailed answer explanations**

- **Personalized recommendations for further practice and study**

Log in to the LearningExpress Practice Center by using this URL: **www.learnatest.com/practice**

This is your Access Code: **6888**

Follow the steps online to redeem your access code. After you've used your access code to register with the site, you will be prompted to create a username and password. For easy reference, record them here:

Username: _____ **Password:** _____

With your username and password, you can log in and access your additional practice materials. If you have any questions or problems, please contact LearningExpress customer service at 1-800-295-9556 ext. 2, or e-mail us at **customerservice@learningexpressllc.com**.

NOTES

NOTES

NOTES

NOTES

NOTES